H, *v*. & O
The poetry of Tony Harrison

MANCHESTER
UNIVERSITY PRESS

H, *v.* & O

The poetry of Tony Harrison

SANDIE BYRNE

MANCHESTER UNIVERSITY PRESS

MANCHESTER AND NEW YORK

distributed exclusively in the USA by St. Martin's Press

The right of Sandie Byrne to be indentified as the author of this work as been
asserted by her in accordance with the Copyright, Designs and Patents Act 1988

Published by Manchester University Press
Oxford Road, Manchester M13 9NR, UK
and Room 400, 175 Fifth Avenue, New York, NY 10010, USA

Distributed exclusively in the USA by
St. Martin's Press, Inc., 175 Fifth Avneue, New York,
NY 10010, USA

Distributed exclusively in Canada by
UBC Press, University of British Columbia, 6344 Memorial Road,
Vancouver, BC, Canada V6T 1Z2

British Library Cataloguing-in-Publication Data
A catalogue record for this book is available from the British Liberary

Library of Congress Cataloging-in-Publication Data applied for

ISBN 0 7190 5294 7 *hardback*
     0 7190 5295 5 *paperback*

First published 1998

05 04 03 02 01 00 99 98   10 9 8 7 6 5 4 3 2 1

Typeset by Action Typesetting Limited,
Northgate Street, Gloucester
Printed in Great Britain
by Bell & Bain Ltd, Glasgow

CONTENTS

ACKNOWLEDGEMENTS

The author is grateful to Tony Harrison for kind permission to quote from his work, and to Harrison's agent, Gordon Dickerson, who commissioned the portrait of Tony Harrison used as the cover illustration of this book from the artist Christopher Stevens.

Cover illustration © Christopher Stevens, 1993.

ABBREVIATIONS

WORKS BY TONY HARRISON

Banquet	Tony Harrison, *The Blasphemers' Banquet*. In *Bloodaxe 1* and *Shadow*. Quotations are from *Shadow*.
Big H	Tony Harrison, *The Big H*. In *TW*.
Black Daisies	Tony Harrison, *Black Daisies for the Bride*. London: Faber and Faber, 1993.
Bow Down	Tony Harrison, *Bow Down*. London: Rex Collings, 1977. Also in TW. Quotations are from *TW*.
Chorus	Tony Harrison, *The Common Chorus*. London: Faber and Faber, 1992.
Coming	Tony Harrison, *A Cold Coming: Gulf War Poems*. Newcastle-upon-Tyne: Bloodaxe Books, 1991. Two poems, also in *Gorgon*. Quotations are from *Gorgon*.
Continuous	Tony Harrison, *Continuous: Fifty Sonnets from 'The School of Eloquence'*. London: Rex Collins, 1981. Collection also in *SP*. Quotations are from SP.
Earthworks	T. W. Harrison, *Earthworks*. Leeds: Northern House, 1964.
Fire-Gap	Tony Harrison, *The Fire-Gap: A Poem with Two Tails*. Newcastle-upon-Tyne: Bloodaxe Books, 1985. Also in *SP*. Quotations are from *SP*.
Gorgon	Tony Harrison, *The Gaze of the Gorgon*. Newcastle-upon-Tyne: Bloodaxe Books, 1992.
Kaisers	Tony Harrison, *The Kaisers of Carnuntum*. In *Plays* 3.
Kumquat	Tony Harrison, *A Kumquat for John Keats*. Newcastle-upon-Tyne: Bloodaxe Books, 1981. Also in *SP*. Quotations are from *SP*.
Labourers	Tony Harrison, *The Labourers of Herakles*. Performed 1995. In *Plays* 3.
Loiners	Tony Harrison, *The Loiners*. London: London Magazine Editions, 1970. Some poems also in *SP*. Quotations from those poems are from *SP*.
Misanthrope	Tony Harrison, *The Misanthrope*. London: Rex Collings, 1973. Also in *TW*. Quotations from text are from *TW*. Quotations from introduction are from *Misanthrope*.
Mysteries	Tony Harrison, *The Mysteries: The Nativity, The Passion, Doomsday*. London: Faber and Faber, 1985.
Newcastle	Tony Harrison, *Newcastle is Peru*, second edn. Newcastle-upon-Tyne: Northern House, 1974. Also in *SP*. Quotations

Abbreviations

	from the poem are from *SP*. Quotations from the introduction are from *Newcastle*.
Palladas	Tony Harrison, *Palladas: Poems*, second edn. Newcastle-upon-Tyne: Bloodaxe Books, 1984. Some poems also in *SP*. Quotations from those poems are from *SP*.
Phaedra	Tony Harrison, after Racine, *Phaedra Britannica*, third edn, with introductory essay. London: Rex Collings, 1976. Also in *TW*. Quotations from the text are from *TW*. Quotations from the introductory essay are from *Phaedra*.
Plays 3	Tony Harrison, *Plays 3*: London, Faber and Faber, 1996.
Shadow	Tony Harrison, *The Shadow of Hiroshima and Other Film/Poems*. London: Faber and Faber, 1995.
School	Tony Harrison, *From 'The School of Eloquence' and Other Poems*. London: Rex Collings, 1978. Also in *SP*. Quotations are from *SP*.
SP	Tony Harrison, *Selected Poems*, second edn. London: Penguin Books, 1987.
Trackers	Tony Harrison, *The Trackers of Oxyrhynchus*. London: Faber and Faber, 1991.
TW	Tony Harrison, *Theatre Works 1973–1985*. London: Penguin Books, 1986.
v.	Tony Harrison, *v.: New Edition with Press Articles*. Newcastle-upon-Tyne: Bloodaxe Books, 1989. Also in *SP*. Quotations are from *v.*

OTHER WORKS

Bloodaxe 1	Neil Astley, ed., *Bloodaxe Critical Anthologies 1: Tony Harrison*. Newcastle-upon-Tyne: Bloodaxe Books, 1991.
'Conversation'	Richard Hoggart, 'In Conversation with Tony Harrison', in *Bloodaxe 1*.
'Interview'	John Haffenden, 'Interview with Tony Harrison', in *Bloodaxe 1*.
'Introduction'	Rosemary Burton, 'Tony Harrison: An Introduction', in *Bloodaxe 1*.
'THL'	Rick Rylance, 'Tony Harrison's Languages', in Antony Easthope and John O. Thompson, eds, *Contemporary Poetry Meets Modern Theory*. Hemel Hempstead: Harvester Wheatsheaf, 1991. Also in *Bloodaxe 1* as 'On Not Being Milton'. Quotations are from 'THL'.
Poetry TH	Luke Spencer, *The Poetry of Tony Harrison*. Hemel Hempstead: Harvester/Wheatsheaf, 1994.
TH: Loiner	Sandie Byrne, ed., *Tony Harrison: Loiner*. Oxford: Clarendon Press, 1997.

NOTE ON THE TEXT

The Penguin paperback edition of Tony Harrison, *Theatre Works 1973–1985* is cited rather than the Bloodaxe Tony Harrison, *Dramatic Works 1973–1985*, which was published a year before, as the texts are identical, and the former is more readily available. The second edition of Harrison's *Selected Poems* is cited throughout, other than for references to *v.*, which are to the second edition ('with press articles', 1989), also containing commentary, reprinted articles, and illustrations. The third edition of Harrison's *Phaedra Britannica* (1976) is cited because it contains a longer version of the introductory essay by the author. The second edition (1991) of Harrison's *The Trackers of Oxyrhynchus* is cited rather than the first edition (1990), because the later work includes two versions of the play, one written for performances in the ancient stadium at Delphi in 1988, and the other for the National Theatre in London in 1990. References are to the National Threatre text unless stated. Harrison's *Newcastle is Peru* (1969), *A Kumquat for John Keats* (1981), and *Looking Up* (1979) were first published as illustrated leaflets or booklets, but, as these are now scarce, references are given to the poems' appearances in *SP*. Harrison's *The Fire-Gap* was also published as a poster/book by Bloodaxe Books in 1985, but as this consists of a single leaf, concertina-folded, references are given to *SP*. In quotation, all typographic conventions follow the styles of the texts cited, unless stated otherwise.

TO PHYLLIS, WITH LOVE

INTRODUCTION

Most reviews of Harrison's work begin by saying that it is concerned with division, or that it is dialectical. The aim of this book is to look at that division and dialectic through three important concepts represented by the letters 'H', '*v.*', and 'O'. H is 'the Big H' of the play of that name, the aspirant whose presence or absence (e.g. 'Unslet and 'Alifax) marks the division between the aspirational language of Standard English and Received Pronunciation (see Chapter 2, note 7) and the 'second-class' dialects and registers of [uz]. The lower-case italic *v.* (followed by a full stop as in the poem and film of that name) stands for 'all the versus of life'; both public and personal divisions and the unity and reconciliation which Harrison sometimes finds within them. The O is as polyvalent in Harrison's poetry as in *Hamlet*; as black O it is the abyss – of oblivion, death, and extinction – but also the star-filled night sky; as a circle it is the celebratory dance, and the light-filled acting-space of many of Harrison's plays; as a cry it proclaims lovers' pleasure, and as a drawn-out sung note it affirms the love of this fleeting life.

The common theme behind these three emblematic letters is articulation and its opposite, not only in the sense of meaningful utterance, but also of ligature and organisation. Linguistic articulation in Harrison's work both reinforces and is produced by social articulation, and personal identity. The divisions – social, personal, linguistic, cultural – are not a matter of equal halves, of dominant versus oppressed, or of self versus other, but of unequal, unreconciled segments, often as linked as they are opposed, and bound in relationships of tension, resistance, negotiation, and interpenetration.

Harrison's poetry is remarkably diverse. It is written in elegiac, lyric, narrative, and dramatic modes; for newspapers, periodicals, television, the theatre (metropolitan, provincial, operatic, musical, and amphi-), and public readings (though the texts are not necessarily exclusively dedicated to any one medium); it contains voices ranging from the didactic, the polemical, and the protesting to the contemplative and tender. Nor is it all straight-faced. The humour ranges from comic harangue to irony, vituperative epigram, and limerick.

Many of the poems' protagonists also seem to abound in ambi-

1

guities, inconsistencies, and paradoxes, and the images we have of the poet himself, through prefaces to the poetry, interviews, and secondary sources, do not add up to an unproblematical, easily-identified persona. Harrison makes a living from poetry, though much of his income is provided by royalties from libretti and theatrical scripts. By English standards he is a popular poet, yet his work is not populist. His position in the canon is uncertain; he is the subject of study in schools, and of much critical, but (relatively) little academic attention. He seems to typify urban man, yet produced some of his most admired poetry on themes suggested by life in rural Florida.[1] He is cosmopolitan and wide-ranging, yet inalienably urban Yorkshire. He has been President of the Classical Association, a champion of high culture, but depicts education as a process of rote-learning, ritual humiliation, and cultural kidnap. His language is usually accessible and often demotic, but his references and allusions are anything but parochial. Notoriously pessimistic and sceptical, he writes love poetry of calm security. He demands a radical voice for poetry, but imagines peace and unity achieved through personal relations, with the proviso that we should leave 'with the worn UNITED, one small v'.[2] Though he often seems to be writing from the margins and pushing at boundaries, he is not part of an avant-garde, and many of his forms and themes are rooted in the traditions of English poetry. It is tempting to see a mirror of his poetic persona in the character of Thomas Theophilus: 'a "half caste", embodying the tensions between Britain and India within himself',[3] but Harrison's network of connection and disconnection embodies more complex tensions than those between equal halves.

Writing of 'The Grey Rock',[4] Louis MacNeice describes 'Yeats's peculiar dialectic – eternity in love with the productions of time, the antagonism between gods and men who are divided by a gulf which demands to be bridged so that upon that bridge they can fight or love each other'. He suggests that in different poems 'Yeats appears to take different sides, an ambiguous partisan because he believes in the final resolution of the rivalry'.[5] Though Harrison's

---

1 See, for example 'Following Pine', *SP*, pp. 220–9.
2 *v.*, p. 41.
3 *Phaedra*, preface, pp. xxii–xxiii.
4 W. B. Yeats, *Responsibilities* (1914), in *The Variorum Edition of the Poetry of W. B. Yeats*, eds Peter Allt and Russell K. Alspach (London, 1957), pp. 270–6.
5 Louis MacNeice, *The Poetry of W. B. Yeats* (London, 1941), p. 112.

poetry does maintain a consistent commitment to certain precepts (his atheism and anti-war stance are most obvious examples), some of his allegiances (for example, to 'the lads') are more ambivalent. He could thus be described as 'an ambiguous partisan', but his poems do not predict an inevitable resolution to the conflicts they describe. Such resolutions and unifications as are offered are almost always conditional and temporary constructs. Like Seamus Heaney, Harrison could be seen as an 'amphibian'. He invokes the artists of eastern Europe: 'because there is something in their situation that makes them attractive [...] an unsettled aspect to the different worlds they inhabit, and one of the challenges they face is to survive amphibiously, in the realm of "the times", and the realm of their moral and artistic self-respect'.[6] Harrison's poetic 'I' is amphibian, but not because he adapts to suit his environment, each avatar suppressing or concealing the other. This is the bard who despises poetry as 'poncy',[7] and reminds himself that literacy is a privilege which has been an instrument of oppression,[8] and of 'the whole fatuity of the belief that writing poetry will *do* anything'.[9] Many of the poems are stories told against the poet.[10]

Yeats suggested that 'We make out of the quarrel with others, rhetoric, out of the quarrel with ourselves, poetry',[11] but Harrison blurs the distinctions between each half of those two pairings. Rhetoric, the persuasive function of language, associated with 'eloquence', is always a two-edged sword in Harrison's work. It can enlighten and preserve, but also deceive and control, and Harrison seems aware that in attempting the one he has to work hard to avoid being complicit with the other. For Yeats, 'the pursuit of one's opposite is also connected [...] with reincarnation'. The poet 'is always quarrelling with himself, perhaps because he half remembers himself in a past life as having been someone different', and those quarrels are 'partly, but only partly, resolved in [...] poetry'.[12] Harrison makes no claim to serial reincarnation, but he has been metamorphosed, 'translated' from one class to another, and in any

---

6 Seamus Heaney, *The Government of the Tongue* (London, 1988), introduction, p. xx.
7 See *Trackers*, p. 127.
8 See 'Interview', p. 231.
9 'Introduction', p. 14.
10 See 'Interview', p. 232.
11 MacNeice, *Poetry of W. B. Yeats*, p. 127.
12 MacNeice, *Poetry of W. B. Yeats*, p. 128.

case offers a complex (fictional) poetic identity which quarrels within itself and which, like his poetic arguments, is similarly unfixed and unresolved. The distinction between selves is, however, perhaps less clear in Harrison's poetry than in Yeats's. Yeats externalises the quarrel through a series of masks; his 'self' summons its opposites, alter egos and counterparts in order to deal with 'all / that I have handled least, least looked upon'.[13] Harrison's quarrel is, generally, between the various voices of his poetry, whether younger self, alter ego, or projection, but those oppositional voices do not exceed a discrete and encompassing single voice, of the narrative I.

Language and self, then, poetry and poet, and all the divisions they explore and encompass, as well as those things that silence them, are the subject of Harrison's work, and of this study of that work.

---

13 W. B. Yeats, 'Ego Dominus Tuus' (1919), *The Wild Swans at Coole, Variorum Edition*, p. 367.

CHAPTER 1

Divisions: some themes of Harrison's poetry[1]

Tony Harrison has famously stated that 'Poetry is all I write',[2] and he is, of course, first, last, and foremost, a poet, whether he is writing for the page, the stage, the screen, or any other medium. So it may seem perverse to begin with his prose. Though his poems generally speak for themselves, he has reflected on them in interviews, essays, and prefaces. In the introduction to his adaptation of Sophocles's satyr play *The Ichneutae*, he recaps the discovery at Oxyrhynchus of some four hundred lines, about half of which were complete or nearly complete. He discusses the problem of textual reclamation, the basic plots of satyr plays, the Homeric hymn to Hermes, in Classical Greek and nineteenth-century English versions, and variations on the myth of Apollo's acquisition of the lyre – a theme of satyr plays. Pursuing this erudite matter with awesome scholarly acumen, Harrison writes:

> there is an alternative version to this story of the tranquil takeover of the lyre [...] In the Valley of the Muses, near Askra, the birthplace of Hesiod, in Euboea [...] there was once, according to Pausanias, who saw it, a bronze of Apollo and Hermes *fighting* for the lyre [...] There were also other cautionary bronzes. There was a statue of Thamyris shown blind, with his lyre shattered at his feet. He was blinded for his presumption in offering competition on the lyre. Near by was a statue of Linus, killed by Apollo for offering him rivalry in singing. Pausanias doesn't mention that there was a bronze of Marsyas, the satyr, flayed alive for competing on the flute against Apollo's lyre. For the divine patron of music and poetry, the Parnassian supremo, this is appalling savagery, but this pugnacity and paranoid possessiveness are

---

1 For a chronological survey of Harrison's work to 1996, and an examination of his publications as material artefacts, see *TH: Loiner*, introduction, pp. 1–27.
2 *Tony Harrison*, Contemporary Writers Series (London, 1987), reprinted in *Bloodaxe 1*, p. 9.

characteristic of Apollo's early transition from macho cowpoke to cultural impresario. Rival lyre players, singers, upstart satyr flautists, flayed, butchered, blinded, were set up as deterrents in the Valley of the Muses and elsewhere.[3]

The language of scholarship is suddenly subverted by demotic, humorous, even facetious throwaway remarks which make the material newly striking, newly accessible. The themes are characteristically Harrison as well: Classical drama, Classical mythology, Classical aggro; the satyrs, the flaying of Marsyas, class struggle, art; machismo. The introduction goes on to recount a (possibly apocryphal) story (and this juxtaposition of the anecdotal and mythical with the historical is also typical) which links past and present, myth and history, and everything and Harrison, in a very characteristic way.

> The Roman emperors Augustus and Nero both loved to dress up as Apollo and it was probably the lyre of Apollo that Nero 'fiddled' on while Rome went up in flames, a cool behaviour long endorsed by Apollo himself. A few months ago in Nicosia I saw a sign saying 'Apollo: Quality Underwear' and I suppose the Y-front endorsement is appropriate, as the male ego has had eons of Apollonian support. His contemporary endorsements include an answering machine and a particularly repellent form of torture used in the prisons of Iran. In some manifestations Apollo would not have shied away from the vast statue that Hitler had planned for him in Berlin. And yet, everywhere, his image is at the apex of the pediment of our palace of art.[4]

Manifestations of Apollo, the embodiment of Olympian high art, and his/its relationship to oppression, to torture, and to Y-fronts (or male ego and its supports) are central to Harrison's version of Sophocles's satyr play, *Trackers*, and to much of his writing. Like this introduction, *Trackers* itself uses heavy-handed humour and slapstick which is abruptly cut up by a serious or horrific image.

Like a Tarantino film which switches genres in mid-scene, and ends up unclassifiable, a Harrison poem or verse-play may be any combination of tragic, comic, anecdotal, historical, tender, bruising, moving, didactic, intimate, lyrical, satirical, and sickening. The conventions of forms as well as themes are transgressed or

---

3 *Trackers*, introduction, p. xix.
4 *Trackers*, introduction, p. xx.

combined. The 'School of Eloquence' poems have the sixteen lines of the Meredithian sonnet, and are concerned with love and loss, but few sonnets include references to tattoos, brown ale, and Newcastle United, or to 'Teenage dole-wallah piss-up'.[5] Nor are sonnets usually broken up into 2, 2, 5, 3, 1, 1, 1, 1 in order to ironise and make painfully poignant their title, as 'A Close One' does.[6] 'Deathwatch Danceathon' has impeccable iambic tetrameter couplets, but how many grand odes to the activities of Royalty would rhyme 'infested infrastructure' with 'bugger's fucked yer'?[7] Not many break words across the line to rhyme 'solitary Chair- / o-planes through whistling air',[8] or:

> Swirled detritus and driftwood pass
> in state the 1880 *Sas-*
> *inena Cold Storage Co.*[9]

Harrison's mature poetry is not difficult. It might cite specialist or scholarly works; it might quote in Latin, Greek, or other languages; it might contain obscure references; it might use long words; but it always has an obvious subject, and always makes a series of clear statements. Many of the early poems are difficult. Those collected in *Earthworks*, sprinkled with references to life (in abstract, conception, birth), death in abstract (suicide, stillbirth), and earth (tangled growth, roses, waste lands) are both claustrophobic and unfocused; their clusters of referents enigmatic. The earliest poems (published in the Leeds University School of English magazine *Poetry and Audience*) are ponderous, prolix, and opaque. The subject of 'When Shall I Tune My "Doric Reed"?', for example, is not immediately obvious.

> These fumbling mistrals, cymbal sharp and sudden,
> Recklessly trundled from No-man's North,
> Grind in a frozen list the cindered wood's deep tree,
> As green diapason shrivels the tinsel horns; rind
> And saurian fingers grip the raving hermit in each root,
> And darkly in the frost rancid earth
> The aching colours harden [. . . .]

---

5 'Divisions', *SP*, p. 173.
6 *SP*, p. 160.
7 *Guardian* (12 October 1998).
8 *Newcastle*, p. 64.
9 *Newcastle*, p. 65.

I shun the malingering of wind on frost
Nor hope when from Dog-days gutted sound
Limp old myths of hot slipseed ground in gristle querns,
But, a Nestor of bricks, as life leaps in venal fits,
I poise in steel, a quadrant above the cradled season.
I watch for red or pallor of soil,
The mean I have sometimes lost[10]

The poems published after Harrison had 'thawed out my tongue on a Nigerian version of *Lysistrata*',[11] and visited Prague[12] are no longer mystifying. They are sometimes complex, and always rich, but they have a directness, a crispness, and an energy which bears the reader on and over words which would have been obstacles in the earlier works. It's as much a matter of metre as of lexis or syntax. Harrison had arrived at the varied iambic pentameter or tetrameter couplets or alternately rhymed lines that were to be his theme tune. Three poems published in *London Magazine* in July 1967 were subsequently collected in *Loiners* and, rightly, set in the concrete of *SP*.[13] The three themes: H (divisions of class and race, language), *v.* (opposition, dialectic, energy/aggression), and O (the nothingness of the black O, and its opposition – life, memory, art – in the *orchestra* of the white O) are already present in these relatively early poems. Like a series of postcards, each depicts an event or encounter, or is an encounter, with a memorable character, and thus has a focus and concentration that the *Earthworks* poems lack.

'The Curtain Catullus' has all the *brio*, insouciance, and confidence of Harrison's later work.

Your fat, failed ballet dancer's calves
Bulge left, right, left. I'm out of breath and stop
To get a peep in at the skirted halves,
Those pale four inches past the stocking top.
That sight's more in my line. I'm not so sold
On all this Gothic and this old Baroque.[14]

---

10 T. W. Harrison, 'When Shall I Tune My "Doric Reed"?', *Poetry and Audience*, 4, no. 11 (25 January 1957).

11 'The Inkwell of Dr Agrippa', in *Bloodaxe 1*, p. 34. (First published in Jeremy Robson, ed., *Corgi Modern Poets in Focus: 4* (London, 1971) but without its title.)

12 He taught at the University of Ahmadu Bello from 1962 to 1966, and at Charles University, Prague, from 1966 to 1967.

13 'The Curtain Catullus', 'The White Queen I', and 'Thomas Campey and the Copernican System', *London Magazine*, new series, 7, no. 4 (July 1957).

14 *SP*, p. 52.

'Thomas Campey and the Copernican System' introduces other avatars of the mature poet; the one who can induce feelings of pity, guilt, impotence, and embarrassment in the space of two lines; the local poet who uses Leeds and other northern locations,[15] named characters, and specific objects; the poet of the material.

> Thomas Campey, who, in each demolished home,
> Cherished a Gibbon with a giltworked spine,
> Spengler and Mommsen, and a huge, black tome
> With Latin titles for his own decline:
>
> *Tabes dorsalis*; veins like flex, like fused
> and knotted flex, with a cart on the cobbled road,
> He drags for life old clothing, used
> Lectern bibles and cracked Copeland Spode,
>
> Marie Corelli, Ouida and Hall Caine
> And texts from Patience Strong in tortoise frames.
> And every pound of this dead weight is pain
> To Thomas Campey (books)[16]

The first section of 'The White Queen' not only introduces Harrison the observer of sexuality, ex-pat grotesques, and imperialism in decay, but also shows that the powerful personality of the poetic 'I' can also extinguish itself in order to ventriloquise the first of many Loiners' voices.

> I hang about *The Moonshine* and *West End*,
> Begging for pure sex, one unembarrassed friend
> To share my boredom and my bed – *One masta want*
> *One boy – one boy for bed* ... and like an elephant
> That bungles with its trunk about its cage,
> I make my half-sloshed entrances and rage
> Like any normal lover when I come
> Before I've managed it.[17]

During his time in Nigeria, Harrison had collaborated with James

---

15 An earlier protagonist kicks stalks of London Pride on 'half-built sites the length and breadth of Leeds', but the cityscape of the poem could be any urban wasteland. See 'The Flat Dweller's Revolt', *Earthworks*, pp. 5–6. For a discussion of the poem, see Desmond Graham, *TH: Loiner*, pp. 29–41.
16 *SP*, p. 13.
17 *SP*, pp. 21–2.

Simmons to produce an adaptation of the *Lysistrata* of Aristophanes. *Aikin Mata*[18] is not a literal translation, rather it translates the specific circumstances of fifth-century Athens to those of twentieth-century Africa, and Attic and Doric Greek to Standard and Pidgin English but keeps intact the structure, themes, and bawdy energy of Classical comedy. Translation, adaptation, importation, and cross-fertilisation – intertextuality, to use a much over-worked word – became Harrison's element, and the means by which he produced some of his best poetry. In 'The White Queen', Harrison brings this heterogeneous quality to non-dramatic poetry, setting reference against reference, form against form, and genre against genre, as he also sets voice against voice and stance against stance. Fourteen lines of 'The White Queen' are modelled on part of Sir Thomas Wyatt's ('They flee from me').

> They flee from me that sometime did me seek
> With naked foot stalking in my chamber.
> I have seen them gentle, tame, and meek
> That now are wild and do not remember
> That sometime they put themself in danger
> To take sometime they put themself in danger
> To take bread at my hand; and now they range
> Busily seeking with a continual change.
>
> Thanked be fortune it hath been otherwise
> Twenty times better, but once in special,
> In thin array after a pleasant guise,
> When her loose gown from her shoulders did fall,
> And she me caught in her arms long and small,
> Therewithal sweetly did me kiss,
> And softly said, 'Dear heart, how like you this?'[19]
>
> Things can be so much better. Once at least
> A million per cent. Policeman! Priest!
> You'll call it filthy, but to me it's love,
> And to him it was. It *was*. O he could move
> Like an oiled (slow-motion) racehorse at its peak,
> Outrageous, and not gentle, tame, or meek –
> O magnificently shameless in his gear,
> He sauntered the flunkied restaurant, queer

---

18 Ibadan, 1966.
19 *Sir Thomas Wyatt, The Collected Poems*, ed. Kenneth Muir (London, 1949), p. 28.

As a clockwork orange and not scared.
God, I was grateful for the nights we shared.
My boredom melted like small cubes of ice
In warm sundowner whiskies. Call it vice;
Call it obscenity; it's love; so there;
Call it what you want. *I just don't care.*[20]

The technique used here is neither straightforward imitation nor adaptation. The narrative voices of the canonical poem of conventional heterosexual courtly love and of the modern (and at the time) little-known poem of homosexual rented sex in one sense could hardly be more different, but their tones – salivating reminiscence, bitter protest, and self-pity – are the same, as their relationship to the beloved is the same. The section

> mirrors Wyatt's own inversion of Petrarchan images of the idealized love-object (as huntress rather than hind). Just as the conventions of courtly love depict an only apparent inversion of a power relationship in the servitude of the courtier and the imperious indifference of the Lady, so Harrison's Queen depicts a beautiful object of desire whose superficial power of accepting or rejecting his clients masks far greater inequalities between them.[21]

Both the Queen and Wyatt's narrator take it upon themselves to declare the feelings of their lovers; the Queen insisting that it was love, Wyatt implying that his lover pursued him willingly, and quoting her seductive speech (*'dere hert, howe like you this?'*). In each case, the [white] man tells the story:

> the narrative voice enables him to attribute thoughts and feelings to the characters [...] just as his coins give [the Queen] the power to manipulate the actions of the rent boys [...] Though at first we share the narrator's bitterness, sympathizing with the steadfast lover against the newfangled, changeable woman in her 'straunge fasshion of forsaking', on a second reading we might wonder whether the two are so neatly opposed as victim and perpetrator, hero and villainess. We realize that the narrator is reproaching the woman for ceasing 'to take bred' from his hands, and thus provide the occasions when for him it was 'twenty tymes better', and for her, and perhaps him as well, there was danger [...] Harrison handles our sympathies as skilfully as Wyatt. When the Queen shouts 'And to him it was. It *was.*' he protests too much –

---

20 'The White Queen 1: Satyrae 1', *SP*, p. 22.
21 Byrne, 'On Not Being Milton, Marvell, or Gray', *TH: Loiner*, p. 58.

almost – just as when Wyatt's narrator insists: 'It was no dreme: I lay brode waking', though he is clearly convincing himself; we do believe him, or at least believe that he believes it.[22]

One other poem which survived into *Loiners* and *SP* was published before Harrison went to Nigeria, and even before *Earthworks*, but though the title remained the same, the 'Ghosts: Some Words Before Breakfast' in *Poetry and Audience*[23] is very different from that in *Loiners*.[24] The epigram to the *Poetry and Audience* version, 'I gave you life', sets the theme. At the centre is a narrator divided between an ardent lust for life and the filial duty which demands that he repress the instinct which makes him feel most alive – the sexual impulses owed by youth to a man 'not twenty three'. Thus, the woman who reminds him that 'I gave you life' also denies him the ability to give life himself, to bring 'love and peace' to 'wife and children'. This putative wife, the narrator's lover, appears only as 'you', the other in the secret trysts, the subject of the suspicions which surface in the mother's dreams, and the vehicle of the narrator's fantasy of love and peace in his dreams.

> I used to dream of murder, war
> And rape behind that solid door
> You closed against the night and hate
> When we together long and late,
> Two lovers of more ardent kind,
> To all but blinded love were blind.
> My mother dreamt you bore a child;
> Accused me, said that I defiled
> Myself and you with thoughtless lust
> My conjured senses, call from dust
> Made war, and peace; I had to say
> We would not meet again that way.

In the revised version she becomes more tangible, and the whole poem has expanded, just as the epigraph has been replaced by a dedication, '*for Jane*', and two quotations, an inscription from the *League of Friends* rest room in the Royal Victoria Infirmary, Newcastle-upon-Tyne, and '*C'est mon unique soutien au monde, à*

22 Byrne, Introduction, *TH: Loiner*, pp. 21–2.
23 *Poetry and Audience*, 7, no. 22 (20 May 1960), pp. 6–7. The poem was subsequently included in *Poetry and Audience 1953–60*, ed. A. R. Mortimer *et al.* (Leeds, 1961).
24 *Loiners*, pp. 91–6.

Divisions

présent!' (It's my only support in the world, at present!') from Rimbaud's *Oeuvres*. The poem's centre has become a threefold relationship: between the narrator and his mother, wife, and daughter. The crisis which has occasioned the poem and determined its location, a terrible accident which has left the daughter in a critical condition, links the three generations of women, female fertility and sexuality (active or repressed), Newcastle, and the past, through the poet. 'Ghosts' becomes, like *Newcastle*[25] and 'Durham',[26] a circular journey through a city, in this case the wards of its hospital, and through a nightmarish day/night, but mostly through the memories and preoccupations of a psyche. In this second poem, the dream has come true; the child, 'the one we married for', has been conceived, but also lost, in stillbirth; another child has been born, and nearly lost to the accident. The long-desired peace has not come (the narrator refuses even the oblivion offered by Newcastle Brown from 'this newest sorrow'), and love is no longer an uncomplicated consummation greatly to be desired, but something much more polyvalent.

> I stoop to kiss away your pain
> through stuff like florist's cellophane,
> but my kiss can't make you less
> the helpless prey of Nothingness –
> *ring-a-ring-a-roses* ... love
> goes gravewards but does move.
> Love's not something you can hoard
> against the geriatric ward.

All that's preserved from the first version is the location in the 'no man's land' 'Between night and dawn', when the ghosts of memory form a *ring-a-roses* chain, which is the same whether entered from Leeds bedroom or Newcastle waiting room, and one phrase, 'the next descent of night', about which the narrator is still afraid. The longed-for peace has not been achieved; the ghosts still walk; but some kind of accommodation has been made with the dead, the guilt, the women.

> An orderly brings tea and toast.
> Mother, wife and daughter, ghost –
> I've laid, laid, laid, laid
> you, but I'm still afraid,

25 See *SP*, pp. 63–8.
26 See *SP*, pp. 69–71.

> though now Newcastle's washed with light,
> about the next descent of night.

If Harrison's mature poetry is not incomprehensible or opaque, it is difficult in other senses. The forms he chooses are, of course, difficult to compose. As he says: 'I still find it all almost impossibly difficult, but the difference is now that [...] in the words of Yeats, "difficulty is our plough".'[27] The physical appearance of the poems is also difficult, in that it retards smooth and easy reading, and sometimes represents the pained and laboured articulation which is its subject.

> The forms I taught myself [...] are now enactments of unresolved existential problems, of personal energies in ambiguous conflict with the stereotype, sexual, racial, political, national. The themes, like Zarate's *History of Peru*, are about discovery *and* conquest; celebration and defeat.[28]

Widely spaced lines, broken lines, a mixture of typographical styles (italic, bold, Gothic, small caps, large caps, the phonetic alphabet ...) and languages (English, French, German, Latin, Greek ...), acronyms, abbreviation, parentheses, asterixes, footnotes ... ensure that the poems are never homogenised, pre-digested verse purée.

> A *Scottish & Newcastle* clops
> past the RVI and traffic stops [....]
> Red splashes on a LADIES floor ...
> *inter urinam et faeces nasc-*
> *imur* ... issues of blood [....][29]

> αἰαῖ, ay, ay! ... stutterer Demosthenes
> gob full of pebbles outshouting seas -

> 4 words only of *mi 'art aches* and [....]

> All poetry (even Cockney Keats?) you see
> 's been dubbed by [ʌs] into RP [....]

> 'We say [ʌs] not [uz], T.W.!'[30]

> What ur-𝔖𝔭𝔯𝔞𝔠𝔥𝔢 did the labour speak?
> ur ur ur to t'master's 𝔖𝔭𝔯𝔞𝔠𝔥𝔢

---

27 'Inkwell of Dr Agrippa', p. 33.
28 'Inkwell of Dr Agrippa', pp. 33-4.
29 'Ghosts', *SP*, p. 72 ('[Man is] born between urine and faeces').
30 'Them & [uz]', *SP*, p. 122.

the hang-cur ur-grunt of the weak
the unrecorded urs of gobless workers[31]

I've left some spaces (   )[1]
benumbed by morphia and Methadone
until the (   )[2] of April, (   )[3]
When I began these lines could I have known
that the nurse's registration of the time
you let your spirit go with one last groan
would help complete the first and third line rhyme [....]

   1.   How you stayed alive
   2.   4th
   3.   10.05[32]

These never slip down so easily that their message is missed, or their production taken for granted. The effort required to read these poems, especially for RP readers hurtled down an exuberant couplet at whose end is the Beecher's Brook vowel (Stick to the southern pronunciation and ally yourself with [ʌs], as well as spoil the rhyme? Try to produce a natural northern [æ] and risk sounding affected or – horrors – patronising?) is great. Harrison has said that, when he is 'conscious of satisfying the literate, cultured reader of poetry', he knows that 'my next temptation is take away his satisfaction by evoking the ghosts of the inarticulate, and by quoting them in the scale against poetry'.[33]

'Book Ends I' exploits typographical and phonetic obstruction and retardation to reinforce its meaning.

> Baked the day she suddenly dropped dead
> we chew it slowly that last apple pie.
>
> Shocked into sleeplessness you're scared of bed.
> We never could talk much, and now don't try.
>
> *You're like book ends, the pair of you*, she'd say,
> *Hog that grate, say nothing, sit, sleep, stare* ...
>
> *The 'scholar' me, you, worn out on poor pay*,
> only our silence made us seem a pair.
>
> Not as good for staring in, blue gas,
> too regular each bud, each yellow spike.

31 'The Bonebard Ballads 1: The Ballad of Babelabour', *SP*, p. 102.
32 'The Heartless Art', *SP*, p. 208.
33 'Interview', *Bloodaxe 1*, p. 232.

A night you need my company to pass
and she not here to tell us we're alike!

Your life's all shattered into smithereens.

Back in our silences and sullen looks,
for all the Scotch we drink, what's still between 's
not the thirty or so years, but books, books, books.[34]

The first two lines, with no simile, metaphor, or other poetic device, seem straightforward enough, but their syntax is not quite ordinary, and it imposes a slightly strained reading. In everyday speech, they would probably become something like: 'We slowly chew the final apple pie that she baked the day she suddenly dropped dead,' or 'That final apple pie she baked the day she suddenly dropped dead, we chew it slowly', because we don't usually substitute the pronoun 'it' for a noun-phrase (such as 'apple pie') before we have introduced the noun-phrase. The word choice imposes a grammatical structure; the sentence is divided into clauses: 'Baked the day she suddenly dropped dead' and 'We chew it slowly, that last apple pie'. The first poetic line leads us to expect a subject – the thing that has been baked – but postpones fulfilling the expectation by moving to the protagonists of the poem: 'we'. 'We chew it slowly' again defers giving us the information we expect: what is 'it'? The line is jointed by 'that', and the break reinforced by the pause we make as we muster our tongue and lips to move from the lateral followed by short front close vowel to the voiced dental fricative (i.e. from 'slow*ly*' to '*th*at'; from spread lips and raised tongue to the tongue on the teeth and the lips closer together). So the whole weight of grammatical, sound, and information stress is therefore on 'that last apple pie'. This in turn sets up another weight, of significance, which will fall on the words to be linked with 'dropped dead' and 'apple pie' in lines 3 and 4: 'scared of bed' and 'now don't try'. The parallel established through the repetition of sound emphasises another series of parallels.

Lines 1 and 2 depict a group, a 'we' doing something together. Given that the 'we' from 'now' don't try to talk, they must have tried 'then', the immediate past of the poem, before the death. Thus the baker of the pie, 'she', whose voice is about to be heard in lines

---

34 *SP*, p. 126. Compare Philip Larkin, 'An April Sunday Brings the Snow', *Collected Poems*, ed. Anthony Thwaite (London, 1990), p. 21.

5 and 6, was the agent of connection. Her absence removes the binding, disconnects the 'book ends' who themselves were parallel not through identicality but through a gratuitous common posture: their silent symmetry on either side of the fire, which *to her* made them *seem* a pair. The structure of the poem echoes its theme of connection and disconnection, and impels us to make connections retrospectively. Thus, 'blue gas', which we would expect to be the subject of the verb-phrase 'is not as good for staring in', is positioned like an adjunct in line 9, making us think back to just what it was that the flame is, as well as forward, to its qualities ('too regular, each bud'). Similarly, *'like book ends'* in line 5 echoes and helps to explain the title of the poem, and is further parallelled by the repetition of the word 'books' three times in the last line. This final image gives a retrospective gloss to the title, and to the poem. The two men are not twinned as a pair, and thus represented as close; the focus on the things *between* book ends puts the emphasis on what holds them apart.

I called 'Ghosts' a journey, but of course it has no destination. The poem is both narrative and dramatic monologue; a drama played out between the life- force (will, memory, libido, creativity) of the narrator and the darkness which threatens to destabilise or overwhelm it. The location is the *orchestra*, the acting or dancing space of the narrator's mind literalised, here, as the poem, and elsewhere as the light-filled O of the Greek theatre, and by extension Harrison's stages and screens. He describes:

> the creation of what I call my 'orchestra' in the sense I later learned for that Greek word meaning 'circular dancing place'. This 'orchestra' became my first brooding ground and, I think, the first intimation of what for me is the basic struggle of art [....] we were celebrating [...] VJ (Victory over Japan) night with a large bonfire in the back street outside our house. The atmosphere was more celebratory than I can ever remember [....] It went on all night [....] when the space was cleared the celebratory bonfire had left a black circle of scorched cobbles with thick scars of tar [....] Looking into that circle I once thought of it as the nightsky globe totally devoid of stars, an annihilated universe [....] It was in this starless shape [...] that I learned to relate our celebratory fire [...] to that terrible form of fire that brought about the 'VJ' when unleashed on Hiroshima and Nagasaki in August 1945.[35]

35 *Trackers*, introduction, p. vii.

The struggle, then, is between light and dark, or life and all that opposes it, but it is also a struggle to contain both. 'One element for celebration and terror. One space for the celebrant and the sufferer.'

If Harrison creates consolations and refuges from antagonisms and divisions, he does not suggest that division can be healed, or neutralised, by poetry, by revolution, or by anything else; and this, I think, is one of his strengths. If art, as *Trackers* asserts, enables opposites to inhabit the same space, it does not make one dilute the other. Art carries out its function of filling the void (the black O) by creating a meeting space for the contradictory aspects of humankind (*v.*). The public space of the *orchestra* becomes the site of the co-existence of irreconcilable opposites: celebration and tragedy; cruelty and love; creative art and destructive war. This notional circle filled with light, opposing the black O, is realised in *Bow Down* by the actors and musicians standing in a ring which becomes the acting space. Thus the empty circle has come to mean not just annihilation but the place where art can bring together cause and effect, suffering and celebration, condemnation and affirmation, and the 'struggle of art' is to find a style which 'permitted the sufferer and the celebrant to share the same space'.[36]

'Life', in Harrison's work, has the same sort of mystical over-tones as it does for Leavis and D. H. Lawrence. Like Keats, Harrison appears to seek a life (or poetry) of that complex thing sensation,[37] but to love this 'fleeting life'[38] is not just to seek height-ened experience; it becomes a kind of imaginative hedonism, and a sense of the individual's being in a continuum with both the natural world and other people. Discussing the 'shared light' of the Greek theatre, Harrison writes: 'since the expression "to see the light" in Greek means to live, the final sense is that of shared *life*'.[39] 'Life' is equated with an individuality, openness to experience and engage-ment with ideas, refusal of repression, and a vigorous physicality. The opposite of 'life' is that which renders silent, still, empty, or

---

36 *Trackers*, introduction, p. viii.
37 See *The Letters of John Keats, 1814–1821*, ed. Hyder Edward Rollins (Cambridge, Mass., 1958), vol. 1, p. 185, and *John Keats's Anatomical and Physiological Notebook*, ed. Maurice Buxton Forman (Oxford, 1934), pp. 55–6. For an excellent analysis of Keats's use of the term, see Stuart M. Sperry, *Keats the Poet* (Princeton, 1994), p. 29.
38 See the refrain in *Banquet*, e.g. p. 54.
39 *Trackers*, introduction, p. x.

uniform – in Harrison's poetry, age, poverty, oppression, ignorance, fire, snow, war, femininity (in some aspects), and death. By implication this is extended to adherence to the formal and thematic conventions of literature.

The protagonists of Harrison's poems are often artists or others who love, or are full of, 'life', or whose work has in some way immortalised their lives. In *Banquet*, for example, Voltaire's bust could stand for an immortalised Voltaire, or at least the life-affirming spirit of his work. Harrison uses busts and statues in several plays and poems. Byron's statue in Hyde Park joins Voltaire at the banquet, and there are Queen Victoria in *Newcastle*, and 'Ghosts', Goethe, Schiller, Heine, Achilles, and the Gorgon in *Gorgon*, and a golden Prometheus in the film of that name. Even *Trackers'* Kyllene in her pediment head-dress resembles a caryatid, while in 'Me Tarzan' the 'bodiless head' of the boy leaning out of the attic window brings to the scholar's mind the bust of Cicero which very likely graced the library of Leeds Grammar School. Perhaps there is an opposition here between the individual distinguished from the masses by birth, achievement, or as an artistic re/creation, whose image, name, and thus individuality is preserved by posterity, and the worker whose literal insignificance condemns him or her to oblivion as part of an undistinguished mass, preserved, if at all, only in piles of bones.[40] In *Poetry or Bust*, depiction in marble becomes a literalised emblem of immortalisation and canonisation.

Francis Chantrey
Everyone wants fame. The whole world's queuing.
All the most powerful, those nearest to the throne,
queuing for Chantrey to carve them out of stone.
(*The sound of chisels is heard again.*)
They know their mortal face is just to moulder
unless Chantrey charms their likeness from a boulder.[41]

The 'Airedale bard', John Nicholson, craves this mark of posterity's approbation of his work, but has to pay for it himself, and acquires only the cut-price version: 'Not marble, mind. Just plaster'.[42] The ersatz likeness which he is cozened into paying for is not even his

40 See 'The Ballad of Babelabour', *SP*, pp. 102–3, and 'The Earthern Lot', *SP*, p. 179.
41 *Poetry or Bust, Plays 3*, p. 30.
42 *Poetry or Bust*, p. 34.

own, but a chiselled-down reproduction of Walter Scott. Besides the guineas, the play shows the other cost of the bust, the baby which starves while its father pursues fame. Nicholson's second wife, Mary, says:

> She isn't plaster,
> though she's as cold as marble and as white.
> She was warm flesh and blood till t'other night.
> Call your Francis Chartrey, maybe – maybe
> he can knock you up a marble baby.[43]

The statues perhaps perform the same function as the stylised characterisations of Harrison's pantomime/magic show plays such as *Square Rounds*, allowing him to avoid the problems of ventriloquising more evidently 'real' characters. Though the Iraqi soldier whose death inspired 'Coming' was real, the very nature of his death, in fire which renders all distinguishing marks down to the common denominator of charred meat, made him a universal soldier, an Everyman, on to whom Harrison's feelings on war could be displaced.

Similarly, the dessicated corpse in *Mimmo Perrella Non è Piu*, one of the programmes in the *Loving Memory* series written and presented by Harrison for the BBC, is endowed with his wife's displaced emotions, and those of the poet, both of whom watch the exhumation.[44] Another programme in the series, *Cheating the Void*, could be interpreted as an acknowledgement of the poet's inability to fill or to escape the big O. An early scene shows Harrison running an old film (the first moving picture, he tells us), in which the doors of a large building open to release a group of people. They spill on to the pavement, talking, laughing, weaving between companions, bicycles, and dogs. 'These people are all dead, and yet they walk', Harrison's voice-over says.[45] The spurious life given to images, negatives, and shadows by cinematic art is accorded the spurious status of immortalisation. The film's reiterated bald statements suggest an already lost, futile struggle:

---

43 *Poetry or Bust*, pp. 39–40. There may be an echo here of Ezra Pound's opposition of true alabaster and ersatz plaster in 'Hugh Selwyn Mauberley: Life and Contacts', *Collected Shorter Poems* (London, 1968), p. 206.
44 *Loving Memory: The Muffled Bells; Mimmo Perrella Non è Piu; Cheating the Void; Letters in the Rock*, BBC TV (July–August 1987). Mimmo Perella is a Neopolitan man whose body we see exhumed after five years in the caustic volcanic soil of his city has dried and preserved it like a leathery mummy.
45 *Cheating the Void, Shadow*, p. 93.

> Oblivion that all our art defies.
> Oblivion where all of us must go.[46]

The title, however, suggests that it is none the less compulsive:

> Oblivion is darkness, memory light.
> They're locked in eternal struggle. Which
> of these two forces really shows its might
> when death's doors are thrown open by a switch?[47]

Perhaps there is a tension here between Harrison's dark and light sides; the working-class Yorkshireman with the Anglo-Saxon sense of impending night, winter, death, and anonymous, unrecalled oblivion, and the light-loving, life-affirming poet who knows that his image and artistic creations will, in a sense, cheat that oblivion.

Nowhere is Harrison more characteristically life-affirming and simultaneously keenly aware of the inevitable end of life than in *Kumquat*. This embodiment of all Harrison's divisions (other than class) is enriched by, but does not require, comparison with D. H. Lawrence's 'Medlars and Sorb Apples' and 'Figs',[48] as well as Keats's 'Ode to a Nightingale' and 'Ode on Melancholy'.

---

46 *Cheating the Void*, p. 94.
47 *Cheating the Void*, p. 93.
48. D. H. Lawrence, *Selected Poems* (Harmondsworth, 1950), pp. 43–8.

CHAPTER 2

The Big H: Tony Harrison's translation class

> The ladder of aspiration, the more you aspire
> the more your aspiration will take you higher.
> Those who drop their aitches fall and break their necks.
> But those with proper aspirations end up REX and LEX!
>
> End to end laid aitches are a ladder to the top,
> so never never let me hear your aitches drop.[1]

Herod, the 'h-fiend' incarnate,[2] brings home the lesson to the schoolchildren of Leeds: power (Latin: *rex*), the law (Latin: *lex*), and the word (Greek: *lexis*) are inextricably linked. *The Big H*'s association of those who disparage the dropped 'h' with those who drop the 'H' bomb indicates the significance with which Harrison invests the theme of language and power.[3] Word-power, for Harrison, is not just a matter of *how* words are spoken, but also of *which* words, and *whether* they are articulated 'properly', or at all. *'My father still reads the dictionary every day. He says your life depends on your power to master words.'*[4] In Harrison's poetry, the illiterate or inarticulate have no defence against the injustice brought about by legalese, bureau-babble, and other mystification.

> The dumb go down in history and disappear
> and not one gentleman's been brought to book:

---

1 *The Big H*, p. 336. *The Big H* was commissioned by BBC Television as a nativity play for December 1984.
2 See Richard Mutimer's 'struggles with the h-fiend' in George Gissing's *Demos* (London, 1886).
3 Harrison's 'h'-dropping boy hero redeems the three Herods, 'curing' Leeds of the pernicious 'h' so that the city's sign posts point to 'Unslett', 'Alifax', and 'Ull', and, appositely, a linguist has suggested that the loss of 'h' in some types of English could be viewed 'as therapy' because it 'is wiping out an exception in the otherwise symmetrical organization of fricatives'. Jean Aitchison, *Language Change: Progress or Decay?* (Cambridge, 1991), p. 210.
4 Arthur Scargill, used as the epigraph to *v.*, p. 5.

The Big H

Mes den hep tavas a-gollas y dyr

(Cornish) –
'the tongueless man gets his land took.'[5]

Articulacy is not, of course, confined to native speakers of Standard English, but in Harrison's poetry the mnemonic feats of illiterate workers, verbal dexterity of 'turns' such as 'Professor' Leon Cortez,[6] and literacy fostered by the Mechanics' Institutes and Workers' Education Associations, are discounted by, if not inaudible to, [ʌs]. In 'Them & [uz]', [ʌs], represented by the schoolmaster governed by the precepts of Daniel Jones,[7] silences the young T. W. Harrison's essay (in the Leeds demotic he calls [uz]) into canonical poetry.

> 4 words only of *mi 'art aches* and ... 'Mine's broken,
> you barbarian, T. W.'

This 'School of Eloquence' taught that standards of living were largely determined by (and determined) the extent to which Standard English was interiorised. It need not be absorbed as a first language, of course; the 'Scholarship Boy', for example, could acquire Standard English from school, in which case it might, for him, remain a register with a distinct field, or his native regional and social dialect might be marginalised as a register inappropriate outside the home.[8] In Harrison's work, attaining linguistic privilege entails a severance from the cultural heritage of dialect. Prescribed language, whether Classical Latin or Standard English, extracts a price for the access it gives to high culture:

---

5 'National Trust', *SP*, p. 121.

6 A dedicatee of the two-part poem 'Them & [uz]', *SP*, pp. 122–3.

7 Author of *The English Pronouncing Dictionary* (1917), who gave further currency to the term 'RP' (Received Pronunciation), first used in the late nineteenth century, and offered as a standard of 'correct' speech that of public school-educated natives of the south of England. Jones also used the term 'Public School English', or PSE, to describe the form of English he presented but, to do him justice, he did assert that he did not believe in 'the feasibility of imposing one particular form of pronunciation on the English-speaking world', and that he took the view 'that people should be allowed to speak as they like' (seventh edn (New York, 1946)) preface, p. x. The phonetic symbols indicate the sounds in the word 'us'. [ʌs] stands for the collective of Received Pronunciation speakers, while [uz] stands for those who speak with a northern or other accent.

8 See Richard Hoggart, *The Uses of Literacy* (London, 1971), especially pp. 291–304.

And so the lad who gets the alphas works
the hardest in his class at his translation
and finds good Ciceronian for Burke's:

a dreadful schism in the British nation.[9]

The last line embodies Harrison's equivocal attitude to and use of language. His poetry shows someone who did work hard at both literary translations and a literal translation from 'barbarian' outside the pale to resident in the *civitas* of the 'School of Eloquence', but using the linguistic skills which he mastered in the process to describe the dreadful schism he had thereby encountered. The catch is that the protest is part of the problem. The medium which exposes the cultural hegemony is a product of it when the poet has 'put it down in poems, that's the bind'.[10]

Demands for the standardisation of spoken and/or written English have occurred during times of political or cultural crises, when the English language was offered as evidence of a national unity underlying differences of religion, political affinity, customs, and habits. 'Standard' English, from the literate Chancery English of Chaucer's time, was the emblem of a projected national (and, later, imperial) identity. Literature which denied the notion of a unified or 'pure' English language based upon the contemporary abstraction of Standard English thus challenged a political hegemony.[11] To reinforce the assertion that there was, or could be, a 'correct' form of English, it was necessary to establish an institution composed of Gramsci's 'organic intellectuals',[12] with the authority to rule on doubtful or disputed usage. The project to found a British Academy on the lines of the *Academia della Crusca* and the *Académie française*, however, failed again and again, as George McKnight records:

> The need of official control in language had been felt by Gabriel Harvey, who felt that the only way to arrive at uniformity in English spelling was to have the orthography 'publickely and autentickly established, as it were by a general Counsel, or act of Parliament.' Elaborate

---

9 'Classics Society', *SP*, p. 120.
10 'A Good Read', *SP*, p. 141.
11 See Tony Crowley, *The Politics of Discourse: The Standard Language Question in British Cultural Debates* (London, 1989), pp. 74–9.
12 See Antonio Gramsci, *Selections from Prison Notebooks*, eds and trans. Quentin Hoare and Geoffrey Nowell-Smith (London, 1971), p. 5.

plans for a literary 'Corporation Royal' to bear the title 'King James his Academe or College of Honour' proposed by Edmund Bolton in 1617, met with royal favor, but came to naught on account of the death of King James in 1625.[13]

A proposal for the founding of an English Academy was made by Sir Francis Kynaston in 1635, and R. H. Esquire's *New Atlantis* of 1660 described an '"Eminent Academy of selected wits" one of whose duties it was "to purifie our Native Language from Barbarism or Solecism, to the height of Eloquence, by regulating the termes and phrases"'.[14] Not long after, Dryden was calling for 'a more certain Measure' of the language,[15] and complaining that though by the age of Aeschylus 'the Greek tongue was arrived to its full perfection' with 'an exact standard of writing and speaking', the English language 'is not capable of such a certainty; and we are at present so far from it that we are wanting in the very foundation of it, a perfect grammar'.[16] His suggested remedy for this was the English Academy, for which he solicited patronage from the Earl of Sunderland, expressing his desire 'that we might all write with the same certainty of words, and purity of phrase, to which the Italians first arrived, and after them the French'.[17] In 1693 he was still advocating reform, if without much hope, describing the English language as 'in a manner barbarous', and observing: 'and what government will encourage any one, or more, who are capable of refining it, I know not'.[18]

In the late eighteenth century, theories of language were still, Olivia Smith finds, 'centrally and explicitly concerned with class division' and, she emphasises, 'they cannot be entirely understood without their political component being taken into account'.[19] This

---

13 George H. McKnight, *The Evolution of the English Language from Chaucer to the Twentieth Century* (New York, 1928), p. 279.
14 McKnight, *Evolution of the English Language*, p. 280.
15 John Dryden, *The Rival Ladies*, dedication (1664), quoted by McKnight, *Evolution of the English Language*, p. 279.
16 John Dryden, *Troilus and Cressida* (1679), preface, in *John Dryden: Selected Criticism*, eds J. Kingsley and G. Parfitt (London, 1970), p. 159.
17 John Dryden to the Earl of Sunderland, quoted by McKnight, *Evolution of the English Language*, p. 279.
18 John Dryden, 'Discourse Concerning the Original and Progress of Satire', in *Selected Criticism*, p. 276.
19 Olivia Smith, *The Politics of Language 1791–1819* (Oxford, 1984), preface, p. viii. The evidence which Smith musters in support of her argument is impressive

was the great age of the dictionary and grammar, the palpable authorities which were to 'fix' the barbarous diversity of rude English – yet also, as Harrison appears to acknowledge in the three 'Wordlists' poems,[20] labours of love by philologists who were truly lovers of words. By the late 1940s and 1950s (during which Harrison was attending Leeds Grammar School), in the post-Newbolt-Report era,[21] education could be depicted as part of a refining process much to be desired. Even as recently as 1987, it was possible for a government think-tank to publish a document which stated unequivocally that Standard English was 'superior to dialect', and advocated the teaching of grammar on prescriptive lines.[22] A year later, the government-appointed Kingham Committee reported that children have a 'right' to learn Standard English, and that it is the responsibility of the school to enable them to do so.[23] The status of Standard English as the superior and appropriate literary language is in some ways parallel to that once attributed to Classical Greek and, especially, Latin, which, having undergone the imposition of standard forms and ceased to be subject to the changes and variations of living languages, were regarded as intrinsically and functionally superior to 'rude' and diverse English.[24] For many years the *lingua franca* of international scholarship and literacy, they remain so, to an extent, for elements of scientific discourse and the liturgy, and retain an almost sacred status.[25] Standard English, and

---

and too complex to be summarised here, but of especial relevance to Harrison's position on language are her introductory section, 'The Problem', pp. 1–34, chapter II, '*Rights of Man* and its Aftermath', pp. 35–67, and chapter VI, 'Variations of the Languages of Men: Rustics, Peasants and Plough-Boys', pp. 202–51.

---

20 *SP*, pp. 117–19.

21 Henry Newbolt, *The Teaching of English in England: Being the Report of the Departmental Committee Appointed by the President of the Board of Education to Enquire into the Position of English in the Educational System of England* (London, 1921).

22 John Marenbon, *English Our English: The New Orthodoxy Examined* (London, 1987), extract in Tony Crowley, *Proper English? Readings in Language, History and Cultural Identity* (London, 1991), pp. 245–60.

23 Cited by John Algeo, 'Sociolinguistic Attitudes and Issues in Contemporary Britain', in Tim William Machan and Charles T. Scott, eds, *English in its Social Contexts: Essays in Historical Sociolinguistics* (Oxford, 1992), p. 174.

24 Living Greek was not, of course, homogeneous, and Harrison shows that he is aware of the inferior status of Doric Greek. See *Aikin Mata* (Ibadan, 1966), foreword, p. 10.

25 For example, the use of Latin prayers and incantations to drive out demons and vampires in popular horror films.

the Latinate grammar sometimes imposed upon it, came to function as the superior touchstone, while dialects acquired the status of shifting, unfixed elements in an inferior rag-bag. Reflecting upon this, the 'School of Eloquence' sequence both bitterly opposes and endorses the sentiments of Waller's 'Of English Verse':

> But who should hope his lines should long
> Last in a daily changing Tongue?
> While they are new, envy prevails,
> And as that dies, our language fails;
> [....]
> Poets that lasting marble seek
> Must carve in Latine or in Greek,
> We write in Sand, our Language grows
> And like the Tide, our work o'erflows.[26]

Ironically, the school which Harrison records as imposing Latin as a cultural standard attempted, in what became known as the 'Leeds Grammar School Case' of 1805, to break free of the traditional grammar school curriculum. The school's application to use its endowment to teach modern, living languages such as French (and, presumably, eventually, English), was refused by the Lord Chancellor, Lord Eldon, on the grounds that it would contravene the original purpose for which grammar schools had been founded, i.e. 'for teaching grammatically the learned [as opposed to the acquired] languages'.[27] Tony Crowley notes that the 'wide-ranging effect of this case was to enshrine the classical languages and literatures in the grammar and public schools as the main subject of the curriculum at the expense of "modern subjects"'.[28] Harrison describes the schoolboy experience of the attempt to model Standard English (in the form of stilted literary high Victorian) on Classical Latin:

> Apart from a weekly chunk of Johnson, Pitt the Younger and Lord Macaulay to be done into Ciceronian Latin, we had to turn once living

---

26 Edmund Waller, 'Of English Verse', *Poems* (1668), in Herbert Grierson and G. Bullough, eds, *The Oxford Book of Seventeenth-century Verse* (London, 1934) p. 446.

27 J. Lawson and H. Silver, *A Social History of Education in England* (London, 1973), quoted in Crowley, *Politics of Discourse*, p. 84. The 'Leeds Grammar School Case' is discussed on pp. 83–4. John Lucas also discusses this case, and other issues discussed in this chapter, in his *Romantic to Modern Literature: Essays and Ideas of Culture, 1750–1900* (Brighton, 1982), chapter 2, pp. 7–29.

28 Crowley, *Politics of Discourse*, p. 84.

authors into a form of English never spoken by men or women, as if to compensate our poor tongue for the misfortune of not being a dead language.[29]

The practice had persisted in spite of scorn poured upon it by Horne Tooke's *The Diversions of Purley*, which, as long ago as 1786, 'as Hazlitt recognized [...] perform a wonderfully neat demolition job on those who believe that if you formally translate the Latin Grammar into English you have written an English grammar'.[30]

The practice of Leeds Grammar School was in accordance with the contemporary philosophy of education expressed in social history and teaching manuals which describe dialects not as variations within a complex language system, but as defective deviations from the 'pure' standard form (which itself, of course, originated as a dialect). From this perspective, it 'was but natural that the fully articulate class, among whom discussion is fast and fairly free, should concentrate their attention chiefly upon the very apparent diseases of the less articulate classes'.[31] For Leeds Grammar School to 'cure' Harrison of Leeds demotic, and instil Standard English and RP, was to set him on the ladder of aspiration. Harrison's choice of the aspirant as an emblem of so-called 'poor' speech is not random. 'Mis-application' of the 'big H' is the focus of middle-class disgust in several mid-nineteenth-century works advocating the imposition of Standard English, for example:

> First and foremost let me notice that worst of all faults, the leaving out of the aspirate where it ought to be, and putting it in where it ought not to be. This is a vulgarism not confined to this or that province of England, or especially prevalent in one county or another, but common throughout England to persons of low breeding and inferior education, particularly to those among the inhabitants of towns.[32]

One character in Harrison's poetry treats aspiration (in both senses) with contempt:

---

29 'Jane Eyre's Sister', preface to *Misanthrope*, in *Bloodaxe 1*, p. 139.
30 William Hazlitt, The *Spirit of the Age*, in *Hazlitt's Works*, ed. W. Carew Hazlitt (1886), p. 94, paraphrased by Lucas, *Romantic to Modern Literature*, p. 16.
31 Stephen Reynolds and B. and T. Wooley, *Seems So! A Working Class View of Politics* (London, 1911), quoted in Crowley, *Politics of Discourse*, p. 215.
32 Henry Alford, *A Plea for the Queen's English* (London, 1864), quoted in Crowley, *Politics of Discourse*, p. 153.

Aspirations, cunt! Folk on t'fucking dole
'ave got about as much scope to aspire
above the shit they're dumped in, cunt, as coal
aspires to be chucked on t'fucking fire.[33]

That he does, however, register the continued significance of aspiration is perhaps suggested by the capitalisation of the 'h' in '*Get thee beHind me, Satan*',[34] which could suggest an over-emphasis, and thus a parody of the speech of 'vicar and cop' which he mimics. Harrison does not omit final 'g' from the gerund endings in his typographical representation of the Leeds dialect, though surely [n] rather than the velar nasal [ŋ] (the sound at the end of 'ing') is characteristic of most English twentieth-century non-RP usage.[35]

Nearly sixty years after Dean Alford's plea, the perceived differences between the English of those who investigated dialect-speakers and that of the subjects of their investigation were still great enough to lead not only to incomprehension but to the relegation of the dialect to mere noise:

> Come into a London elementary school and see what it is that the children need most. You will notice, first of all, that in a human sense, our boys and girls are almost inarticulate. They can make noises, but they cannot speak. Linger in a playground and listen to the talk and shouts [...] you can barely recognise your native language.[36]

Such works describe meaningful and orderly utterance as the prerogative of the ruling classes; theirs to give, if they choose, to the under-classes. 'Plainly, then, the first and chief duty of the Elementary School is to give its pupils speech – to make them articulate and civilised beings, able to communicate themselves in speech and writing, and able to receive the communication of others.'[37] As in the eighteenth and early nineteenth century, the vernacular is relegated to the status of a disorderly system unfit for systematic study, and

---

33 *v*., p. 17.
34 *v*., p. 21.
35 A useful model for the examination of dialect in literature is provided by Patricia Ingham, 'Dialect in the novels of Hardy and George Eliot', in George Watson, ed., *Literary English Since Shakespeare* (Oxford, 1970), pp. 347–63.
36 Newbolt, *Teaching of English*, quoted in Crowley, *Politics of Discourse*, p. 242.
37 Newbolt, *Teaching of English*, in Crowley, *Politics of Discourse*, p. 241.

rarely acknowledged in conventional theories, grammars, and dictionaries written after 1750. A vulgar language was said to exist, a refined language was said to exist, and others were not recognized. Such extreme concepts dismissed everyone except the classically educated as an identifiable group characterized by their incapacity for refined thought and moral behaviour.[38]

The wording of prescriptive works on dialect (in the style of Victorian anthropological papers placing aboriginal tribes not far above the apes on the evolutionary tree) bring to mind the Classical Greek attitude to foreigners, and the Newbolt Report does make the logical progression from non-possession of the privileged register to non-participation in approved manners and mores, to existence outside the rule of 'rex and lex', to 'barbarianism'. 'For such people life has no emphasis, no significance. They have no dance, no Helicon, no Muse.'[39] Harrison's Rhubarbarians are these despised hordes. They don't make poetry.

> What t'mob said to the cannons on the mills,
> shouted to soldier, scab and sentinel
> 's silence, parries and hush on whistling hills,
> shadows in moonlight playing knurr and spell.
>
> It wasn't poetry though. Nay, wiseowl Leeds
> *pro rege et lege* schools, nobody needs
> your drills and chanting to parrot right
> the *tusky-tusky* of the pikes that night.[40]

They are not given the leading parts, important soliloquies and arias; they only make up the crowd scenes, the mob.[41] A short poem by (perhaps surprisingly) Robert Graves touches on themes which we associate with Harrison, and suggests an association for the emblematic letter 'H' with which Harrison might well concur.

> H may be N for those who speak
> Russian, although long E in Greek;
> And cockneys, like the French, agree
> That H is neither N nor E

---

38 Smith, *Politics of Language*, preface, p. x.
39 Harrison cites, from an unattributed papyri source, 'an appeal to a Roman general to come and save the inhabitants of Egyptian Thebes from a barbarian tribe'. 'Facing up to the Muses', *Bloodaxe 1*, p. 445.
40 'The Rhubarbarians I', *SP*, p. 113.
41 See 'The Rhubarbarians II', *SP*, p. 114.

> Nor Hate's harsh aspirate, but meek
> And mute as in *Humanity*.[42]

Unlike Seamus Heaney, Harrison does not write about the occasions on which dialect can be exclusive of Standard English speakers. There is no equivalent in Harrison's Leeds to the 'strangers' who 'found difficult to manage' the Derry 'gh' ([x]) in Heaney's 'Broagh',[43] only an exile whose diluted first language has to be recalled to the tongue. No RP speaker tries to manage the Loiners' dialect, though speaking it denotes inclusivity with [uz]. No one born outside is shown wanting to get in.[44]

Echoing the style of prescriptive and proscriptive grammars and guides to pronunciation,[45] Harrison describes Leeds speech in physical terms which suggest phlegm and a literal impediment to 'proper' speech: 'all stuffed with glottals, great / lumps to hawk up and spit out' ('Them & [uz]'). His teacher-villains find the dialect intrinsically inferior and physically repellent as well as socially disabling. Its use disqualifies the young Harrison from performing the words of poets who themselves did not speak Standard English.

> All poetry (even Cockney Keats?) you see
> 's been dubbed by [ʌs] into RP

Though there were dissenting voices,[46] for Harrison's teachers in the 1940s, orthodox thinking on language may still have been

---

42   Robert Graves, 'H', *Collected Poems* (London, 1975), p. 441.
43   Seamus Heaney, 'Broagh', *Wintering Out* (London, 1972), p. 27.
44   The use of dialect as a marker of inside, outside and borderline is, of course, not new. See, for example, Thomas Hardy's *Tess of the D'Urbervilles*.
45   Such grammars themselves echoing a disparagement of northern dialects which has been going on for at least six hundred years. In his Latin *Polychronicon*, Ranulf Higden (d. 1364), himself born in Cornwall and a fellow of Exeter and Queen's Colleges, Oxford, describes the speech of Yorkshire as 'stridet', i.e. whistling or hissing. John Trevisa's translation and adaptation of the work (1387) describes 'the language of Northumberland, and especially of York' as 'so sharp, slitting [like the sound of ripping cloth?], and froting [strident or harsh?] and unschape [unshapely], that we southern men may not understand it' (passage modernised). See John Trevisa, *Polychronicon Ranulphi Higden, Monachi Cestrensis: together with the English Translations of John Trevisa and of an Unknown Writer of the Fifteenth Century*, ed. Churchill Babington (London, 1869), vol. 2, p.163.
46   For example, F. E. Palmer, who regretted that 'the chimerical idea of a standard dialect still persists'. *A Grammar of Spoken English* (1924), third edn (Cambridge, 1969), quoted in Richard W. Bailey, *Images of English* (Cambridge, 1992), p. 9.

represented by the Society for Pure English and writers such as Henry Wyld and R.W. Chapman. 'If I were asked among what class the "best" English is most consistently heard at its best', Wyld wrote, 'I should say among Officers of the British Regular Army.'[47] Chapman concurred, noting that Standard English was 'now the language of a class far more than it is the language of a region', for 'Phonetically, England is not a democracy', and therefore correct speech was both inherited and reinforced, at 'the schools which we call public [...] recruited [...] from our least indigent classes'.[48]

The imposition of RP, it was sometimes suggested, would dissolve (some) class divisions. A nineteenth-century guide asserts that when 'a firm control of pronunciation has thus been acquired, provincialisms and vulgarisms will at last be entirely eliminated and some of the most important barriers between the different classes of society will thus be abolished'.[49] For Harrison, like Richard Hoggart, this Arnoldian attempt at (selective)[50] Hellenisation of the working classes and their language was no social leveller but a form of kidnap.[51] Instead of imbibing middle-class attitudes with the standardised tongue of middle England, and gratefully accepting the key to the temple of culture, Harrison, in 'Them & [uz]', informs his despised oppressors ('yer buggers') of his resolve to occupy their province: 'your lousy, leasehold poetry'. Whilst reasserting William Cobbett's belief that the division of the population into those who knew the grammar of Standard English and those who did not was a means of class manipulation, Harrison here seems to invert Cobbett's social mission. Cobbett 'considered grammar [...] as an integral part of the class structure of England, and the act of learning grammar by one of his readers as an act of class warfare'.[52] Harrison depicts his own recollection of the grammar of the Leeds

---

47 Henry Cecil Wyld, *The Best English: A Claim for the Superiority of Received Standard English,* Society for Pure English Tract 39 (Oxford, 1934), p. 614.
48 R. W. Chapman, 'English Pronunciation', *Saturday Review of Literature,* 7, pp. 841–2.
49 Henry Sweet, *A Handbook of Phonetics* (Oxford, 1877), quoted by Crowley, *Politics of Discourse,* p. 154.
50 The scholarship which Harrison won to Leeds Grammar School was one of only six for the whole of the West Riding.
51 Harrison's experience of the English educational system was not one of unalloyed misery, repression and enforced consciousness of class division. Romana Huk describes what she sees as the positive influence of Leeds University in '*The Loiners* and the Leeds Renaissance', in *Bloodaxe 1,* pp. 75–8.
52 Smith, *Politics of Language,* p. 1.

dialect, and substitution of it for the grammar of literary English, as an act of class warfare. His embracing the 'colloquial barbarisms, licentious idioms, and irregular combinations' which Dr Johnson wanted to purge from the language,[53] in a personal poetic which he substitutes for the 'grammar' of both Standard English and canonical poetic conventions, could be seen as a similar act.

The ladder of aspiration could lead not only to higher social status, but to the means of literary production. These include the printing presses, the mechanisms of theatrical performance, the word-processor and wholesale distributor, but also the complex system of agencies and forces which influence the production and reception of texts. That system includes education, publishing, reviewing, academic criticism, and bookselling. John Guillory calls the literary syllabus 'the institutional form' of 'cultural capital', the practice of reading and writing which gives access to the means of literary production. For Guillory, this is first

> *linguistic* capital, the means by which one attains to a socially cred-entialed and therefore valued speech, otherwise known as 'Standard English'. And second, it is *symbolic* capital, a kind of knowledge-capital whose possession can be displayed upon request and which thereby entitles its possessor to the cultural and material rewards of the well-educated person.[54]

The institutions which control linguistic and symbolic capital and its dissemination are secular inheritors of the functions of the churches of the Book described by Jack Goody:

> If the teaching of the skills of reading is an intrinsic part of religions of the Book, its specialists inevitably acquire control of the input and output of a considerable segment of available written knowledge. But in addition they need the means to maintain the schools in which this instruction is given. Such maintenance requires not just a building, a temple, but personnel [...] who have to be supported not by daily offerings alone, but by more substantial, more permanent endowments [....] literacy is not only one of the ends but the means too, being crit-ically involved in the process of acquisition itself since the making of written wills and deeds often accomplishes, indeed legitimises, the alienation of property from family or lineage to church [....] there

---

53 Samuel Johnson, *The Rambler* (15 January 1752).
54 John Guillory, *Cultural Capital: The Problem of Literary Canon Formation* (Chicago, 1993), preface, p. ix.

seems to be a close association between literacy and variable inheritance.[55]

The literate, as Harrison suggests, inherit the earth, or at least its cultural capital, but:

> Ambition! Dual parentage frustrates
> all hopes he might have had in both his states[56]

and 'obviously by being a poet I've moved into another class anyway'.[57]

Harrison's first tangible production of cultural capital, his first published poems, 'When Shall I Tune My "Doric Reed"?',[58] 'When the Bough Breaks',[59] and others published in *Poetry and Audience*, the Leeds University English School magazine, are the work of 'T. W.', still steeped in the register of [ʌs].

> Plato might have said that
> Here was the spark's near victory
> As the dog with interlocking teeth
> Snapped at the mucous coil of you,
> Transferred the leash of clay,
> And from concord night ran you to birth.
>
> Not long after they held a mirror
> To your maple smile,
> And saw the mother's tears
> Unclouded in the glass.
> Plato might have said that
> Your smile was part of some triad more purely
> Severed and strung out,
> Unclasped, apart from me,
> Who, bare as any stillborn syllable
> On this page, flitted
> To your closed deaf face,
> Migrating to your death[60]

---

55 Jack Goody, *The Logic of Writing and the Organization of Society* (Cambridge, 1986), p. 18.
56 *Phaedra*, p. 28.
57 'Interview', p. 233.
58 Discussed in Chapter 1.
59 *Poetry and Audience*, 4, no. 15 (22 February 1957), p. 5.
60 'What Plato Might Have Said', *Poetry and Audience*, 4, no. 22 (22 May 1957), pp. 4–5.

By the time *Newcastle* was published, in 1969, Harrison's diction
had become more relaxed, his lexicon had widened to include slang
('I faff with paper chips and coal'), and he was breaking words
across lines:

> Newcastle got its motto: FORTIT-
> ER TRIUMPHANS DEFENDIT[61]

(though he had not yet adopted his characteristic use of elision, such
as 's and t'.)[62] Dialect is used in several of the 'School of
Eloquence' poems, but is often italicised, bracketed off from the
narrative voice.[63] The status of dialect in such poems is thus not
equivalent to the 'norm' of the native speech of the narrative 'I', but
has the effect of an importation or linguistic borrowing (if only from
memory).[64] Harrison is not a dialect writer, in either the patronising
mode of nineteenth-century 'rustic' verse, or the bilingual mode of,
for example, W. N. Herbert.[65] Rather, he uses dialect in a similar
way to Hardy or Lawrence, creating sympathetic characterisation by
suggesting either deprivation and outsiderliness (Lawrence's
Mellors, Harrison's Rhubarbarians), an old-fashioned milieu or
mind-set (Hardy's Jack Durbeyfield, Harrison's Harry Harrison), or
group membership and (sometimes) masculinity (the miners
addressed by Sir Clifford Chatterley, the 'lads' in several of
Harrison's poems, including 'Me Tarzan'). Vernacular dialogue is a
feature of some of Harrison's plays, but, other than *Big H* and
Chorus, none has a contemporary setting which calls for modern
English dialect, and the logistics of those plays restrict the extent to
which it can be used.[66] Even if it were possible to reproduce the
spoken language verbatim, or to make poetry from it, 'how I speak

---

61 *Newcastle*, p. 63.

62 An early example of the use of this device outside the dramatic poetry is in 'Me
Tarzan', *London Magazine*, new series, 12, no. 5 (December 1972/January
1973), *SP*, p. 116.

63 For example, 'Me Tarzan' and 'Wordlists I', *SP*, p. 117.

64 See M. M. Bakhtin, *The Dialogic Imagination, Four Essays*, trans. Michael
Holquist and C. Emerson, ed. Michael Holquist (Austin, Texas, 1981), p. 287.

65 See, for example, *Forked Tongue* (Newcastle-upon-Tyne, 1994).

66 The dialect-speakers in *Big H* are played by children who might find long
speeches difficult to memorise, and the story dictates that eleven out of the
twelve boy speakers must abandon the most obvious characteristic of Leeds
pronunciation featured in the dialogue, the dropped 'h', when they become
Herod's 'Prel'. The lines given to the twelfth boy, who retains his Leeds accent,
do not use specifically dialect words.

at home' ('Classics Society') is no longer pure Leeds. The recollected Leeds pronunciation of 'my' as 'me': '*mi 'art aches*' which marked the Scholarship boy T. W. becomes Tony Harrison's 'my' ([mai]).[67] He performs his own words with an unexcited deliberation and authority. *Trackers* perhaps satirises such bilingualism. When the haughty Kyllene is offended by the satyrs' 'uproar foul' (i.e. working-class dialect, earthy comments, and wheedling obsequiousness), they switch to an exaggerated 'high' tragic diction:

SATYR 1
(Joining in 'tragic' tone)
Stay thine anger, nymph of the deep zone.
We are no bringers of disruptive strife.
Nay, all that we humbly wish is that you disclose
the meaning of that hidden sound we heard.

Evidently the satyrs intend no insult. This is not mockery but their attempt at the suitable language in which to address a nymph. Encouraged when, soothed by their respectful address, Kyllene responds more affably: 'That is a better way to learn what you desire',[68] they launch into an even more convoluted style:

SATYR 1
Ruler of this region, Kyllene, Queen,
our purpose later will I you explain.
But this voice we heard, what is it, pray?
It frayed our nerves and set our teeth on edge.
Who is it that bringeth the gooselumps on our flesh?
What is it that raiseth the spine hairs on our back?[69]

The comic effect of this gentility issuing from the mouths of the heavily-built, clog-dancing satyrs, geranium latex *phalloi* flapping, can be imagined, but the scene is not entirely humorous. Though Silenus and the satyrs are treated more sympathetically than Apollo and Kyllene, they are not heroic figures. Released from the prison of

---

67 See, for example, 'Initial Illumination', *Gorgon*, p. 46.
68 Compare: 'Tragedy does not deserve to blurt out trivial lines, but she will modestly consort a little with the forward satyrs, like a respectable lady dancing because she must on a feast day.' Horace, *The Art of Poetry*, in *Classical Literary Criticism*, eds and trans. D. A. Russell and M. Winterbottom (Oxford, 1989), p. 104.
69 *Trackers*, Delphi text, p. 40.

words, not so much gods in the machine as genii in the papyri, they represent both escape from the stultification (imprisoning) of 'dead' languages and that which unthinkingly destroys linguistic value; as both the power of carnival and an undiscriminated, destructive pack.

In his enterprise of giving a voice to the voiceless, and disinterring from history's indifference the unheard dead (and, sometimes, the living), Harrison takes as his theme not only language but the physical act of speech-production. *'Some could articulate, others not.'*[70] 'Articulate', like 'eloquence', is, via the eighteenth century, a key word in his work, rather as 'newfangylnes' is for Wyatt, from, perhaps Chaucer and Malory.[71] Harrison declares his 'obsessive commitment to all forms of articulation' and returns again and again to the mechanisms of pained and difficult articulation.[72] In 'Fire-eater' and 'Study' it is physical impediment:

> Dad's eldest brother had a shocking stammer.
> Dad punctuated sentence ends with but ...
> Coarser stuff than silk they hauled up grammar
> knotted together deep down in their gut.[73]

> Uncle Joe came here to die. His gaping jaws
> once plugged in to the power of his stammer
> patterned the stuck plosive without pause
> like a d-d-damascener's hammer.[74]

In 'On Not Being Milton' it is regional articulation – allegedly unmelodic and unpleasing to RP ears:

> The stutter of the scold out of the branks
> of condescension, class and counter-class
> thickens with glottals to a lumpen mass
> of Ludding morphemes closing up their ranks.
> Each swung cast-iron Enoch of Leeds stress
> clangs a forged music on the frames of Art,
> the looms of owned language smashed apart![75]

---

70 'The Earthen Lot', *SP*, p. 179.
71 See, for example, *School*, preface, p. 9.
72 Tony Harrison, interviewed by Clive Wilmer, 'Poet of the Month', BBC Radio 3, February 1991, transcript published in Clive Wilmer, ed., *Poets Talking* (Manchester, 1994), p. 99.
73 'Fire-eater', *SP*, p. 168.
74 'Study', *SP*, p. 115.
75 On Not Being Milton', *SP*, p. 112.

In 'Wordlists II' it is eloquent inarticulacy:

> The *Funk & Wagnalls*? Does that still survive?
> Uncle Harry most eloquent deaf-mute
> jabbed at its lexis till it leaped to life
> when there were Tory errors to confute.[76]

In these poems, Harrison is not only the champion and redeemer of the inarticulate but the beneficiary of their inspiration and motivation:

> *How you became a poet's a mystery!*
> *Wherever did you get your talent from?*
>
> I say: *I had two uncles, Joe and Harry -*
> *one was a stammerer, the other dumb.*[77]

Harrison presents his own painstaking acquisition of articulacy and eloquence as a lesser achievement, and one which, like the scholarship, is double-edged, a password into one world, a banishment from another. The same poem closes with regret:

> but not the tongue that once I used to know
> but can't bone up on now, and that's mi mam's.

Stress, in both senses, is an essential element of Harrison's poetry, and reflection on language provides most of the tensions and strained correspondences which produce that stress.

> Words and wordlessness. Between the two
> the gauge went almost ga-ga.[78]

Heaney similarly pays his dues of acknowledgement and respect to inarticulate ancestors, but in Heaney's poetry the inarticulate are silent rather than silenced, grudging of speech, and their economy makes the poet feel garrulous in his eloquence.[79] Heaney describes the silences and curtailed utterances of his father and their lineage of farmer and cattle-dealer in idealised, almost romanticised terms. Harrison's more remote ancestors (actual and metaphorical) are shown fighting, struggling for articulation and a desired, if unattain-

---

76 'Wordlists II', *SP*, p. 118.
77 'Heredity', *SP*, p. 111.
78 'Wordlists I', *SP*, p. 117.
79 See, for example, Seamus Heaney, 'The Outlaw', *Door into the Dark* (London, 1972), pp. 16–17 and 'The Forge', *Door into the Dark*, p. 16.

able, aspiration,[80] and his immediate progenitor is given speeches which are not inarticulate, but clumsy, disjointed and unheroic. In 'Wordlists I':

> Sometime ... er ... there's summat in that drawer ...

– and in 'Next Door IV':

> Pork's gone west, chitt'lins, trotters, dripping baps!
> And booze an' all, if it's a Moslem owns t'new shop.[81]

A sense of stress is invested in every line of 'Marked With D.', in which Harrison writes of his father's cremation:

> When the chilled dough of his flesh went in an oven
> not unlike those he fuelled all his life,
> I thought of his cataracts ablaze with Heaven
> and radiant with the sight of his dead wife,
> light streaming from his mouth to shape her name,
> 'not Florence and not Flo but always Florrie'.
> I thought how his cold tongue burst into flame
> but only literally, which makes me sorry,
> sorry for his sake there's no Heaven to reach.[82]

It is not only the reflection that his father, tongue-tied throughout his life, will never have a tongue of fire, and that death is a leveller only to the lowest common denominator, the corpse, and not an uplifter to an equality of articulacy, which makes the narrator 'sorry'. With the grief and anger is something else, central to Harrison's work, a reflexiveness, here on his own eloquence. 'I get it all from Earth my daily bread', in the same poem, is a refutation of idealism, and an acknowledgement that both the matter of Harrison's poetry and therefore the 'bread' it earns for him come from 'the foul rag and bone shop of the heart' he left in working-class Leeds. Intelligence and education, however, gave him the freedom of another city: the mythology and imagery of the world's cultures, and the pleasure he takes in the imaginative play of connection, congruence and opposition. The poem is made out of a tension between the materialist and the metaphysician. The regret is not only that the father's tongue ignited 'only literally', but that the son, atheist, realist, possessor of many tongues, none the less, half stunned by grief, fell

---

80 See, for example, 'On Not Being Milton' and 'The Rhubarbarians'.
81 'Next Door IV', *SP*, p. 132.
82 'Marked With D.', *SP*, p. 155.

back into the register of Christian imagery, and 'thought how his cold tongue burst into flame', and 'thought of his cataracts ablaze with Heaven and radiant with the sight of his dead wife'. Furthermore, with that rueful sense of intellectual regression is the suggestion of an apology to Harrison's parents for the insincerity, perhaps blasphemy, of the non-believer's use of these sacred images, and for his inability to use them referentially rather than figuratively. In Accordance with Authorised Version convention, the ashes of the baker become the flour to make a loaf, but his son appropriates and reverses the image to get from the dust of Earth his daily bread. He thinks in metaphysical images, of the transcendency of love and art, even when his subject is mortality, and, 'I believe life ends with death, and that is all'.[83]

'Punchline' broods on some of the same preoccupations.

> No! Revolution never crossed your mind!
> For the kids who never made it through the schools
> the Northern working class escaped the grind
> as boxers or comedians, or won the pools.[84]

Harrison did not fight, strum or joke his way out of the under-class, but made his escape by working the hardest in his class at both kinds of translation; into and through Barthes's 'class of rhetoric'. For Barthes, rhetoric is: 'that privileged technique [...] which permits the ruling classes to gain *ownership of speech*. Language being a power, selective rules of access to this power have been decreed, constituting it as a pseudo-science, closed to "those who do not know how to speak" and requiring an expensive initiation.'[85] The privileged technique is the ability to articulate the resulting division. The price is the division.

> I'm guilty, and the way I make it up's
> in poetry, and that much I confess.[86]

Poems such as the two 'Currants' sonnets[87] may represent apology and expiation for past insensitivity. Harrison has evidently come to value, even to sentimentalise, the habits which once embarrassed him, so why does he accuse himself of being a busker who lives by entertaining the privileged? Perhaps because, though revolution has crossed

---

83 'Long Distance II', *SP*, p. 134.
84 'Punchline', *SP*, p. 150.
85 Roland Barthes, *The Semiotic Challenge* (Oxford, 1988), pp. 13–14.
86 'Confessional Poetry', *SP*, p. 128.
87 *SP*, pp. 151–2.

Harrison's mind, it is not advocated in the forms of his poetry, and his story is one of escape from an oppressed into a privileged class (as however ambivalent and conditional a member) and not of a struggle to change the system which creates the inequality.

Rick Rylance points out that Harrison is writing within a tradition of English elegy which expresses sympathy for the dispossessed, but not in the language of the dispossessed.[88] Demotic in Harrison's poetry is usually in the form of another character's (sometimes the child T. W.'s) direct or indirect speech, in inverted commas, italicised, or otherwise bracketed off from Harrison's (current) voice: '*Off laikin', then to t'fish 'oil*' ('Me Tarzan'), '*th'art knobbut summat as wants raking up*' ('Working').[89] In this way they are isolated as objects of investigation rather than directly used as signifiers.[90] When, in 'Currants I', the young Harrison and his father exchange words, in italics, 'h' is made a powerful signifier by its juxtaposition as presence in the son's and absence in the father's speech.

> Sweat dropped into the currants from his nose:
>
> *Go on! 'ave an 'andful. It's all free.*
>
> *Not this barrel though. Your sweat's gone into it.*
> *I'll go and get my handful from another.*

'No modern English poet has shown more finely [than Harrison] how the sign is a terrain of struggle where opposing accents intersect, how in a class-divided society language is cultural warfare and every nuance a political valuation.'[91] Similar claims have, of course, been made for other poets. The editors of *The New Poetry* suggest that Carol Ann Duffy, Jackie Kay, Ian MacMillan, and Geoff Hattersley have strengths which are located 'in a tension between ironic social naturalism and confrontational political work'.[92] Perhaps, but if their writing, and that of the other New Poets, needs the twenty-eight-page polysyllabic introduction from which the

---

88 'THL', p. 57.
89 *SP*, p. 124.
90 The use of 'mi mam' and 'Mi aunty's' in, for example, 'Wordlists I' and 'Study' seems to signify that the language is that of the voice represented in the poem, the T. W. who still belonged to the family and linguistic group, rather than the enunciation of the poem, the contemporary poetic I.
91 Terry Eagleton, 'Antagonisms: Tony Harrison's *v.*', *Bloodaxe 1*, p. 349.
92 Michael Hulse, David Kennedy, and David Morley, eds, *The New Poetry* (Newcastle-upon-Tyne, 1993), introduction, p. 17.

quotation is taken, can it really have 'attack and access', and does it support the claim that Duffy's poems 'popularise complex ideas about language and its political role and meanings'? The editors single out for special praise Duffy's 'Poet for Our Times', which they call 'a bitterly funny indictment of the Thatcher years',[93] but also of 'the abuses that come with a debasement of language and syntax'. (The suggestion that language can exist and be debased independently of syntax is strange, unless 'language' here means lexical selection.) The expression of fear and loathing of contemporary debasement of language by Americanisms, dialect and 'sloppy usage' seems incongruously reactionary in the context of this anthology. Further, given that Duffy's poem is directed at the 'Workshop of the World',[94] its apparent unawareness that headlines *are* today's 'punchy haikus', that *Sun* English is an extant working-class register, like it or not, is likely to alienate many readers. The sub-editors who produce tabloid headlines may or may not be native speakers of working-class dialects, and they may or may not be cynical exploiters foisting on to their readers a synthetic demotic – it makes no difference. To try to undo 'debasement' and to restore 'proper syntax' is to kill language, an endeavour usually attributed to 'the enemy' whom the editors suggest Duffy's work aims 'to take on'. It seems significant that Hulse, Kennedy and Morley place this endeavour within the project to 'help preserve a liberal society and humanist culture'.[95]

'Poet for Our Times' resents the popularity of headline journalism which 'kids will know [...] by heart' in an age when most children memorise little poetry, and perhaps none of Duffy's, and it acidly parodies 'the poems of the decade ... *Stuff 'em! Gotcha!*'[96] This is a different use of the demotic from Harrison's, which 'mourns the loss' of ancient languages, but does not participate in the hypocrisy of supporting campaigns to preserve the 'noble' classical languages and 'pure' Standard English, or 'quaint and folksy' languages such as Cornish, 'exotic' languages such as Hausa, or better classes of dialect whilst despising the argot of urban teenagers, or journalese. 'Classics Society' reminds us that yesterday's

93 Hulse *et al.*, *New Poetry*, introduction, pp. 17–18.
94 The cover illustration of *The New Poetry* is Ken Currie, 'Workshop of the World: Hope and Optimism in Spite of Present Difficulties', 1987.
95 Hulse *et al.*, *New Poetry*, introduction, p. 18.
96 Duffy, 'Poet for Our Times', *New Poetry*, p. 229.

Rhubarbarians are today's occupying army.

> The tongue our leaders use to cast their spell
> was once denounced as 'rude', 'gross', 'base' and 'vile'.

Quite early in Harrison's writing career, he began to utilise a medium untrammelled by associations of high culture, and fit to carry the demotic message which might occupy the leasehold poetry. In *Phaedra*, imaginary graffiti are a projection of personal guilt:

> I see the hand of judgement start to scrawl
> graffiti of my guilt on every wall.[97]

In, or rather on, *Continuous*, it occupies the cover of a poetry book, and, on publication of the book form of *v.*, it has taken centre stage. The combination of graffiti and slim volume marks an ambivalent attitude to text, but especially, perhaps, a suspicion of the privileged text enshrined in a 'work of art'. Harrison does not appear to recognise a process in poetry parallel to the appropriation of the novel by (self-styled) working-class writers in the 1940s, but writes as though poetry, especially confessional poetry, imposes on the writer the valorised forms of 'high' culture. It is likely that many of the 'School of Eloquence' poems were written before the 'Martian invasion'[98] and the influx of demotic in the (new) New Poetry, but Harrison does not acknowledge the effect either of those poets who might be considered his immediate literary forebears, such as Alvarez, Lowell, MacCaig, and Larkin, or of his (near-) contemporaries Silken, Porter, Dunn, and Gunn.[99] Rather than celebrating the revisionist efforts of contemporary social and cultural historians, sociologists, and linguists, he chooses to remember the lexicographer James Murray.[100] It is as though regional accents are still binding their speakers as firmly to the bottom of the ladder of aspiration as in Murray's time.

Does the recension of the wording of 'Classics Society' after its publication in *School* indicate a change in Harrison's attitude to the Loiners' way of speaking? The opening lines, other than a few changes to the punctuation, remain the same, but the central section

---

97 *Phaedra*, p. 30.
98 I.e. the work of poets such as Craig Raine and Christopher Reid.
99 Though he does address poets as friends in the dedication of 'The Act', *Gorgon*, p. 19: 'for Michael Longley & James Simmons'.
100 'Wordlists III', *SP*, p. 119.

of the poem is altered. Version one (*School*) is:

> We boys can take old Hansards and translate
> the British Empire as S.P.Q.R.
> but nothing demotic or too up-to-date,
> and certainly not how I speak at home.
> Not Hansard standards, and if Antoninus

Version two (*Continuous*) is:

> We boys can take old Hansards and translate
> the British Empire into S.P.Q.R.
> but nothing demotic or too up-to-date,
> and *not* the English that I speak at home,
> not Hansard standards, and if Antoninus[101]

The revision produces a more crisp rhythm, but it also suggests that up-to-date colloquial Leeds dialect, instead of being 'how I speak at home', a language distinct from the Standard English of Leeds Grammar School, is at least a species of the mother-language.

'*E-nun-ci-ate!*' commands the teacher in 'Them & [uz] I':

> 'Poetry's the speech of kings. You're one of those
> Shakespeare gives the comic bits to: prose!'

Does poetry require, or enforce, particular enunciation? Antony Easthope suggests that iambic pentameter, the archetypal metre of English verse, is especially compatible with RP because 'it legislates for the number of syllables in the line and therefore cancels elisions, making transition at word junctures difficult'.[102] ('All poetry [...] you see / 's been dubbed'.) Easthope cites Epstein's attribution of 'the cancellation of elision in formal style to "a reader's socially inherited competence in the reading of poetry"', and suggests that this competence is 'motivated linguistically by pentameter because it requires full pronunciation to be given to every syllable, thus discouraging elision and demanding cessation of phonation between similar sounds at word boundaries'.[103] Having occupied their 'lousy leasehold Poetry', Harrison subverts enunciation by abbreviation, elision and emphasis:

> *It won't be long before Ah'm t'only white!*

---

101 *Continuous*, p. 17. In *SP* (p. 120) the wording remains the same, but the full points are omitted from 'S.P.Q.R.'.
102 Antony Easthope, *Poetry as Discourse* (London, 1983), p. 68.
103 Easthope, *Poetry as Discourse*, p. 69.

Or t'Town Hall's thick red line sweeps through t'whole street.[104]

Or does he? The pattern of alternating unstressed/stressed beats in an iambic line may demand careful attention to diction, but it privileges RP no more than a working-class accent. Harrison's subversion is only at eye level. All that happens is that the reader takes care to enunciate the elisions, giving 't'', or ''s' syllabic weight when necessary. Without literary competence, a native speaker of the working-class Leeds dialect would probably not produce the lines above as iambic poetry, but Harrison, producing northern vowels and elisions in the reading of his poetry, does not produce either the rhythm or the natural stress of ordinary Leeds speech. His careful diction and almost metronomic accuracy of rhythm is the same whether he is speaking Standard English or dialect lines.[105] Harrison does, however, demonstrate that poetry, not only verse or the patronising pseudo-native poetry he satirises in 'The Queen's English', can be made from dialect, for example in his *Mysteries*,[106] *U.S. Martial* and 'Next Door IV':

> *Ay, t'Off Licence, that's gone Paki in t'same way!*
> (You took your jug and bought your bitter draught)
> *Ah can't get over it, mi dad'll say,*
> *smelling curry in a pop shop. Seems all daft.*

As 'Confessional Poetry' says: 'Mi dad's did scan, like yours do, many times!' What he does not do is translate the 'high' diction of canonical literature into demotic in his shorter poems. Although 'one of my culture heroes' is 'the comedian "Prof." Leon Cortez who offered his own cockneyfications of Shakespeare, reducing the high flown poetry of kings to an earthy demotic',[107] Harrison does not translate, say, Milton, into demotic, but quotes him in Latin.[108] His heteroglossia is more

---

104 'Next Door I', *SP*, p. 129.
105 As in, for example, his narration of *Banquet* in the production by Peter Symes for the BBC, and of *v.* in the Channel 4 film directed by Richard Eyre.
106 The collected edition of Harrison's adaptations of *The Nativity*, *The Passion*, and *Doomsday*, from the York, Wakefield, Chester and N-Town cycles of Mystery Plays, written, to an extent, in a northern dialect (London, 1985).
107 *Phaedra*, preface, p. xviii.
108 Part of Milton's 'Ad Patrem' ('To the Fathers') (*c.* 1637) is placed immediately after the prefatory poem 'Heredity' in *Continuous*, presumably as an epigraph to the 'School of Eloquence' sequence. It retains that status in *SP*, where it appears on p. 110, before 'Heredity' on p. 111.

generally confined to forms of speech appropriate to their contexts (for example, the satyrs/football hooligans in *Trackers*). When Harrison does translate, for example, 'high flown' lines of Racine or Aeschylus, he does not 'loinerise' them in the way Cortez 'cockneyfies'. The example below is intelligible and demystifying, and to the average theatre-goer and poetry-reader probably straightforward and simple, but it is not Cockney, Leeds, or other regional dialect.

> LEMNOS! Its very name is vile
> Clytemnestra should have been
> of that murderous and manless isle
> the killer queen.
>
> Queen of women who wield knives
> or slaughtered husband's sword.
> The Lemnos husband-killing wives.
> LEMNOS – name to be abhorred.[109]

In much of Harrison's work, RP and Standard English form the base against which regional and social dialects stand out.

Harrison's adaptation of medieval mystery plays provided a chance to undo the north/south, poetry/prose, high/low, Standard English and RP/regional and social dialect oppositions. Bernard O'Donoghue finds the use of northern dialect in Harrison's mystery cycle 'a highly significant contribution to that geographical decentring which has been one of the most important movements in contemporary English poetry' and 'a very ambitious project [which . . .] attempts to achieve effects of theatrical power and dignity in a dialect of English usually associated with marginalisation and even unseriousness'. The dialect itself has intrinsic linguistic merit. O'Donoghue writes of the 'vibrant literary language' at T. W.'s command; of the 'power and skill of the Yorkshire alliterative language',[110] of its 'vigour and integrity'.[111] He quotes from 'the very first page of this Faber (London) book' an instance of

> the occupation of the 'leasehold poetry' in the name of communal northern language [. . . .]
> In loving aye lasting to lout me.   [praise][112]

---

109 *Oresteia, TW*, p. 249.
110 Bernard O'Donoghue, '*The Mysteries*: T. W.'s Revenge', *Bloodaxe 1*, pp. 316–17.
111 O'Donoghue, '*Mysteries*', p. 322.
112 O'Donoghue, '*Mysteries*', p. 320. Original underlining and gloss.

And, from a little later in the play, examples of 'vigorous elements of the corresponding modern Yorkshire register',[113] including Cain's speech:

> Farewell. When I am dead
> Bury me in Wakefield by t'quarry head.
> Damned for my deed I now depart.
> By men set I not a fart.[114]

This is neatly reminiscent of Middle English secular verse[115] as well as drama. The demotic elements of Cain's speech, other than 't'quarry', do not derive exclusively from northern English, though Harrison himself regards his work as northern in character:

> Now the Northernness was useful, not only useful, it's necessary to *The Mysteries*. I was angered when I went to see them at York, and God and Jesus were played by very posh-speaking actors from the south, and the local people again played the comic parts. The whole marvellous quality about the Mystery plays is that they have a homogeneous language, that God, Christ, and everybody else speak in the language of the time, which is also colloquial.[116]

Middle English may be *'par excellence*, the dialectal phase of English, in the sense that while dialects have been spoken at all periods, it was in [Middle English] that divergent usage was normally indicated in writing',[117] but the dialect transcribed in the play books – either the form spoken by the cast and taken down by the scribe, or the form written by the author(s) and copied by subsequent scribes – was not necessarily the only one to be heard in York at that time, nor did the extant varieties necessarily have equal status, even though regional dialects could be the norm; parallel rather than inferior to the developing national standard. While the parts of Christ and his mother, and Biblical characters, were taken by the local guild members, speaking their native dialect (and presumably employing their respective craft registers), there is no reason to assume that in a large trading centre such as York they

---

113 O'Donoghue, *'Mysteries'*, p. 321.
114 *The Nativity, Mysteries*, p. 30.
115 See, for example, ['How Death Comes'] Index 3998. Trinity College, Cambridge, MS B. 1.45 (43), f. 73b, in C. Brown, ed., *English Lyrics of the Thirteenth Century* (Oxford, 1932), p. 130, no. 71.
116 'Conversation', p. 44.
117 Barbara M. Strang, *A History of English* (London, 1970), p. 224.

would all have been native to the area. Other members of the cast or audience (the clergy, guild Masters, and other officials) would have been exposed to the written form of Chancery Standard (as well as French and Latin) through education and documents emanating from the south, and many would have encountered spoken southern English. Jeremy J. Smith charts the growth of 'standard' written English in the fourteenth and fifteenth centuries, and, citing M. L. Samuels, *Linguistic Evolution*,[118] describes Chancery Standard as the form which, after 1430, continued to be used outside its area of origin, and became the basis of modern English spelling.[119] Though allowing a range of variation, this form became 'a kind of mean' analogous to 'socially prestigious varieties' in Modern English. 'Given the social developments [...] the basis of this standardisation had to be the form of the language current in London. The prestige of the capital had a linguistic effect of the kind commonly recorded in modern sociolinguistic surveys.' Harrison's text does preserve an encounter between two socially marked Middle English accents. In *The Second Shepherd's Pageant* (part of *The Nativity* in Harrison's version), the northern First Shepherd responds to Mak (the sheep stealer)'s affecting of a posh accent:

> Mak, now take out that Southern tooth
> And put in a turd.[120]

Smith argues that the gradual spread of the Chancery Standard was more a matter of lexis than accent or syntax.[121] The dialect of the York cycle, like all dialects, includes many registers, some denoting the recognition of social difference. Thus, the style of the speeches of welcome for Christ's entry into Jerusalem, delivered by the Burgesses (with, perhaps, an eye for social mobility), 'is unmistakeably that favoured for pageants celebrating the formal royal entry into the medieval city'; formal and formulaic, almost liturgical, and drawing on the national Biblical rather than specifically local lexicon:

> Hayll domysman dredful, that all schall deme,
> Hayll that all quyk and dede schall lowte,

---

118 Cambridge, 1972.
119 Jeremy J. Smith, 'The Use of English: Language Contact, Dialect Variation and Written Standardisation During the Middle English Period', in Machan and Scott, eds, *English in its Social Contexts*, pp. 55–6.
120 *The Nativity*, *The Mysteries*, p. 61.
121 Smith, 'The Use of English', p. 61.

Hayll whom worschippe most will seme,
Hayll whom all thyng schall drede and dowte.
We welcome the,
Hayll and welcome of all abowte
To owre ceté.[122]

Although Harrison speaks of his desire to 'restore Yorkshire's great classic to itself', his plays were developed from the *Ludus Coventriae* (or N-Town) and Chester, as well as the York and Towneley (Wakefield), cycles, so he was drawing upon the dialects of East Anglia[123] and the West Midlands as well as Yorkshire, and his own text is not strikingly Yorkshire but rather a sort of modernised ur-Middle English. It would have been difficult for him to produce recognisably northern Middle English dialogue intelligible to modern audiences, particularly as some of the main features which distinguished the northern dialects were grammatical (for example, the third person plural pronoun set 'thai', and 'thei', 'thame', 'thare' and 'ther') and, of course, dialects depend upon differences of articulation unrepresentable in a play book, as well as upon dialect words. Certain lexical features were and are characteristically northern, however, and either Middle or Modern English examples could have been introduced to the play, perhaps the Middle English usage 'strange' for 'strong', which appears in the York *Play of the Crucifixion*, or a word such as 'thole' (put up with, bear) which remains in use, or, perhaps in the Nativity scenes, some northern words associated with farming (for example 'twinter', a sheep which has lived two winters, or 'shippon' and 'mew', the parts of the barn which house, respectively, animals and feed). Instead, Harrison uses speech-forms which, though not specifically northern, produce an 'old', 'foreign' flavour and might be taken as northern by a southern audience. The dialogue in the examples below, though northern in character, is neither specifically Yorkshire nor entirely Middle English.

ANGEL

Unto thee maker unmade that most is of might.
Be loving ay lasting in light that is lent.

---

122 Richard Beadle, 'The York Cycle', in Richard Beadle, ed., *The Cambridge Companion to Medieval Theatre* (Cambridge, 1994), p. 87.
123 Following the attribution by Alan J. Fletcher, 'The N-Town Plays', in Beadle, *Medieval Theatre*, p. 164.

Thy Father that in heaven is most, He upon height,
Thy sorrows for to sober, to thee has me sent.[124]

Bursar was I, balancing t'brethren's budgeting book.
[....]
In t'best of all alabaster was t'balm brought in [....][125]

Perhaps the angel's speech represents a kind of Received Standard Heavenish, and the elisions used by Judas an earthly demotic, but they are both, of necessity, hybrid.

Harrison's methods can lead to a kind of cod-northernness which invites the mixed or southern audience to mark its presence, in a way unthinkable for the original. Compare, for example, the speeches below:

3 Sold.   Sen ilke a thyng es right arrayed,
          The wiselier nowe wirke may we.
4 Sold.   þe crosse on grounde is goodely graied
          And boorede even as it awith to be.
1 Sold.   Lokis þat þe ladde on lengthe be layde
          And made me pane unto þis tree.
2 Sold.   For alle his fare he schalle be flaied;
          That one assaie sone schalle ye see.[126]

          KNIGHT 3
Since ilka thing is right arrayed
The wiselier now work may we.
          KNIGHT 4
The cross on t'ground is goodly spread
And bored even as it ought to be.
          KNIGHT 1
Look that the lad on length be laid,
And made be tied unto this tree.
          KNIGHT 2
For all his brag he shall be brayed:
(Turning to crowd/audience)
Stay stood there and you shall see.[127]

---

124 *The Passion, Mysteries*, p. 108.
125 *The Passion, Mysteries*, p. 99.
126 The York *Play of The Crucifixion*, in A. Burrow and T. Turville-Petre, *A Book of Middle English* (Oxford, 1992), p. 251.
127 *The Passion, Mysteries*, p. 136.

Writing, of course, is not identical to performance. At least one critic heard God say 'Nowt is but I' in 'a thick Yorkshire accent',[128] when the printed text has 'and nought is but I'.[129]

Despite his assertion that the articulate rule the world, Harrison never suggests that power over words confers a concomitant power to change society. Blake Morrison describes him as 'a sort of prole-Prince of Elsinore'[130] with Hamlet's predilection for procrastination. For Harrison, effectuality is not guaranteed by political, cultural, or artistic ability. His poetry can seem to echo the equation of advanced intellectual power with diminished masculinity implicit in certain novels written by working-class intellectuals in the 1950s.[131]

> All this is booktalk, buddy, mere En-
> cyclopaedia know-how, not for men!)[132]

If graduates from the school of eloquence are sissy procrastinators, then it is hard to see who in Harrison's universe does get anything done, because the 'dumb go down in history and disappear', and the voluble but ineloquent do not seem to want to achieve anything. In *Trackers*, dialect is given to characters who are both protagonists/victims and hooligans/destroyers; the demotic speaker of *v.* is emphatically anti-intellectual, but not specifically for anything other than a win for Leeds United and a comprehensive racism. Characters in Harrison's poetry resemble the non-militant, grumbling, but imperceptive working class of Hoggart's *Uses of Literacy*. They are not fighting, are not even aware that there is a fight. Thomas Campey, Uncles Joe and Harry, like Patience Kershaw, are victims, oppressed and powerless. Harrison's father is worn out on poor pay, 'broken' by the ruling classes. Young working-class men, usually hunting in packs, are 'All aggro in tight clothes and skinhead crops'; off to 'aerosol the walls, then go get pissed'.[133] They may vent their personal and local grievances, but their rage is generally undirected and impotent.

---

128 Michael Ratcliffe, *Observer* (27 January 1985), reprinted in *Bloodaxe 1*, p. 325.
129 *The Nativity*, *Mysteries*, p. 11.
130 Blake Morrison, 'The Filial Art', *Bloodaxe 1*, p. 54.
131 For example John Wain, *Hurry on Down* (London, 1953) and John Braine, *Room at the Top* (London, 1957).
132 'The Lords of Life', *SP*, p. 213.
133 'Divisions I', *SP*, p. 173.

> Some sort of pattern seemed to exist,
> get a bit pissed on, then go and get pissed.[134]

Women, as discernable characters, rarely appear, even though in his poems it is 'the mams' who push their (male) children up the social ladder.

> A box like a medal case went round the lads
> as, one by one, their mams pushed them as 'bright'.[135]

Mothers are 'carriers' of articulacy in Harrison's work, pushing their sons to speak 'nicely', teaching them nursery rhymes:

> T. H. [...] my love of rhyme [...] came from that close family upbringing. Because my mother did tell me poems.
> R. H. What poems?
> T. H. Nursery rhymes and things of that kind. I think of one poem now, sitting on her knee.[136]

These bridged the gap between the older men gagged by repressive social structures and the younger men disenfranchised from their native voices, but not necessarily articulating their own voices. Most of the poets and other language-heroes to whom Harrison refers are male (e.g. Leon Cortez, Roget, Wordsworth, Keats, MacNeice and Marcelinos Dos Santos), as are the 'acts' he follows, his uncles.[137] Women are also victims of the derailment of articulacy. The disruption of syntax caused by Alzheimer's disease, depicted in *Black Daisies*, is reminiscent of the 'babble' of Julia Kristeva's semiotic,[138] and the insanity (hysteria) which is said to be the natural state of the unrepressed female unconscious for the phallocentric society.[139]

Just as 'the lads' despise the bright scholarship boy for his studiousness, and the older generation is suspicious of those who read 'too many books', so Harrison writes scathingly of the fruits of cultural sophistication:

---

134 *Trackers*, Delphi text, p. 69.
135 'Breaking the Chain', *SP*, p. 153.
136 'Conversation', p. 41. Compare Harrison's 'Blocks' and Lawrence's 'Piano', *Selected Poems*, p. 30.
137 See 'Fire-eater', *SP*, p. 168.
138 See *La Révolution du langage poétique* (Paris, 1974).
139 For a study of the patterns of linguistic disintegration in senile dementia, see Luce Irigaray, *Le Langage des déments* (Paris, 1973). For the ways women relate to phallocratic discourse see 'Women and Madness, the Critical Phallacy', in Catherine Belsey and Jane Moore, eds, *The Feminist Reader* (London, 1989), pp. 133–53.

The Big H

Ah, the proved advantages of scholarship!
Whereas his dad took cold tea for his snap,
he slaves at nuances, knows at just one sip
Château Lafitte *from* Château Neuf du Pape.[140]

Though the epigram projects bitter self-mockery, it reinforces an image of Harrison built up through a succession of poems. That 'he slaves' at nuances suggests physical effort. He also 'slaved to speak or read' Latin, Greek, Czech, French, Swahili, Afro-Cuban, Hausa, Yoruba.[141] The badges of manual labour, grime, sweat, spittle, grease, which once offended his fastidiousness,[142] become badges of retrospective solidarity, of *working*-classness and of masculinity. They show that, although Harrison went 'up a rung or two' to a position from which he could 'wear [his] own clothes to work' and would not make 'oilstains in the wash', he did 'not go posh' ('Breaking the Chain'). Even the metre he frequently employs as an alternative to iambic pentameter, the robust line of a variable number of syllables with four dominant stresses, suggests strength and controlled power.

Harrison uses oppositions to represent the social gulf in poems published at various stages of his career, but the touchstones have changed. In 1970, emblems of deprivation include illiteracy, cheap clothes, a second-class dialect, and having nowhere to make love but waste ground near an abattoir.[143] In 1978, in 'Social Mobility', the opposition is between fine wine and cold tea. By 1992, the privileged are represented by first-class passengers who drink from glass at the front of the plane, while deprivation is drinking Californian Chablis from a ring-pull can in a rear seat,[144] a situation described with none of the irony of 'Social Mobility'. That poem seems to endorse T. S. Eliot's suggestion that the acquisition of a new language entails the adoption of a new (secondary) personality. Thus, 'one of the reasons for not acquiring a new language *instead* of our own is that most of us do not want to become a different person'.[145] It is presumably in the interest of any polyglot poet to

---

140 'Social Mobility', *SP*, p. 107.
141 See 'Wordlists II', *SP*, p. 118.
142 See, for example, 'Currants I', and 'Still', *SP*, p. 140.
143 See, for example, 'Allotments', *SP*, pp. 18–19.
144 'Y', *Gorgon*, pp. 22–3.
145 T. S. Eliot, 'The Social Function of Poetry', in *On Poetry and Poets* (London, 1957), p. 19.

retain his or her first language and personality, together with as many supplementary languages and personae as possible.

If 'Social Mobility' and 'Y' depict someone high on the ladder of aspiration, the process of social metamorphosis has not been unidirectional. The cover of the paperback edition of *Continuous* put the poet into the urban landscape of his poems and prefigured, stylistically, his better-known work of four years later. *Tony Harrison* as aerosol-sprayed graffiti on a wall is outside the traditional literary canon and inside the skin of *v*.[146] Harrison's description in *v*. of an act of vandalism committed by a younger avatar is a demonstration of solidarity with the skinhead's sense of oppression.

> Herman Darewski's band played operetta
> with a wobbly soprano warbling. Just why
> I made my mind up that I'd got to get her
> with the fire hose I can't say, but I'll try.
>
> It wasn't just the singing angered me.
> At the same time half a crowd was jeering
> as the smooth Hugh Gaitskell, our MP,
> made promises the other half were cheering.

Gaitskell's assumption of his audience's complicity in their own suppression by his myth of better times provokes a violent reaction in the young Harrison, and the political promised land becomes identified with art's promises of the sublime.

> What I hated in those high soprano ranges
> was uplift beyond all reason and control
> and in a world where you say nothing changes
> it seemed a sort of prick-tease of the soul.
>
> I tell you when I heard high notes that rose
> above Hugh Gaitskell's cool electioneering
> straight from the warbling throat right up my nose
> I had all your aggro in *my* jeering.

When the soprano siren leads him on with tantalising allusions to transcendent beauty, but does not deliver the climax of ultimate sublimity, his anger erupts, and he ejaculates over her with a fire extinguisher.

---

146 See *v*., p. 22.

And I hit the fire extinguisher ON knob
and covered orchestra and audience with spray.
I could run as fast as you then. A good job!
They yelled 'damned vandal' after me that day ....[147]

The identification with the skinhead is, however, significant in other ways. The skinhead is an effective concrete poet. He sees his words made instantly manifest, and they gain an immortality perhaps more secure than the poet's. Moreover, the language he uses could be taken for a parody of all that Harrison desires to convey in his poetic register, and at the same time the antithesis of what poetry can achieve. It may largely consist of profanity, and be both repetitive and unoriginal, but it is striking, vigorous, 'manly', vernacular and, above all, effective. While the sprayed messages bring about no political change, they do succeed in leaving a permanent, or at least long-lasting, record of the skin's existence; they do succeed in recording the anger of working-class Leeds youths (if not its causes); they do succeed in affecting the poet, who is shocked, and they do effect a change, in Harrison's attitude – he chooses not to erase them. The poem (among so much else) could be an illustration of the poet's envy of someone who can do something in and with language. Ronald Butt missed the point when he reproached Harrison for choosing 'to victimize those who, without being silly, ignorant, or prudish, do not wish to find themselves and their families faced with obscenity on the breakfast table, in what was clearly a gratuitous taboo-breaking exercise'.[148] The exercise was not, I would argue, clearly gratuitous, and the poem conveys a sense both of outrage *and* relish for the skin's language.

One poem depicts Harrison as an inheritor of rather than ambivalent about culture high and low, and indeed suggests that inherited 'culture', the great tradition, can be a 'culture', like a Petrie dish of agar jelly, on which his own cultural contribution will grow.

W. Martin's work needs its restorer,
and so from 1891 I use
the paperhanger's one known extant line
as the culture that I need to start off mine

---

147 *v.*, pp. 20–1.
148 Ronald Butt, 'Disdain versus Manners', *The Times* (22 October 1987), reprinted in *v.*, p. 55.

Harrison allies himself with the paperhanger rather than with the owner of the papered walls, Wordsworth, but unlike the paper-hanger, and in spite of the promise of his lines, does not 'hide our combined labours underground', and:

> so once again it might be truly said
> in words from Grasmere written by the dead:
>
> *our heads will be happen cold when this is found.*[149]

Like 'On Not Being Milton', which belies his claim to have read and committed to the flames the poem's sixteen lines, this poem illustrates the tension between an affiliation with the unsung, the dumb, and the forgotten, and a desire to articulate for them and, through fame and a place in the canon, to be the 'restorer' of their words.

'Them & [uz] II' belligerently declares:

> You can tell the Receivers where to go
> (and not aspirate it) once you know
> Wordsworth's *matter/water* are full rhymes,
> [uz] can be loving as well as funny.

In *Poetry or Bust*, however, a dialect poet, John Nicholson, is given a speech in which 'water' rhymes not with 'matter' but with (wool) 'sorter'.

> The Aire seems like a mass of heaving fleeces –
> all those I ever fingered as a sorter.
> Something's dragging me into the water.
> I feel some awful power pull
> my body into depths of greasy wool.[150]

As an Airedaleman, John Nicholson would not have spoken either Wordsworth's or Harrison's dialect, but he would have had the northern [æ], which Barrie Rutter, in the role of Nicholson, used in the Salt's Mill performance of the play. Given the weight of significance with which the matter/water opposition is invested for anyone acquainted with Harrison's work, such a variant was bound to be striking, and is perhaps a measure of Nicholson's social ascent and moral descent.

Harrison's poetry is not concerned solely with physical, social, and political disablement – the dumb, the gagged, the inarticulate,

---

149 'Remains', *SP*, p. 180.
150 *Poetry or Bust, Plays 3*, p. 55.

and the ineloquent – but shows even native speakers of Standard English silenced, or at least severely restricted in the carrying power of their words, by the curtailing of freedom of expression and by the non-existence of an audience, or of a medium to reach an audience. *Banquet* is 'v' intolerance, especially organised and institutionalised intolerance, racial, religious, intellectual, or ideological, which leads to censorship. The burning of *Satanic Verses* by Islamic fundamentalists is described in the same breath as the unreceptiveness of the contemporary French Academy to Racine.[151] The canonic ranking of literary texts is thus equated with the laws on censorship, the rules and mores of religious orthodoxy, and moves to keep a city district 'all-white', a province 'racially unmixed', or a nation genetically 'pure'. It may seem an exaggeration, but, we are reminded:

> A boy in Abbeville for having sung
> a mildly blasphemous ballad had his tongue
> ripped from its roots, and on his blazing body
> my *Philosophical Dictionary* was flung.

Thus Harrison equates this particularly horrifying, powerfully effective image with political strangulation and linguistic imperialism.

The randomisation of the memories of the patients of High Royds Hospital in *Black Daisies* is akin to the supposed policing of memory by the unconscious, conditioned by the conventions learned on the subject's entry into the symbolic order. Those who suffer from Alzheimer's disease do not censor their memories, however; their loss is not voluntary, nor are the suppressions motivated by guilt or shame. Indeed, the position is reversed: 'The monstrous misadventure / Of Alzheimer's dementia'[152] often dislocates the most cherished memories of beloved people, familiar names and places, habitual occupations:

> All life's brightest moments, filling hearts and heads,
> Alzheimer's, like a blizzard, rips up into shreds.[153]

Sometimes, though the ability to produce the signifier has gone, the signified concept remains:

---

151 *Banquet*, p. 53.
152 'The Therapist's Song', *Black Daisies*, p. 8.
153 *Black Daisies*, p. 9.

Kathleen played piano, played accordion too,
sometimes her hands remember what they used to do.[154]

The play is not, then, the departure from Harrison's usual
subject-matter that it might seem. In *Black Daisies*, linguistic
competence, freedom of the tongue, language, *is* life. Linguistic and
physical deterioration are made parallel both there and in 'The
Mother of the Muses':

There's one with mashed dinner who can't summon
yet again the appetite to smear
the food about the shrunk face of a woman
weeping for death in her 92nd year.
And of the life she lived remembers little
and stares, like someone playing Kim's Game,
at the tray beneath her nose that fills with spittle
whose bubbles fill with faces with no name.

Another

tries to find
alternatives ... *that long thing where you lie*
for words like coffin that have slipped her mind
and forgetting, not the funeral, makes her cry.[155]

Just as in *Gorgon* war dehumanises and ossifies, and in *Banquet*
extremism and intolerance brutalise, so in *Black Daisies* Alzheimer's
disease infantilises and depersonalises, stripping its victims of their
identities:

I'm the Muriel who wed
but your memories of being me are fled.[156]

Their control of language broken, the women exist in a featureless
living death. The songs representing dialogues between the old
women and their former selves are reminiscent of Rosie Probert's
chilling indifference to her fading memories in *Under Milk Wood*.[157]
Literature is offered as a saving grace of fanatic, violent humanity in
Banquet, and rhythm – in tunes, dances and verse – remains in the
High Royds inhabitants as a last grace note of all that distinguished

---

154 *Black Daisies*, p. 15.
155 *Gorgon*, p. 40.
156 'The Song of the Bride III', *Black Daisies*, p. 25.
157 Dylan Thomas, *Under Milk Wood* (London, 1962), pp. 69–71.

them as individuals and, passing, leaves only uniform blankness.

> Muriel Allen's days have all gone astray,
> life's bright blossoms clutched in one black bouquet.
> The music in her still lingers
> In twisting, twitching fingers,
> and in the beat of sneakered feet
> that she drums in the ward all day.[158]

Schism, then, both social and individual, is a major theme in Harrison's work, and language is both the sign of difference and that which maintains it. The polyglot poet inhabits many divided sides, and in his heteroglossic poetry indexes the distance between them.

---

158 'The Therapist's Song', *Black Daisies*, p. 8.1

CHAPTER 3

v.: opposition, antagonism, blasphemy

> all those Vs – against! against! against!
> *v.*

Unusually, *Banquet* (a television film inspired (or inflamed) by the burning of Salman Rushdie's novel *The Satanic Verses* in Bradford) is a more or less unequivocal statement of position. The poet asserts:

> It's blasphemy enabled man
> to break free from the Bible and Koran[1]

He appears to be suggesting that, if the function of art is 'to open the prisons and give a voice to the sorrows and joys of all',[2] then it is the job of poets to oppose suppression and censorship with antagonistic poetry – versus/verses. Voltaire is the first blasphemer to arrive at the banquet. He speaks 'v' organised religion, not necessarily specific beliefs or faith *per se*, but religions which claim a monopoly on knowledge of 'truth' or 'right', and enforce their version of it.

> When I see bigots wanting Rushdie dead
> burning a book I'm sure they've never read,

---

1 *Banquet, Bloodaxe 1*, p. 406. I have quoted from *Bloodaxe 1* here rather than from *Shadow* (p. 64), as elsewhere, because, as well as including the two stanzas removed by the BBC, the Shadow version contains a small but significant variation. The stanza preceding the one quoted addresses Salman Rushdie:
> Where you're in hiding, tuned to the BBC
> I hope you get some joy in watching me
> raise my glass to *The Satanic Verses*,
> to its brilliance and, yes, its blasphemy.
> The opening line of the following stanza in *Shadow*, 'Its blasphemy enabled man', suggests that the blasphemy of *The Satanic Verses* has enabled man 'to break free from the Bible and Koran', whereas the *Bloodaxe 1* version quoted above suggests that it is blasphemy *per se* which enables man to break free.
2 Albert Camus, quoted by John Lucas, *New Statesman*, reprinted, *SP*, back cover.

> marble bust or not, Voltaire's got stored
> a much more critical book in this old head.[3]

(For a dead person summoned to speak for those who reject the idea of an afterlife, Voltaire manages to say quite a lot in *Banquet*. Perhaps 'Voltaire', represented in the film by a marble bust, stands for the 'spirit' or 'message' of Voltaire's writing, the embodiment of the Enlightenment.)

Omar Khayyam is similarly invoked as a blasphemer who was 'v' religions' promises of paradise hereafter in exchange for conformity now.

> Omar Khayyam, who also loved his wine and had no care
> for those cascade-crammed castles in the air
> the Koran promises to those who sacrifice
> 'this fleeting life' for afterlife up there.[4]

Like his guests, Harrison is 'v' dogma:

> And of the afterlife I have no heed.
> What more could a godless mortal need
> than a samosa and a can of beer
> and books, like Rushdie's, to sit here and read?[5]

His work consistently maintains an atheist case. No immortality, not even the Truth and Beauty of art, in this poem, is offered as a consolatory substitute with which we can plug the void of the fear of death:

> In Arthur Symons' *St Teresa* Nazaréth
> is stressed on the last against its spoken flow
> to engineer the contrast Jesus/Death.
> Do I endorse the contrast? I don't, no![6]

If this is blasphemy, it is a mild example. If there ever was a requirement for congruence between the values expressed in canonical literature and the values of established cultural institutions such as the Christian religion, clearly there is no longer, though, given

---

3 Specifically, in Voltaire's case, the bigotry of *L'Infâme* in eighteenth-century France.
4 *Banquet*, p. 54.
5 *Banquet*, p. 55.
6 'The Heartless Art', *SP*, p. 207. The comma is significant in signalling a pause which clarifies meaning. Without it, in performance the sentence could be 'I don't know'.

the actual proportion of non-Christians in England, rather than their cultural hegemony, the poem could be said to be representative of the majority. Though insistent on his godlessness, Harrison does set up certain shibboleths:

> Priests may turn to piety and prayer,
> I turn to poetry and plays by Molière.
> 'Theatre', said Hugo, 'is a place for forming souls',
> but the only gods it knows are those up there.
>
> Believing only in this life below,
> these are the only Gods I'll ever know.[7]

'The gods' are not only cheap theatre seats but poetry and plays, the vehicles of liberatory blasphemy. Harrison's blasphemy is not so much against an establishment as for a form of humanism which regards all religions as constraints on human development, and involves an anti-theism which worships 'life' – the whole-hearted entering into sensuous appreciation of the material world:

> The Koran denounces unbelievers who
> quote 'love this fleeting life' unquote. I do.
> I'm an unbeliever. I love this life.
> I don't believe their paradise is true.[8]

Harrison notes that Rushdie's book, like Racine's, has been flung into 'Inquisitorial *Auto da Fés*', and that by

> reading it, where fools had it cremated
> I bring it whole again, out of the air.[9]

Even if the *fatwa* ceased to exist, however, would Rushdie become 'a monument with Molière'? Voltaire tells us that his work was excluded from the contemporary canon of French literature on the grounds of irreverence:

---

7 *Banquet*, p. 56. *Bloodaxe 1* has some minor variants:
   Priests may turn to piety and prayer,
   I turn to poetry and plays by Molière.
   Theatre, said Hugo, is a place for forming souls
   but the only gods it knows are those up there.

   Believing in this life below,
   these are the only Gods I'll ever know.
   See p. 398.
8 *Banquet*, p. 54.
9 *Banquet*, p. 54.

> I too heard bigots rant, rave and revile
> books of mine which after a short while
> were canonised as classics[10]

Literary merit preserved Voltaire from oblivion. The supposed blasphemy of Rushdie's book led to its burning, and its notoriety led to its becoming a best-seller, neither of which would exclude it from a twentieth-century literary canon, but neither are indices of merit. Harrison does not address the question of whether literary value, either as an immanent quality or in terms of the text's function and effect, will keep *Satanic Verses* out of the academic or popular canons,[11] though his characters do speak as though it were possible to apply absolute criteria to texts:

> ORONTE.
> [...] but still I'm at a loss
> to know what's in my poem ...
> ALCESTE.
> Jesus wept!
> It's bloody rubbish[12]

Banquet does acknowledge that literary evaluation and literary canons are as fleeting as other cultural constructs:

> Time, that gives and takes our fame and fate
> and puts say, Shakespeare's features, on a plate
> or a Persian poet's name on a Tandoori
> can cast aside all we commemorate[13]

It could, however, be read as equating literary value and blasphemousness of subject matter, and as treating the destruction of a material work as the determinant of the survival of the conceptual text.

In general usage, the meaning of blasphemy has broadened from profane speaking, offering impious irreverence to God or sacred things, to include any challenge or refusal of accepted dogma, rather as the meaning of *fatwa* (which Harrison associates with Ayatollah Khomeini[14]) has shifted in general usage from edicts on Islamic law

---

10 *Banquet*, p. 53. We should, of course, bear in mind that Voltaire's work included didactic plays, biased histories, and lampoons studded with scurrilous and unsupported accusations.
11 He does 'raise my glass' to its 'brilliance' as well as its 'blasphemy', *Banquet*, p. 64.
12 *Misanthrope*, p. 17.
13 *Banquet*, p. 61.
14 See *Banquet*, pp. 54, 63.

and practice to the terrorist acts of religious zealots. Harrison proposes a toast to blasphemers: 'all those, then or now, damned by some priest',[15] and can seem to assume that blasphemy, mere challenging of orthodoxy, is intrinsically good. The function of the blasphemers, then, is primarily to oppose not specific doctrines and regimes, but intolerance; to oppose that which suffocates life rather than affirms it.[16]

> The thorny whys and wherefores, awkward whences,
> things that seduce or shame or shock the senses
> panic the one-book creeds into erecting
> a fence against all filth and all offences.[17]

The 'one-book creeds' are representative of more than the tunnel vision which enforces an orthodox reading of one canonical text within a plethora of discourses. That religions are founded on books, sacred texts, hallowed canons, and the *Logos*, is a significant aspect of our cultural baggage. John Goody believes that these creeds begin in opposition. 'The articulation of dissent in written form leads to the formulations of dissent groups: the Manifesto, the Party Programme, the Writings of the Prophet, each can form a point on which dissenters can focus, giving rise to a social aggregate, a collectivity of protest.'[18] Within this somewhat reductive view of religions, the 'one-book creeds' direct and repress the energies of those less sexually charged, less physical, less in touch with 'life', than Harrison, away from enjoying 'life' to fighting for their respective consolatory fictions:

> fear of that big O that swallows whole
> both the human body and the soul,
> fear of time that makes us live and die,
> fear of transience that takes its daily toll,
>
> fear of living, fear of being dead,
> fear that what we love most's soonest fled,
> fear of loving what is fleeting for itself
> our fear of what false prophets make us dread[19]

---

15 *Banquet*, p. 53.
16 The life-affirming and life-opposing in Harrison's poetry, especially the dramatic poetry, are discussed in more detail in Chapter 8.
17 *Banquet*, p. 59.
18 Goody, *Logic of Writing*, p. 122.
19 *Banquet*, pp. 59–60.

Literary art, then, is a redirection of writing from its perversion in upholding the repression of 'one-book creeds':

> writing is connected with the distribution of power to the other semi-autonomous 'great organisations', especially the church. For it sets down beliefs and practices, ideologies and programmes, as well as demanding the attention of specialists. The autonomy of the church and hence, to some extent, its power within the society, is predicated upon the written word.[20]

And, *Banquet* suggests, if the different ways of explaining away the fear of death are not divisive enough, the prophets and priests invent different kinds of damnation to keep people frightened – and divided. Through the figure of Voltaire, *Banquet* affirms that art can save humankind from the tyranny of religion by stripping bare its hypocrisy and making it the object of laughter:

> When a small boy bellows *Mort! Mort! Mort!*
> for Salman Rushdie and fanatics roar
> *Death* to the imagination a revival's due
> of work I wrote two centuries before.[21]

Later, Harrison became

> doubtful, in these dark days, what poems can do,
> and watching the mists round Lindisfarne receding
> my doubt extends to Dark Age Good Book too.[22]

The blasphemy, if any, of these lines is surprisingly mild, and the unqualified use of the phrase 'the word of God', with despair at its misappropriation rather than protest about claims for its existence and authority, is striking in the context of the rest of Harrison's work.

> The word of God so beautifully scripted
> By Eadfrith and Billfrith the anchorite
> Pentagon conners have once again conscripted
> to gloss the cross on the precision sight.
> Candlepower, steady hand, gold leaf, a brush
> were all that Eadfrith had to beautify
> the word of God much bandied by George Bush
> whose word illuminated midnight sky

---

20 Goody, *Logic of Writing*, p. 122.
21 *Banquet*, p. 61.
22 'Initial Illumination', *Coming*, p. 4.

Neither Islam nor Christianity is attacked as in itself duplicitous, or as the cause of intolerance. Religion, in the sense of the word of (the Christian) God, is rather the object of sympathy. This, I suggest, is because 'the word' in the first part of the poem is not the abstract faith or dogma but its manifestation in the material gospel. The word is not only objectified but also almost personified, and feminised. Eadfrith's and Billfrith's work is described as a luminously beautiful golden thing begemmed *and* jewelled (suggesting gem-embroidered clothes and personal jewellery[23]), and 'graced' with cormorants, stolen from Lindisfarne. Histories of despoiled monasteries and convents are invoked by

> Billfrith's begemmed and jewelled boards got looted
> by raiders gung-ho for booty and berserk

– and the theft becomes imaginatively associated with the rape of a gracious and lovely woman by the rude and licentious soldiery. Religion, here, is the victim. The power of the conventional image of Church as woman here draws attention to a structural weakness in the poem, the slippage of meaning between the first use of 'the word' and the second. The 'word of God much bandied by George Bush' is not a book or an illuminated manuscript – an artefact of blended material and spiritual value – but quotation or attribution (and, it could be inferred, misattribution). More importantly, the looting of the gospels is not really equivalent to Pentagon conners' conscription and George Bush's bandying about. Vikings only stole the manuscripts, they did not use them to justify their wars.

Harrison's 'Satanic poems' and 'Satanic play[s]'[24] blaspheme against totalitarian creeds which oppose or censure tolerance, imagination, and somatic pleasure. It is these which presumably justify his right to a seat in Bradford's Omar Khayyam Restaurant (the Blasphemers' Siege Perilous of *Banquet*). Unfortunately, the reputation for shockingness which for some would get him a place at the round table where blasphemers oppose the black circle appears largely to depend on his use of profanity which is not specifically impious, and in particular on his use of profanity on television.

---

23 This is reminiscent of the reiteration of the rood's adornment in *The Dream of the Rood*. See *Anglo Saxon Poetic Records*, vol. II, *The Vercelli Book*, ed. G. P. Krapp (New York, 1934).

24 *Banquet*, p. 62.

Just as Graham Sykes's photograph of a tomb partly obscures the names of its occupants in order to foreground the sprayed and scratched graffiti,[25] so the 'torrent of four-letter filth'[26] was the foregrounded aspect of the film of *v.* and, later, the poem itself. Publication of the poem in the *London Review of Books* on 25 January 1985, and as a Bloodaxe book in December 1985, generated excited reviews, but sales were not spectacular – about 400 and about 1700 of the cloth and paper first editions. The sum of readers' intense individual reactions did not coalesce into public acclaim or fury. (Harrison's televised reading of extracts from the poem caused the Tyne Tees switchboard to be jammed, but that might have been the rescheduling – viewers were expecting darts.) Then Channel 4 announced its intention to broadcast Richard Eyre's film of *v.* – after which the deluge. The poem's epigraph was wilfully misread as a dedication to, rather than a quotation of, Arthur Scargill,[27] headlines called for the film to be banned, and the *Star* selected the nine most expletive-packed lines, printed them gashed with thick black strokes, and primly advised that they had 'censored' them 'for family reading'.[28] The programme was cleared for transmission by the IBA board only 'after heated debate' and because it would have been 'impossible to "bleep" or cut'.[29] Transmission was postponed from mid-evening after the Booker Prize ceremony, 29 October 1987, to 11pm on 4 November. It seemed as though every journalist in Britain was taking a stance, *v.* or v *v.*, and some perhaps unlikely champions appeared. Bernard Levin quoted from the poem,[30] Auberon Waugh appraised its literary merit,[31] Blake Morrison painstakingly explained it.[32] Others talked only of good taste and the Broadcasting Act. 'This House', appraised by Mary Whitehouse, was 'appalled at plans by Channel 4 to screen with the approval of [the IBA] the poem "v."' in an Early Day Motion of 27 October. Whilst 'recognising that the poem may not be wholly devoid of liter-

25 The William Harrison whose tomb was photographed by Graham Sykes and reproduced in the *London Review of Books* and, later, in *v.*, p. 6, is not related to the poet.

26 John Deans and Garry Jenkins, *Daily Mail* (12 October 1987), reprinted in *v.*, p. 40.

27 *Daily Express* (12 October 1987), reprinted in *v.*, p. 42.

28 *Star* (13 October 1987), reprinted in *v.*, pp. 44–5.

29 *Why Did We Broadcast v.?* (IBA, 1988), extract reprinted in *v.*, p. 73.

30 *The Times* (19 October 1987).

31 *Sunday Telegraph* (18 October 1987).

32 In a preface to the *Independent*'s printing of the poem on 24 October 1987.

ary merit', 121 proposers considered that 'the stream of obscenities' would 'serve to hasten the decline of broadcasting standards'.[33] Seventeen Conservative MPs and one Liberal were further moved to express their concern to the IBA, which before transmission also received fourteen other letters of protest and two of congratulation. When the papers began to cry 'hype' about the coverage they had generated (the *Sunday Telegraph* called the film the 'Most over publicised event of the week'[34] after it and its sister paper had printed four articles about *v.*[35)], there seemed a danger that if the conceptual 'v' had come to stand for 'all the versuses of life', the book/film of *v.* would be appropriated to stand for all the censorship, and like *Lady Chatterley* be frozen as an emblem of an old row instead of resonating on with the flexibility of a live voice. Indeed, Harrison's entry in *Lord Gnome's Literary Companion* suggests that it did.[36] Channel 4's duty officers logged sixty-three calls about the film between 11.29 on 4 November and 21.00 on 5 November. A few callers did comment on the strength and power of the poem; someone rang in tears, moved by its 'compassion'; a boy rang to say that he didn't like poetry at school, but thought this was 'really good'; but most either congratulated Channel 4 on their 'courage', and for 'sticking to their guns', or shouted about that lunatic saying 'C.U.N.T.' and 'F.U.C.K.'.

Harrison is reported as saying, 'The offensive words have been taken out of context by people who have neither seen the programme nor read my poem. It does seem an artificially-created storm'.[37] But by whom? Collected in the 'New edition: with press articles' of *v.* are (among other items) the *Sun* report ('A shocking TV poem – packed with obscene four-letter words – is to be broadcast despite protests by clean-up campaigners [.... it] contains 90 swear words'[38]); the *Star* article with its headline 'FROM BAD TO VERSE ...', and comment: 'Furious Tory MP Gerald Owart [*sic*]

---

33 Reprinted in *v.*, p. 60.
34 8 November 1987.
35 On 13 October 1987, 16 October 1987, 18 October 1987 and 1 November 1987.
36 Francis Wheen, ed., *Lord Gnome's Literary Companion* (London, 1994), p. 240. In a review of Michael Kustow's memoirs, Harrison is mentioned only in the context of his 'bad language', as Michael Clark is represented only as a 'bare bottom'.
37 Harrison quoted by Geordie Greig, *Sunday Times* (18 October 1987), reprinted in *v.*, p. 51.
38 [No by-line], *Sun* (12 October 1987), reprinted in *v.*, p. 42.

has demanded that the Channel 4 programme be banned [...]'; and the House of Commons proposed motion censuring both the film and Channel 4 for wanting to show it. Press releases and previews ensured that the poem had plenty of media coverage, and the title of the book is always prefixed by 'controversial poem'. This seems a flawed marketing strategy, because those whom the shock value would alienate are not likely to be buyers of contemporary poetry anyway, and those whom it attracted would buy the poems for the wrong reasons and, disappointed of sustained skinhead-speak, buy no more – though clearly some people did buy the book either because they had read the poem in the *London Review of Books*[39] or the *Independent*, seen the television film, or come across the publicity. This is a pity, because the more important blasphemy, or disruption, in Harrison's writing is not his use of taboo words.

'What is it that these crude words are revealing?'[40] Most viewers seem to have heard someone describing his feelings about profanities sprayed on his parents' headstone, and either accepted the reiteration of those words as necessary, or found their quotation in a poem gratuitous and offensive. But those were, are, Harrison's words, and not just in his skinhead aspect. He uses them not because his work is a flagship for independent broadcasting, or to *épater les bourgeois*, but because they are the best words for the job. Harrison does not ignore offensiveness, he uses it, but *v.*'s invective is directed less against aerosolling skins than against the policies which deprive them of education and employment. In *Trackers*, satyrs fucked by high culture fuck culture's products, demolishing 'all that poncy Apollonian art'.[41] Elsewhere, *cunt* and *fuck* denote a part and an activity of honest lovers, naked to one another with no need of linguistic fol-de-rols and Sunday-best accent.[42] Harrison's awareness of the convoluted aggro-prudery behind the slippage of meaning from sexual term to generalised signifier marked [+rude] provides just one part of the multifaceted pleasures of reading his work, yet reductive criticism and, even more so, journalism describe his profanity in terms of 'shock-value', and make the issue of *v.* one of its censorship rather than any political content it might profess to have.

---

39 *London Review of Books*, 7, no. 1 (24 January 1985), pp. 12–13.
40 *v.*, p. 17.
41 *Trackers*, p. 127.
42 E.g. 'The Pomegranates of Patmos', *Gorgon*, pp. 28–35.

John Barrell suggests that the 'balance and resolution' which literary texts have sought to achieve

> bear a close resemblance to the political balance which, in England especially, was both cause and effect of the increasing power of the middle class, and which has made the notion of balance itself a term of value with a crucial function in middle-class ideology, underwriting the political authority of 'consensus' or the 'middle ground', by representing as irrational extremism whatever cannot, or whatever refuses to be, gathered into the middle ground.[43]

Harrison's invective, then, can be seen as a refusal of the middle ground, of 'balance', and as a failure 'to manifest the control necessary to the production of a properly literary text', for, 'if the tone of working-class writers is "awkward" or "strident" and so apparently betrays their failure to internalise the linguistic manners of the middle-class, then this is evidently the result of a failure to transcend their particular class situation'.[44] Butt's accusing Harrison of transgressing middle-class boundaries of taste and victimising those with a greater sense of decorum is in keeping with this,[45] as is Derwent May's judging *v*. to be 'an unhealthy poem, in the sense that it seems to emerge from a rather disturbed and unpleasant state of mind'.[46]

The protagonists of *Banquet*, then, are writers who, like Harrison, place life-affirming art in opposition to the black O and the earthly powers which invest it with horror – in this play religious intolerance. No awareness that the work of Molière, Voltaire, and the other blasphemers is entrenched in the divisions which Harrison's own art describes is apparent in *Banquet*, yet it is representative of the kind of literature in which readers have sometimes found the consolations and alternative realities usually offered by religion. In *Banquet*, Harrison 'saves' Rushdie's work by plucking it from the air; in *v*., he destroys a work of (musical) art. *v*. equates both Gaitskell's electioneering and the wobbly soprano's singing with duplicitous promises, and they provoke the young Harrison to an act which in its way is like the burning of Rushdie's books. He warns that 'those who feel excluded from "high" art and relegated to "low" will sooner or later want to destroy what they are not allowed

---

43 John Barrell, *Poetry, Language and Politics* (Manchester, 1988), p. 6.
44 Barrell, *Poetry, Language and Politics*, p. 6.
45 Butt, 'Disdain versus Manners', *v*., p. 55.
46 Derwent May, 'A Note on the Poem', *The Times* (1 November 1987), reprinted in *v*., p. 65.

to inhabit',[47] but the young Harrison tries to destroy the song not only because he is excluded from it, or even because the performance is bad, but because it lies to him. His writing does not attack individual artists or the content of individual works, but the social history with which they are inscribed. It therefore seems contradictory for *Banquet* to ignore the equivalent of book-burning (in the denial of a voice, of publication, to the underclasses) which much of his work describes. If Harrison did 'come round to your position on the Arts'[48] for a time, perhaps this is a sign of a sort of suspension of hostility.

Not only sufferer and celebrant share Harrison's *orchestra*, but aggressor and victim, intellectual aesthete and sensualist, Apollo and Dionysus. Defending the satyr play with which, he says, modern audiences are so uncomfortable, he writes:

> With the loss of these plays we are lacking important clues to the wholeness of the Greek imagination, and its ability to absorb and yet not be defeated by the tragic. In the satyr play, that spirit of celebration, held in the dark solution of tragedy, is precipitated into release [....] Without the satyr play we cannot know enough about the way in which the Greek spirit coped with catastrophe. The residue of a few tragedies might give us the illusion of something resolutely high-minded but it is a distortion [....] The thought of tragedy and satyrs co-existing has not been easy even for the most comprehensive of scholars.[49]

The performance of *Trackers* in the ancient stadium at Delphi dramatised 'a contemporary division in our culture between sports and art. In the Pythian Games [...] such a division would have been incomprehensible. As would the division between tragedy and satyr play, "high art" and "low art"'.[50] The juxtaposition of love and death, celebration and despair, aggression and tolerance, the cerebral and the sensual, in poems such as 'Cypress & Cedar' are thus Harrison's continuation of the wholeness of the Greek theatrical imagination. *Trackers* was performed 'in honour of that ancient wholeness', the producers of that performance becoming, for Harrison, '*Ichneutae*, "Trackers", seeking in fragments of our past and present a common wholeness, a common illumination, a

---

47 *Trackers*, introduction, p. xiv.
48 'A Good Read', *SP*, p. 141.
49 *Trackers*, introduction, p. xi.
50 *Trackers*, introduction, p. xxi.

common commitment to survival'. The opposites in the play are not perfectly balanced. Silenus and his satyrs are sympathetic creatures, characterful and lively, whereas Apollo is a thief not above making sinister reference to his flaying of Marsyas, and Kyllene is pompous and preposterous in her head-gear, as the stage directions indicate:

> KYLLENE *finally emerges from the tent. She is a Caryatid, like those supporting the pediment of the Erectheum in Athens. In as dignified way as possible she places a vast piece of pediment on her head and walks slowly from the tent* [....] *She speaks only 'high' dated Victorian verse of the kind that Greek tragedy used to be translated in.*[51]

She is given pompous dialogue, peppered with Miltonic inversions, archaisms and obfuscation:

> KYLLENE
> Bestial creatures! Wherefore have you brought
> to this secluded spot your uproar foul?
> What novel sports are these? They are not they
> wherewith of old you made your master glad,
> who clad in his fawnskin and with thyrsus high
> was wont to chant of yore the holy hymns
> with, for escort, nymphs and youthful throngs?[52]

In the narrative poems, the central protagonists display 'new man' traits, but do not attain the ideal 'formed continuum of female/male' symbolised by the snake,[53] or the gruesome 'fleshly glory' of love-bugs squashed flat in mid-copulation, their 'twinned remains [...] merged into one mess', though, made visionary by a long journey, sun, giant raindrops, pungent pine, Harrison is momentarily beguiled by

> the vision of our simultaneous death [...]
> that made it seem the two of us were melting
> and in a radiant decay becoming one[54]

Masculine and feminine rarely blend; they remain an opposition. The earlier poems describe a culture in which to be called 'sissy' – girlish – is a deadly insult, and linked to education. Possession of the (pass)word, graduation from the 'School of Eloquence', entails a

---

51 *Trackers*, p. 37.
52 *Trackers*, p. 39.
53 'The Lords of Life', *SP*, p. 213.
54 'Following Pine', *SP*, p. 222.

kind of emasculation, a diluting of the over-abundant testosterone in the stage working-class male, and a concomitant inarticulacy. The correlation of middle-class educated liberalism with ineffectuality – stereotypical feminisation – would amount to a castration fear which could explain Harrison's numerous references to his past loutishness and insistence on his present blokishness.[55] 'Currants I' shows his youthful fastidiousness marking him as unworthy of being '"wi' t'men"', and relegating him to the place of infants and women, the home: '"*Next Sunday you can stay 'ome wi' yer mother!*"'[56] His television film *Arctic Paradise*[57] is, in part, a hymn to frontiersman self-reliance and the hunting instinct. His American neighbours' (imagined) assessment of him as 'fairy', 'sissy', leave him apparently unmoved, in, for example, *Fire-Gap*, yet, in 'The Lords of Life', he forces himself to join 'Bill' in the tests of manhood, 'round 1: the shooting, 2: the boozing match!' and

> His suspicions of me as some city loafer
> I tried, when I felt him watching, to dispel
> by letting him see me working, working well.
> I make sure, when he stares over, my swing's true
> when I heave the axe like I've seen rednecks do,
> both hands well-balanced on the slippery haft

He even postpones the attempt to emulate his host's 'manly' feat of squashing empty beer tins flat until he is at home and safe from possible humiliation:

> and found, to my great chagrin, aluminium
> crushable with pressure from one thumb![58]

The narrator never quite proves his manhood to his own satisfaction. He describes himself as a 'contemplative',[59] but 'effete' scholarly references or cerebral passages are often juxtaposed with descriptions of the emphatically physical: sweat, labour, anger, or fingers fishing in Harrison's 501s[60] – themselves iconic of defiantly physical youth culture which is beyond class, and marketed by images of manual labour, other energetic activities (horse riding, swimming,

---

55 For example *v.* and 'The Act'.
56 *SP*, p. 151.
57 BBC 'World About' Series, October 1981.
58 *SP*, pp. 210–11.
59 'Ghosts', *SP*, p. 75.
60 'The Pomegranates of Patmos', *Gorgon*, p. 34.

motor bike riding), and/or sex. In 'Cypress & Cedar', the cerebral
and mystical or moral is balanced by the physical and sensual; a
description of Harrison writing 'in the margins of a sacred Sanskrit
text' and reading the hymns 'for the little clues they offer to life's
light',[61] is countered by:

> Today I've laboured with my hands for hours
> sawing fenceposts up for winter; one tough knot
> jolted the chainsaw at my face and sprayed
> a beetroot cedar dust off the bucked blade [. . . .]
>
> To get one gatepost free I had to tug
> for half an hour, but dragged up from its hole
> it smelled, down even to the last four feet
> rammed in the ground, still beautifully sweet

Activity which shades into metaphysical speculation is in turn
followed by:

> Bob gave me a cedar buckle for my belt
> and after the whole day cutting, stacking wood,
> damp denim, genitals, 'genuine hide leather'
> all these fragrances were bound together
> by cedar, and together they smelled good.
> It was wonderful the way my trousers smelled.[62]

Philip Dodd suggests that Harrison's work, like that of many
northern novelists and poets, depicts the north as the emblem of all
that is masculine, working-class and physical, while the south stands
for the 'feminine, middle-class and spiritual'[63] (thus ignoring the
great importance in Harrison's poetry of his northern, working-class
mother). Dodd sees in 'Me Tarzan' the scholarship boy's yearning
'for untrammelled masculinity', and such a 'lament for the masculine, physical and classed pleasures which the scholarship boy has to
forgo' as 'not merely a matter of biography but of stance'. Men who
have left the manual working class 'find their own masculinity problematic (sissy, "feminine") and they bestow a settled masculinity on
the men left behind'.[64] This kind of '"Northern writing" not only

---

61 'Cypress & Cedar', *SP*, p. 230.
62 *SP*, p. 231.
63 Philip Dodd, 'Lowryscapes: Recent Writing about the North', *Critical
Quarterly*, 32, no. 2 (summer 1990), p. 20.
64 Dodd, 'Lowryscapes', pp. 20–1.

celebrates but also fixes men at the level of the body; the writer as mind'.[65]

'The Nuptial Torches',[66] because it is partly written in the voice of Isabella of Spain, might be assumed to demonstrate the poet's successful blending of his masculine and feminine attributes. Luke Spencer finds in the poem an exception to Harrison's gender position, 'a sensitive rendering of a woman's experience',[67] but the character of Isabella is a thoroughly male projection. She expresses fear and loathing of an extreme of male sexuality portrayed in the character of Philip II. She is a mouthpiece for male fears about male libido as an aggressive and possibly sadistic, *inflictual* drive; the passive object on which the king's gross sexuality operates, forced, by political and cultural forces, but also by her function as a fictional device, to endure in (more or less) silence. Rather than a successful imaginative leap into a feminine persona, I would suggest that Isabella's experience in the poem is an objectification of the dark side of Harrison's glorification of sexuality in other poems.[68] She represents the victim of the Other of male sexuality, the aggression which Harrison fears is inalienable from the life-affirming, even though, paradoxically, the life-affirming is, elsewhere in Harrison's work, represented by female resistance to war. Philip of Spain is at one extreme and the 'I' of 'The Lords of Life' and 'Cypress & Cedar' at the other of a gender continuum, polarised with the concepts of male and female, aggression and sensitivity, destruction and creation, ignorance and education. Sexuality thus becomes a class issue, and much of Harrison's writing dramatises a tension between the desire to be the sensitive, gentle, intellectual, 'new man' of the American poems, and a feminisation/castration anxiety.

The chorus of six women in *Square Rounds* share a line in three languages:

> I will give my life for peace
> Ma vie je donne pour la paix
> Ich gebe mein leben für frieden[69]

---

65 Dodd, 'Lowryscapes', p. 22.
66 *SP*, pp. 60–2.
67 *Poetry TH*, p. 35.
68 For a discussion of desublimation and pornography, see Herbert Marcuse, *One-Dimensional Man* (Boston, 1964).
69 *Square Rounds* (London, 1992), p. 2. No punctuation. For a splendid discussion of the play, see Gillian Beer, *Open Fields: Science in Cultural Encounter* (Oxford, 1996), chapter 14.

This suppresses both individual and national differences, and suggests an international (or supra-national) archetype, while the fatalistic prophecy implied by the unconditional case ('I will give', not 'I would give') further removes the stage personae from realistic characterisation. Of course none of the characters in *Square Rounds* is presented realistically – it's not realist drama – but the male characters, at least those based on 'real' people, do have personalities and are distinguished from one another linguistically as well as physically. Later in the play, the women's physical differentiation is literally veiled and they enter as 'WOMEN IN MOURNING VEILS', thereafter referred to as 'VEILED CHORUS'. The only character who steps forward and removes the veil, taking on a separate, individual identity, is a man, Fritz Haber, played by a woman, Sara Kestelman in the National Theatre production.[70]

A Bloodaxe Books pressrelease on *Gorgon*, which also promotes the opening of *Square Rounds*, notes as newsworthy that the play is 'performed almost entirely by women', as does the back cover of the Faber book. Out of twenty-eight parts, three were played by men: the shell-shocked man and Chinese Magician by Arturo Brachetti and Lawrence Evans, and Sweeper Mawes, the longest speaking part, by Harry Towb. Most of the women took dual roles; two were 'munitionettes/musicians'; eight both anonymous munitionette/musician and a named character; and the rest were part of the undistinguished groups of either munitionettes or musicians. While evidently valorising the female as the peace-maker, this chorus of peace-protesting women from which one or two might step forward to take on a distinct voice, but into whose collective identity most then return, could suggest a reduction of individual identities to a stereotyping which is the reverse of feminist.

The one distinct female persona in *Square Rounds*, Clara Haber, is a strong character, and is indeed based on a real person,[71] yet even she embodies stereotypical feminine attributes. Self-deprecating, she defers to her husband:

> In that cabin began the crisis for man
> which my husband's genius solved.
> His brilliant mind rather left me behind
> but I was thrilled by his work, and involved.[72]

---

70 *Square Rounds*, p. 40.
71 *Née* Clara Immerwahr, a German chemist.
72 *Square Rounds*, p. 26.

Science and romance are 'intertwined' as the couple 'share every test', and an ideal of peace through science.[73] Clara's pacifism is not developed in defiance of her husband, rather she remains true to their ideals, while Fritz Haber allows himself the comfortable illusion that his scientific discoveries will hasten the end of war. She cannot work against him; her only independent act is one of self-destruction. Rather than see the horrors brought about by Fritz Haber's science, she kills herself.

In *Chorus*, Lysistrata says,

> Sexual identity, what a frightful bore
> When the issue we're debating is the end of War.[74]

Sexual difference, however, is always intact in this play. The pleas for pacifism are sometimes spoken as from purely personal motivation:

> LYSISTRATA
>   aren't you all sore
> seeing your children's fathers going off to war?
> All of us here, in one way or another,
> as lover, wife, daughter, sister, mother,
> have got to the point where we've seen
> too many of our men fed to the war machine.[75]

And sometimes they are spoken as from an altruistic drive:

> LYSISTRATA
> Good! That's wonderful. I always knew
> that I could count every one of you.
> So now I can tell you. I have a dream
> that war will end, and a foolproof scheme.
> Are you committed, are you forward-looking?
> It's quite a sacrifice. It may come as a shock.
> Let's have a show of hands, those who say yes!
> [....]
> LAMPITO
> Well, life's pretty terrible if you don't screw.
> But peace has to come before sex, so yes, OK.[76]

---

73 *Square Rounds*, p. 25.
74 *Chorus*, p. 51.
75 *Chorus*, p. 21.
76 *Chorus*, pp. 22–4.

Rarely do the pleas for pacifism seem to come from a radical perspective or social sense. Sentimentalisation associates a peaceable, tolerant outlook with childish innocence and stereotypically female 'softness':

WORLD WAR I VETERANS
We want to gas 'em and they give us bouquets!
WOMEN
To remind you of your mothers and your wedding days.[77]

The way the women persuade the men to stop fighting is not by rhetoric but by refusing to have sex with their husbands, whilst dressing up in titillating 'glamourwear'.[78] Male voices do refute war in Harrison's poetry, of course, but they use a quite different register from the women.

Sex is another kind of answer to territorialism in 'The Chopin Express',[79] and sexuality as both a private refuge and a public expression of a political stance features in many poems, but it is largely male sexuality. Spencer describes the 'enormous impact' of Marcuse on the politics of private desire and public revolt in the 1960s, and criticises a (female) reviewer of *Loiners* for failing to 'acknowledge that the poems occasionally deal with women's sexuality as well as men's'.[80] The poems deal with women's sexuality not only very occasionally but also very indirectly and partially, however, and Anne Cluysenaar seems to me to be more accurate in describing the presentation of sex in *Loiners* as 'a fundamental test and sample of any man's attitudes to racialism, politics, conventional morality, the terror of dying'.[81] In Harrison's poems male sexuality is life-affirming and life-enhancing, opposed to death and repression. Early poems such as 'The Flat Dweller's Revolt'[82] depict women enclosed in, and enclosing men in, a world of 'claustrophobic voices' and 'suffocated talk', a world of silences, repression, and still-births, 'embodying stereotypical female stubbornness and sexual non-compliance'. Masculinity is outside the flats, connected to the earth and a Lawrentian life-stream. Male procreative sexuality is a

---

77 *Chorus*, p. 43.
78 See *Chorus*, pp. 25–30.
79 *Loiners*, pp. 69–70.
80 *Poetry TH*, p. 22.
81 Anne Cluysenaar, *Stand*, 12, no. 1 (1970), pp. 73–4.
82 *Earthworks*, p. 45.

sort of *tsunami*, overwhelming, unencompassable, dyke-bursting, fertilising. As Spenser goes on to say, the only solution 'that the man can imagine is one in which every bride's defences will simply be overwhelmed in a sort of divinely sanctioned elemental gang-bang'.[83] It may be significant that this poem was excluded from *SP*, but those poems from *Loiners* which are included do not, I suggest, extend Harrison's affinity with female sexuality.

Harrison's retention in his *Oresteia* of Apollo's dismissal of the biological role of the mother was taken to be a shock tactic designed to bring 'an incredulous gasp from the audience',[84] an underlining of Athenian fear of the matriarchy when 'Apollo's misogyny exposes the concealed agenda'.[85] Interestingly, however, the emotional response of the youthful narrator of 'Allotments' (if not his actual knowledge) is not so very different when he cries for 'the family still pent up in my balls'.[86]

Classical Greek drama provides Harrison with a forum within which the male and female can be manifest, as archetypes, certainly, but as powerful, compelling figures pared of the blurring accidentals of modern realist drama. By referring to the pre-Olympian myths of the triple goddess, the Earth, who is usurped and degraded by a *nouveau* pantheon of sky-gods, especially Apollo, Harrison associates woman with passion, irrationality, intuition, the element of earth, nature, blood, blood-grudge and brooding, while Apollo, and Orestes, the Everyman of the play, are associated with the cerebral, spiritual and abstract, with the element of air, with philosophy and rational systems of thought, with (literally) high art.[87] The 'art' of women, here, is not the polished recital on lyre or in poetry, but the primal response – the keening of grief, the dancing of maenads. Medea, in Harrison's *Medea: A Sex-War Opera*, like other Harrison female characters, becomes merely one branch of the hydra-like Woman, as Jason is the archetypal tunnel-visioned mythic hero, Man.

---

83 *Poetry TH*, p. 10.
84 Michael Coveney, review of the National Theatre's performance of *The Oresteia*, *The Times* (30 November 1981), reprinted in *Bloodaxe 1*, p. 292.
85 Carol Rutter, 'Men, Women, and Tony Harrison's Sex-War *Oresteia*', in *Bloodaxe 1*, p. 300.
86 *SP*, p. 19.
87 Rutter describes 'girls' as the 'be-ers', and thus repositories of memory, nurturers of grudge, and men as 'do-ers', and thus possessed of short memories and attention-spans. 'Men, Women, and Tony Harrison's Sex-War *Oresteia*', p. 295.

As part of their hostile campaign
against the old Earth Mother's reign
men degrade her
in whatever form she takes
Goddess brandishing her snakes,
Helen, Leda ... [88]

The confrontation of these archetypes is dramatised as a court case in both *Medea* and the *Oresteia*, enabling the representatives of male and female to state the case for the supremacy of their respective gender. With Jason as judge, however, Medea's fate is fixed, and in the *Oresteia* the binary nature of the court is illusory. The Eumenides are dispossessed, merely titular deities, robbed of their tithe of man's offerings by the new pantheon in the ascendant, whose representative is Apollo.

CHORUS
You new he-gods trample the she-gods of old.[89]

Nor is the chorus of Athenians left to judge for themselves. Athena, advocate and patroness of the matricide Orestes, who orders the judges to come to a just decision, in fact makes the decision herself.

ATHENA
It's my duty to come to a final pronouncement.
I add my own vote to those for Orestes!

Though she is represented as female, Athena is almost an anti-goddess, opposed to everything for which the all-mother stands, in her chastity, her cruelty, her blood-lust, and her male physique.[90] That she is, literally, a creature of the males is made clear by her parthenogenic birth:

I myself was given birth by no mother.
I put the male first, although I'm unmarried,
and I am the wholehearted child of my father,
so I don't count the death of a woman
of greater importance than that of her manlord.

The Olympiad divides the triadic female not into nymph, mother and crone, but into creative and destructive woman. While the mannish

88 *Medea: A Sex-War Opera*, *TW*, pp. 431–2.
89 *Oresteia*, *TW*, p. 284.
90 Though she is described as a reconciliation of the male and female in Richmond Lattimore, *Aeschylus I: Oresteia* (Chicago, 1953), introduction, p. 30.

Athena takes over the attributes of the nymph, denuding her of her latent sexuality, Aphrodite and hag-types such as the Eumenides embody the distinction between sexually/procreatively viable, beautiful woman-as-lust-object, and desexed object of horror. The procreatively non-viable becomes an abhorrence, and, since it cannot bring life, it brings death. As Harrison says:

> The Furies do get an honoured place, but it's in a cavern under the ground. If only I had been able to segregate the audience into men and women, I would have got a tension over the whole piece which would have made it into a contemporary debate [....] It's not an antiquarian concern that made me want only men in the play, it was to lock the play into an all-male statement [....] It's weird too that in Greek art the Furies are always depicted as beautiful, but they're described horrendously, with pus oozing from their eyes: it's like two conflicting views of women.[91]

The confrontation is thus neither balanced in its elements nor fair in its process, and this is typical of Harrison's juxtapositions, which often lead us to expect mirror-images and symmetrical polarities, only to undermine that expectation by enacting a collision of unequal opposites.

Harrison's *Misanthrope* dramatises a dialogue between the civilised restraint of moderation and extreme reaction. Philinte insists:

> A little understanding's what's required.
> Humanity leaves much to be desired.
> I know that very well, but let's not rant
> about its vices. Let's be tolerant.
> Moderation's where true wisdom lies.
> What we should be is *reasonably* wise [....]
> Compromise, accommodate; don't force
> your principles to run too stiff a course.
> It's sheer, outrageous folly to pretend
> you'll change things or imagine you'll amend
> mankind's perversity one little jot.
> You think your anger's wisdom, but it's not [....]
> I've learnt to be tolerant of what men do,
> I take them as they come, put up with them.
> 'Bile' 's no more philosophical than 'phlegm'.
> In social intercourse the golden rule

---

91 'Interview', pp. 244–5.

's not curse, like you, but like me 'keep one's cool'.

Alceste replies:

> So, whatever vast disaster or mishap
> you're philosophical and never flap?
> If you were in my shoes and someone planned
> to gain possession of your precious land;
> betrayed you, slandered you, what then? What then?
> Would you still show 'tolerance' for men?
> Maligned, betrayed, and robbed! You'd be a fool
> to watch all that occur and 'keep your cool'.[92]

This is not, however, an encounter of opposites, of liberal versus radical. Alceste is a 'not-in-my-back-yard' moralist who is offended only by outrages which affect him personally; a dog-in-the-manger. 'True love desires uniquely to possess / its object, not to go shares with other men.'[93] Philinte is a detached, fatalistic cynic who sees 'men swindle, steal, lie, cheat', and feels

> about as much sense of dismay
> as if I'd seen some beast devour its prey.
> or if I'd watched, say, monkeys in the zoo [....]
> That's your humanity. There's no escape.
> These are the antics of the 'naked ape'.[94]

If his divisions are rarely binary, Harrison does deal in correspondences, great chains of metonymic congruity which lead from, for example, the dropped 'h', as in ''Uddersfield', to the reaction of Standard English speakers to the dialect which produces that form, as in hatred; to social injustice and oppression, as in hardship; to intolerance and cruelty, as in H-block; to homicide; genocide, as in the H-bomb, and the incarnation of evil, Herod.[95] Peter Forbes finds Harrison to be 'not an intensely metaphoric poet' and suggests that, because 'names for him come replete with a field of associations (class and history in particular), metaphor would confuse the signals they give off',[96] but, as Forbes's examples show, Harrison's work does depend upon synecdoche and

---

92 *Misanthrope*, p. 8.
93 *Misanthrope*, p. 11.
94 *Misanthrope*, pp. 8–9.
95 See the discussion of *The Big H* in Chapter 2.
96 Peter Forbes, 'The Bald Eagles of Canaveral', in *Bloodaxe 1*, p. 488.

metonymy; in 'Cypress & Cedar' the cypress tree is 'a reminder' of primeval ooze, swamps, stagnation, unevolved nature, and cedar is represented by its good smell.[97] The 'balance' which Forbes finds in Harrison's work[98] is not a harmonisation or unification through metaphor, but a juggling act, precarious in the sense of artificially and temporarily created. Despite his obsessive willing into being strands of continuance, a circuit which can carry currents between himself and his family, the more powerful matter of Harrison's poetry, as John Lucas says, is disconnection.[99] The non-equivalence of Harrison's divisions, and his description of hegemony – of society and culture as sites of tension and unequal struggle between dominant and subordinate classes – suggest a Gramscian spirit in his work, and perhaps we should look at Harrison's *v.*s in terms of Gramsci's 'compromise equilibrium'.[100] Seen through Gramsci's view of culture as a structured terrain of exchange and negotiation between forces of incorporation and resistance, Harrison's depiction of language, art, and social division take on new aspects. The language of Harrison's narrative voice, neither Standard English nor Leeds demotic, is a 'new' language, the result of negotiation between the dominant and the subordinated forms. His disconnection from his roots can be seen as the result of his awareness of such groups' failure to recognise, and therefore their collusion in, the coercive nature of the 'deputies' of dominant groups, who sustain cultural hegemony by determining and organising the reform of moral and intellectual life.[101] Harrison's ambivalent attitude to the vehicles of his own work can be explained in terms of the paradox of anti-establishment words being articulated in a system which supports capitalism, the culture industry, and exclusive art-forms. As Storey explains, the force for change stabilises the power-base of the *status quo*.[102]

Even if moral imperatives are anathema to him, Harrison's poetry does have a moral dimension, though the framework of belief it voices is neither comprehensive nor complacent. Rather than offering his readers moral precepts, he more usually leaves them to

---

97 'Cypress & Cedar', *SP*, pp. 230–4.
98 Forbes, 'Bald Eagles', p. 489.
99 John Lucas, 'Speaking for England?', *Bloodaxe 1*, p. 358.
100 Gramsci, *Selections from Prison Notebooks*, p. 161.
101 See John Storey, *An Introductory Guide to Cultural Theory and Popular Culture* (London, 1993), p. 120.
102 Storey, *Cultural Theory and Popular Culture*, p. 122.

abstract the moral lesson from the horrors he describes. *Big H* depicts the '*Pro Rege et Lege*' motto[103] as leading to divisiveness and a whole series of 'antis' including infanticide, but the play refrains from formally advocating the suppression of all that Herod stands for, other than in the chorus of mams' laments[104] and, obliquely, in the slightly embarrassing 'and the lions lay down with the lamb' speech given to Boy 12 ('Our 'arry') in the penultimate scene.[105] Silenus does make an open appeal to the audience, and to an extent sums up the 'moral' of *Trackers*,[106] but he does it in character, and the audience's response to the victimisation of the satyrs, and to the story of Marsyas, is tempered by the speech's coming from the anti-heroic drunk who wants an easy life. Reading or watching other plays of Harrison's, it is as well to recall Richmond Lattimore's conclusion that it is hard 'to interpret a whole tragedy in terms of one moral proposition. Look for the moral dimension.'[107] Harrison's dialectic is not a liberal willingness to see and debate every point of view: not '*tout comprendre c'est tout pardonner*', but both the exercising of imaginative identification and the diversity and intellectual nimbleness which enable him to enjoy correspondences, juxtapositions, oppositions, and arguments, within a drama of opposing voices none of which is necessarily clearly marked 'right' or 'hero'. (The question of sincerity or 'real' affiliation is irrelevant to this study, though critical reception of Harrison's work has emphasised the texts' generation of the sense of 'clenched, exposed engagement' which Terry Eagleton found in *Gorgon*.[108])

With a clearly defined target to oppose, to be 'v.', *Gorgon*, 'Coming', and *Shadow* should perhaps be the most uncompromising of Harrison's poems, delivering an unequivocal message: war is bad. But in works which acknowledge that war is not an abstraction, but something done by people to people, it's not that easy. The poems don't simplify either to glorify or vilify. They depict the

---

103 The motto is shown in the photo-montage opening scene of the play, carved on the front of Leeds Civic Hall, and on the City of Leeds coat of arms which appears on the wall behind Herod on the dais in the fictitious school classroom. *Big H*, p. 325 and p. 330.
104 For example, *Big H*, pp. 340–1.
105 *Big H*, p. 360.
106 *Trackers*, pp. 130–3.
107 Richmond Lattimore, *Story Patterns in Greek Tragedy* (London, 1964), p. 17.
108 Terry Eagleton, 'Tony Harrison, *The Gaze of the Gorgon*', *Poetry Review*, 82, no 4. (winter 1992/3), p. 53.

propaganda of nationalism as forging a mystificatory connection
between local interest and Right, or God's will, bonding

> our VJ bonfire to Jehovahspeak,
> the hotline Jesus got instructions from[109]

Thus, euphoric festivities of righteous victory lead to a sense of
justification: the association of 'A-bomb blast to celebration'.

Harrison depicts wars from both sides, and if the winners of the
war he lived through as a child are handled sympathetically, but not
heroically, then the victims of wars he has lived through as an adult
are seen with pity, but not through blinkers. The Iraqi soldier of
'Coming', determined to make his own terrible appearance a lesson,
peremptorily forbids our overwhelming urge to turn aside.

> Don't look away! I know it's hard
> to keep regarding one so charred,
>
> so disfigured by unfriendly fire
> and think it once burned with desire.[110]

His tone is neither pitiful nor self-exculpating, but sardonic and
aggressive.

> Excuse a skull half roast, half bone
> for using such a scornful tone.[111]

Finally, he reflects on Harrison, and the kind of poet Harrison has
presented himself as being.

> Isn't it your sort of poet's task
> to find words for this frightening mask?[112]

Harrison has indeed set himself up as the kind of poet who finds
words for the silent and silenced. Here his narrator is ventriloquial,
projecting his own voice into the mouth of someone inarticulate. The
poem makes us squirm at our own keenness to accept the fiction of
the 'exclusive interview', the gadget which can record 'words from
such scorched vocal chords', and reveals itself as of the same genre
as the 'happy soldier' poem so deplored by the likes of Owen and
Sassoon.

---

109 'Snap', *Gorgon*, p. 14.
110 *Gorgon*, p. 51.
111 *Gorgon*, p. 49.
112 *Gorgon*, p. 48.

That's your job, poet, to pretend
I want my foe to be my friend.

It's easier to find such words
for this dumb mask like baked dogturds.[113]

This, of course, makes the lies which the soldier demands the poet make all the more effective.

Lie that you saw me and I smiled
to see the soldier hug his child [. . . .]

pretend they have the burnt man's blessing
and then, maybe, I'm spared confessing

that only fire burnt out the shame
of things I'd done in Saddam's name,

the deaths, the torture and the plunder
the black clouds all of us are under.

Neither a forgiving gilded saint nor a wholly black sinner, the Iraqi becomes another Everybloke:

a mirror that returns the gaze
of victor on their victory days[114]

Thus, he can speak to every other common man without being suspected of a political agenda, and warn them.

Each Union Jack the kids now wave
may lead them later to the grave.

Harrison's refusal of the kind of false balance which would unite the divisions he finds and resolve the oppositions he makes is nowhere better illustrated than in the endings of his poems. The *Aeneid*'s ending, on 'a typically Virgilian ambiguity, a dubious triumph and the shade of Turnus grudgingly leaving the earth',[115] seems to have stayed with Harrison since his early work on translations of the poem. Pairing-off and retribution (in the form of Célimène's condemnation to the loneliness she dreads) lead us at the end of *The Misanthrope* to expect the classic denouement of a

---

113 *Gorgon*, p. 53.
114 *Gorgon*, p. 52.
115 T. W. Harrison, 'Dryden's *Aeneid*', in Bruce King, ed., *Dryden's Mind and Art* (Edinburgh, 1969), p. 159.

marriage party and a speech of summation. In Harrison's version, however, Alceste's declaration to Célimène is swiftly retracted when she refuses to rusticate with him:

> ALCESTE   No, now I hate you, loathe, abhor.
> This beats anything you've done before [. . . .]
> This last humiliation's set me free
> from love's degrading tyranny.[116]

In the space of the same speech, he turns to Eliante, making her a declaration (of admiration) which he undermines by, firstly, failing to produce the conventional hyperbole of romantic love, expressing instead hesitation, and, secondly, stating his expectation of rejection:

> I started to admire you long ago
> and hope you'll let me go on doing so,
> but, please, with all my troubles, understand
> if now I hesitate to seek your hand.
> I feel unworthy of it. It seems that Fate
> didn't intend me for the married state.
> Cast off by one not fit to lace your shoes,
> my love's beneath your notice. You'd refuse.

When Eliante accepts, not the proposal, but the invitation to reject him, Alceste's reply is his last speech of the play. It is neither a gracious benediction on the love of Philinte and Eliante (he feels 'betrayed on *all* sides'), nor quite a valediction:

> For me, betrayed on *all* sides and laid low
> by heaped injustices, it's time to go,
> and leave man floundering in this foul morass
> where vice goes swaggering as bold as brass,
> and go on looking for a safe retreat
> where honesty can stand on its own feet.

Man goes on floundering; Alceste goes on looking.

Similarly, by placing the execution at the beginning of *Medea*, and telling the story of Jason, Medea, Butes, and the others in a non-linear way, Harrison is enabled to cut between the deaths of Medea and Jason at the end of the play.[117] This scene is in turn undercut as a climactic finale by the chorus of women who quote

---

116 *Misanthrope*, p. 68.
117 The end of the version of the play by Euripides is not unproblematical. See Richmond Lattimore, *The Poetry of Greek Tragedy* (Baltimore, 1958), p. 108.

from the Euripidean and subsequent versions of the *Medea*, and reflect upon the play as translation and as unfinished business.

> DOWNSTAGE WOMAN.
> Did you know that what you hear
> is from Euripides *Medea*
> of 431
> that's 431 BC!
> The breaking of male monopoly
> has just begun!

> These words from a women's chorus
> at least 2000 years before us
> weren't much heeded,
> but since what they sung then
> should still be listened to by men
> a translation's needed ...[118]

Kaisers has a sequence of apparent endings as three different people queue up to deal the gladiator-caesar Commodus three successive death blows. Orpheus impales him on the point of a cello, his father, Marcus Aurelius, covers him with a lion-skin pall, then Harrison (playing himself) stabs him through the heart with the sign-post for the amphitheatre in which the production takes place. Even then the play is not over. After a moment's silence, Commodus springs up, brandishes the sign-post, rips off his muzzle, and, laughing, takes a bow. He had crowed:

> Art will have to acknowledge that it's truly beaten
> when he [Orpheus] plays his magic lyre but still gets eaten.[119]

And he is right, in that the artist cannot 'kill' him, and the brutality he represents, but the point of this play is that it should not try, should not ignore, suppress, or 'Disneyfy' ugly chapters in our history.[120]

Perhaps the most characteristic ending of Harrison's plays is *Banquet*. From the opening shot the audience is set up to expect a final scene like the last page of an Asterix adventure – the heroes fêted and feasting. Harrison drinks wine at a restaurant table

---

118 *Medea*, *TW*, p. 447.
119 *Kaisers*, p. 77.
120 See *Kaisers*, p. 75.

prepared for dinner, the 'blasphemers' banquet table', he tells us, where, 'on mirrored cushions will sit', besides Harrison, Voltaire, Molière, Omar Khayyam, Lord Byron, and Salman Rushdie.[121] We know that the first four guests are not going to attend, unless they are played by actors or busts, but it is possible that Rushdie will arrive, or that the camera will go to him in some safe house. He does not appear, however, and no banquet ends the play, only a blank screen, and silence, reminiscent of Harrison's evocation of:

> that most haunting epigraph in the whole of literature, the sentence from Azedinne El Mocadecci, prefixed to Edward Powys Mathers' masterly and beautiful rendering of the Panchasika of Chauras, *Black Marigolds*: 'And sometimes we look to the end of the tale that there should be marriage feasts, and find only, as it were, black marigolds and a silence.'[122]

---

121 *Banquet*, p. 53
122 'Inkwell of Dr Agrippa', *Bloodaxe 1*, p. 34.

CHAPTER 4

A blasphemers' banquet? The critical reception of Harrison's work

The heterogeneity of Harrison's work is matched by the diversity of the ways in which it has been interpreted. Critics have described, among other things, its political agenda,[1] failure of radicalism,[2] sentimentality, post-structuralist intertextuality,[3] mastery of form,[4] 'doggerel' rhymes and 'rumty-tum' rhythms,[5] directness and urgency,[6] generalisation which amounts to class treachery,[7] an over-literal imagination and naivety,[8] and Bakhtinian polyphony.[9] To Mary Whitehouse, *v.* embodied indecency, its transmission raising the question of standards of decency in television.[10] To Sir Gilbert Longden, it embodied the taking-over of art by 'the riff-raff'.[11] To John Lucas, it embodied the struggle of literature against censorship, a struggle to which 'the nation itself' became 'the invited audience'.[12] Similarly, to David Glencross, the poem embodied free-thinking opposition to the 'vendetta' of government against broadcasters.[13]

---

1 See Lucas, 'Speaking for England?', pp. 351–61.
2 See Terry Eagleton, 'Antagonisms: Tony Harrison's *v.*', in *Bloodaxe 1*, p. 350.
3 See 'THL', pp. 53–67.
4 See Douglas Dunn, 'The Topical Muse', The Kenneth Allott Lecture (1990), extract reprinted as 'Formal Strategies in Tony Harrison's Poetry', in *Bloodaxe 1*, pp. 129–32.
5 Martyn Harris, *Daily Telegraph* (16 October 1987).
6 See Jonathan Barker, 'Peru, Leeds, Florida, and Keats', in *Bloodaxe 1*, pp. 46–53.
7 See Ken Worpole, 'Scholarship Boy: The Poetry of Tony Harrison', in *Bloodaxe 1*, pp. 61–74.
8 See Stephen Spender, 'Changeling', *The New York Review of Books*, 29, no. 12 (15 July 1982), reprinted in *Bloodaxe 1*, pp. 221–6.
9 See Huk, 'Leeds Renaissance', pp. 75–83.
10 See Mary Whitehouse, letter to *The Times* (26 October 1987), reprinted in *v.*, p. 59.
11 Sir Gilbert Longden, letter to the *Independent* (2 November 1987), reprinted in *v.*, p. 68.
12 Lucas, 'Speaking for England?', p. 351.
13 David Glencross, 'Censorship: Let the Viewers Decide', *Observer* (1 November 1987), reprinted in *v.*, pp. 66–7. Though Director of Television at the IBA, Glencross was described as writing 'in a personal capacity'.

A blasphemers' banquet?

Harrison's insistence upon the social and historical might seem to dictate the most appropriate approach to his poems. Most kinds of contextual or biographical study would not, however, focus on the multiplicity of discourses in the writing, or its contradictions and paradoxes, nor would they provide the detailed linguistic analysis which the work seems to demand. The poems could be taken to be ill-suited to a traditional critical analysis which devalues contradiction, but, while post-structuralist analysis can embrace paradox, contradiction and irrelevance, it would presumably sit ill with the poems' dependence upon certain givens. Is Harrison's work inconstant, incomplete, and immature, or transgressive and innovative – a hybrid or a maverick? Is its persistent slipperiness to definition and evaluation definitive of its own special nature, or indicative of the inadequacy of the critical apparatus applied to it?

If Harrison's writing would be ill suited to a Leavisite analysis which looked for cohesion and resolution, would it be better served by more recent criticism which 'By contrast [...] has tended to stress textual disarray'?[14] Investigating '"discourse" – the structure of concepts and assumptions which hold together the understanding of social groups and which have derived from relationships of social power', this kind of criticism seems to share many of Harrison's preoccupations. Rylance suggests that the sensitivity of post-structuralist literary critics to 'ideological determination and constructedness' could usefully be applied to Harrison's work, and that its 'verbal and intellectual organisation [...] might lend itself to post-structuralist method', because he has 'a strong sense of the social ground of language, especially its silences and occlusions, and of the suppression of variations across an apparently homogeneous language community'.[15] For Rylance, Harrison's techniques also bear resemblance to those of post-structuralist criticism, in that 'he has a highly self-conscious relationship to earlier literature, and his work is packed with quotation, allusion and intertextual citation'. The poetry could be said to share some of the 'central features associated with postmodernism in the arts', which Maran Sadup describes as including 'the collapse of the hierarchical distinction between élite and popular culture; a stylistic eclecticism and the mixing of codes [...] parody, pastiche, irony and playfulness', and

---

14 'THL', p. 53.
15 'THL', p. 54.

Harrison could be said to partake of the postmodernist tendency to '"textualize" everything', to treat 'history, philosophy, jurisprudence, sociology and other disciplines' as 'optional "kinds of writing" or discourses'.[16]

Rylance's post-structuralist analysis of 'On Not Being Milton' is revealing, but the influence of post-structuralist thought on Harrison's work is perhaps less apparent in the attention it pays to social divisions than in its preoccupation with self-consciousness and self-reflection. Alan Robinson describes the latter as a natural progression from the former, finding in the work of Heaney, Paulin, and Dunn a resistance to 'what they regard as England's continuing political and artistic hegemony over their nations', corresponding to the 'widespread refusal of women poets to accept as "natural" and hence unquestionable their subordination to the existing patriarchal order in society'. Both nationalism and class- and gender-consciousness 'converge in opposition to the Establishment's marginalisation of "the Other"'.[17] Robinson sees parallels between self and political awareness and analysis and style, finding 'an increasing self-consciousness in stylistic matters' both in technical experimentation and in 'ethical introspection about the pragmatic role of the writer's artful "representations" in the social construction of the self'. He asserts that this 'increasing theoretical sophistication (evident in the impact on several poets of varieties of Poststructuralism) will, for better or worse, surely come to be seen as one of the characteristics of late-twentieth-century poetry'.[18] If 'the fragmentation of the political consensus in Britain is paralleled indirectly and complexly in the divergences of contemporary poetry',[19] and in the radical destabilisation of the self, then that de-centred, fragmented, self-conscious, unstable self of the poet has, paradoxically, become central. What precludes Harrison from being a postmodernist poet is precisely that self. Alienated, angst-ridden and complex, but recognisably a central subject, this self has a sense of history, a past to describe and a future which may be changed.

---

16 Madan Sarup, *An Introductory Guide to Post-structuralism and Postmodernism* (London, 1993), p. 132.

17 Alan Robinson, *Instabilities in Contemporary British Poetry* (London, 1988), preface, p. ix.

18 Huk presents the case for classifying Harrison's work as postmodern in her 'Postmodern Classics: The Verse Drama of Tony Harrison', in James Acheson, ed., *British and Irish Drama Since 1960* (London, 1993), p. 202.

19 Robinson, *Instabilities in Contemporary British Poetry*, preface, p. ix

Eagleton explains that the 'depthless, styleless, dehistoricized, decathected surfaces of postmodernist culture are not meant to signify an alienation, for alienation requires a dream of authenticity which postmodernism finds quite unintelligible. Those flattened surfaces and hollowed interiors are not "alienated" because there is no longer any subject to be alienated and nothing to be alienated from.'[20] Harrison seems less at home with Lyotard or Deleuze than 'revolutionary avant-gardism, one of whose major impulses [...] was to dismantle the institutional autonomy of art, erase the frontiers between culture and political society and return aesthetic production to its humble, unprivileged place within social practices as a whole'.[21] For Eagleton, the postmodernist practice is 'the cynical belated revenge wreaked by bourgeois culture upon its revolutionary antagonists', a monstrous perversion of a utopian dream, whose desire for 'a fusion of art and social praxis is seized, distorted and jeeringly turned back upon them as dystopian reality'. From this perspective, it seems as though postmodernism 'mimes the formal resolution of art and social life attempted by the avant-garde, while remorselessly emptying it of its political content; Mayakovsky's poetry readings in the factory yard become Warhol's shoes and soup-cans'.[22] Like Eagleton's 'old-fashioned modernism', Harrison's work 'is still agonizedly caught up in metaphysical depth and wretchedness, still able to experience psychic fragmentation and social alienation as spiritually wounding, and so embarrassingly enmortgaged to the very bourgeois humanism it otherwise seeks to subvert'.[23]

Rylance describes 'On Not Being Milton' as 'engaged in a cultural exchange and borrowing typical of the postwar period', its discourse formed by a *bricolage* of international elements, using techniques of intertextual allusions, punning, self-conscious analogy and juxtaposition characteristic of a certain contemporary manner (as in the ubiquitous postmodernism).[24] Allusion and juxtaposition in Harrison's poems surely make them closer to modernism than postmodernism, and they do not use the characteristic postmodern

20 Terry Eagleton, *Against the Grain* (London, 1986), p. 132.
21 Eagleton, *Against the Grain*, p. 131.
22 Eagleton, *Against the Grain*, pp. 131–2. Compare his remark that the skinhead in *v.* is 'the kind of man you feel Mayakovsky would have got on with' in 'Antagonisms', *Bloodaxe 1*, p. 350.
23 Eagleton, *Against the Grain*, p. 143.
24 'THL', p. 65.

devices of randomness and anarchy, nor seem 'antagonistic to any theory that "goes beyond" the manifest to the latent'.[25] 'On Not Being Milton', Rylance finds, articulates with 'particular regional and generational emphases, engaging with a familiar postwar argument concerning the history of the British working class, and these features are not happily absorbed into post-structuralist theory'.[26] He goes on to discuss the value of theories which are concerned with cultural issues and with both 'human agency and individual experience', finding that because of the suspicions of 'Marxists influenced by French structuralism', theory was 'stressed over history, structure and ideology over agency, the unconscious over willed creativity'. In literature, 'forms which were dislocating rather than representational were valued, as was an abstracted, erudite and generalising language, rather than one that was plain, detailed or emphasised feeling'. Rylance finds that these shifts 'involved gains, but also losses. Among the losses were attention to specific history, and to individual or non-metropolitan experience'. Those losses did not necessarily include popularity and accessibility, of course, nor does post-structuralist analysis necessarily valorise the complex and mystificatory.

Rylance suggests that a thoroughgoing post-structuralism would be inadequate to describe Harrison's work because of its neglect of literature's 'communicative powers, its capacity to intervene and create, and to render human situations and histories meaningful' in favour of the 'emphasis on textual "signification", the epistemological difficulties of sceptical rationalism, and psychoanalytic speculation'. None the less, it is worthwhile to 'preserve and extend some of the responsible guiding insights of this work'. It is clear that 'language does carry the "traces" (to appropriate a Derridean term) of a history within it; and that human identity is often a matter of crisis and dislocation'. Rylance therefore 'considers these ideas in relation to [. . .] "On Not Being Milton"', but tries to 'avoid much of the terminology usually used to discuss them'.[27]

Like other aspects of modern theory, post-structuralist analysis 'has been suspicious of frank appeals to emotion, preferring the complexities of disruption and difficulty'. Barthes is again held up as a culprit, a perpetrator of difficulty, but at least a stylish and vivid

---

25 Sarup, *Post-Structuralism and Postmodernism*, p. 132.
26 'THL', p. 65.
27 'THL', pp. 53–4.

one. 'Even when 'the pleasure of the text" has been stressed, this emotion has been sophisticated and cerebral; and rather chillingly, and often bafflingly, couched in a language which it takes a very sophisticated stylist indeed – like Roland Barthes, for instance – to make at all vivid.' Rylance expresses reservations about theory's ability to express 'the recognisable and openly expressed human situation' described in 'On Not Being Milton', 'which poses interesting questions for our modern sense of how we read as literary critics. It is technically accomplished and verbally dextrous, but its primary impact is emotional. Like much of Harrison's work, it bids for sentiment through its virtuosity.' 'On Not Being Milton'

> invites a response which professionally we are not accustomed to give. It is populist in cast, draws upon the sentimentality of popular entertainment, and wants to make us cry. This embarrasses the tough, conceptualised manner of much recent criticism, which has not wished to attend to such effects.

There are many references to tears, his own[28] and other people's,[29] in Harrison's poetry, and he has expressed an affinity with the novelist of sentiment and pulled heart-strings: 'I got a lot from Dickens. I liked what I think of as something very English about Dickens, also his directness, his vulgarity, his willingness to be almost sentimental.'[30]

We might expect Harrison to concur with a Classical Greek concept of the relationship between sentiment (including sometimes painful emotion) and the pleasure of the text. Malcolm Heath finds it clear that 'a successful performance in Ion's view is a particularly emotive one, i.e. one which leaves the audience in tears'.[31] Heath notes 'the paradox of our taking pleasure in painful emotions like grief', and remarks that 'in *Philebus*, too, Plato observes that at tragic performances the audience takes pleasure in its tears'.[32] This pleasure is not identical to straightforward enjoyment, but better described as 'emotional excitement'. In this sense, tragedy is 'the

---

28 Early references are oblique, for example 'Marked with D.', *SP*, p. 155 and 'Background Material', *SP*, p. 171. Later examples are explicit, for example 'An Old Score', *SP*, p. 139, 'Still', *SP*, p. 140, and 'Isolation, *SP*, p. 142.
29 See, for example, 'Blocks', *SP*, p. 164, 'Bringing Up', *SP*, p. 166, and 'Changing at York', *SP*, p. 154.
30 'Conversation', p. 42.
31 Malcolm Heath, *The Poetics of Greek Tragedy* (London, 1987), p. 8
32 Heath, *Poetics of Greek Tragedy*, p. 9.

kind of poetry which gives most pleasure', a pleasure which Plato regarded as morally harmful. Thus, Heath continues, 'The hedonistic principle is conceded only with a qualification', one which 'utterly transforms it: it is the pleasure of the best educated and morally soundest (that is, of those who will not be beguiled by corrupting emotionalism) which is to provide the criterion by which poetry is judged'. This justification on intellectual and moral grounds seems to be a precursor of the Romantic theory which justified luxuriation in melancholy by regarding it as a fine wine to be best appreciated by those with the most discriminating palate, the finest aesthetic judgement for joyous or melancholy experience.

> Ay, in the very temple of delight
>   Veil'd Melancholy has her sovran shrine.
>   Though seen of none save him whose strenuous tongue
>   Can burst Joy's grape against his palate fine;
> His soul shall taste the sadness of her might,
>   And be among her cloudy trophies hung.[33]

Harrison does not present either the artist or the moral philosopher as the connoisseur of emotion. He does evoke powerful feelings in his poetry, of love and grief, for example, but his audience is not allowed to wallow in them, and, indeed, the emotions are often turned against the audience, particularly in the theatre works. As in Greek tragedy, emotional content is not separable from action, from cause and effect. 'Behind the words of Greek tragedy there is action, behind the action emotion: the abstract and the concrete are made one, the emotion and the meaning are indivisible.'[34]

Rylance also addresses the question of the extent to which Harrison's work has received serious and/or academic interest, and why. Jibes in Harrison's work suggest that he wouldn't care. Silenus appeals to the audience:

> He gets that vicious when he's vexed,
> so you'd better 'elp out and get his lads from 'text.
> Perhaps there's a doctor ... some don from Queen's
> who can tell the uneducated what this means.[35]

---

33 John Keats, 'Ode on Melancholy', *Works*, p. 219.
34 Oliver Taplin, *Greek Tragedy in Action* (London, 1978), p. 1.
35 *Trackers*, pp. 96–7.

Harrison announces: 'I prefer the idea of men speaking to men to a man speaking to god, or even worse to Oxford's anointed.'[36] To what extent, however, does he owe his readership to academic readers, academic reception and criticism? For Astley, the taint of academicism is the kiss of death to poetry aimed at the general market, as though a considered and scholarly review or back cover copy somehow rubbed off on the book.

> The easiest way to put off potential readers is to compose a blurb as if it were a piece of literary criticism, making readers feel that they need a degree in English to understand the poems in the book [.... Editors] make no attempt to understand why a particular book might interest other readers, and in many cases they are robbing their own poets of a much wider readership by tarring them with an academic brush.[37]

Not all academic criticism is mystifying, intimidating or exclusive, and not all of it aims to appropriate poetry for the academy. While Astley is, I should think, right in suggesting that copy sprinkled with trendy jargon and blurbs claiming definitiveness and innovation for their poetry can be off-putting, his editorship and publication of *Bloodaxe 1* suggests that he distinguishes between gratuitous blurb and elucidation, and that he places a value on the scholarly interpretations, assessments, and commentaries of, for instance, Romana Huk, John Lucas, and Bernard O'Donoghue. Harrison acknowledges that without his education he could not produce his poetry, and, as David Trotter points out, 'there can be little poetry published today on which the shadow of an institutional readership does not fall'.[38] The readership for literature, Trotter suggests, is organised and identified largely by the educational system.

The 'academy', the institution of English literature, is not, of course, a straightforward concept, and the argument surrounding the problematisation of this concept, and the related concept of 'canonical text' is too complex to be summarised here. For Leslie Fiedler, almost no novels, 'seem any longer to be ends in themselves', rather,

> 'they represent transitional stages on the way to a final form: if they are adjudged 'high literature', they are represented by a diagram on the black-board; or if classified as 'low literature', they become images on

---

36 In *Bloodaxe 1*, preface, p. 9.
37 Neil Astley, ed. *Poetry with an Edge* (Newcastle-upon-Tyne, 1988), p. 15.
38 David Trotter, *The Making of the Reader: Language and Subjectivity in Modern English and Irish Poetry* (London, 1984), p. 146.

the screen. English majors are taught to deplore the latter transformation as vulgarization, although it is better understood as the democratization of art, which is desirable as well as inevitable in a mass society.

A similar division has been made 'in the realm of poetry'. One kind of verse 'is typically set to music and therefore customarily not read but heard by a mass audience [. . . .] The others are printed, and read as part of a classroom assignment.'[39] Harrison's poetry has, to an extent, crossed those boundaries – broadcast on television and radio, staged at the National Theatre, published in Penguin paperback, and on academic syllabi – but the transgression of the boundaries does not necessarily demonstrate the possibility of a work's being simultaneously academic or 'intellectual' and 'popular'. Rather, it could be a product of the particular profile of the poetry audience in England – broad-range middle-brow, with fairly catholic taste within certain limits.

'Academic is no bad thing to be', Donald Davie wrote in response to criticisms of The Movement, 'and in any case becomes inescapable, as the philistinism of Anglo-American society forces all artists – not just writers – back into the campus as the last stronghold.'[40] Harrison has not retreated back into the campus as a sanctuary, having refused academic appointments and literary fellowships since 1974, and, though his work is popular with sixth-form students and undergraduates, his readership is far from exclusively academic. Trotter borrows Randall Jarrell's phrase 'the Age of Criticism' to argue that our reading of literature has become more firmly directed by discourses produced within the institutions of the schools and universities.[41] Directed, but not entirely determined. 'Despite the power of these institutions, Common Readers – readers identified by assimilation into a "homogeneous culture" rather than by their response to a segregating rhetoric, or by membership of an academy – have not disappeared.'[42] These readers are presumably among those whom writers like Harrison seek to attract. Increased sales following transmission of his television programmes and the publication of journalistic poems such as

---

39 Leslie A. Fiedler, 'Literature as an Institution', in Leslie A. Fiedler and Houston A. Baker Jnr, eds, *English Literature: Opening up the Canon*, (Baltimore, 1981), pp. 77–8.
40 Quoted by Trotter, *Making of the Reader*, p. 136.
41 Trotter, *Making of the Reader*, p. 135.
42 Trotter, *Making of the Reader*, p. 233.

'Coming' in the news pages of newspapers indicate a potential for by-passing the academic in reaching an audience.

Fiedler argues that the 'Republic of Letters' identifies literature 'with the texts – the words on the page they scrutinize together'. For them, 'print is the ultimate medium toward which all preceding mediums represent a slow ascent, and from which all succeeding mediums represent a regrettable decline'. Thus works which prove 'untranslatable into post-Gutenburg forms without loss, or even worse, with some gain of effect and authenticity, challenge the very *raison d'être* of professional teachers of English'.[43] These teachers are no longer battling for modernist works against their 'genteel predecessors and their obsolete notions of what constituted literary excellence', but against 'the mass audience'. Perhaps we should distinguish between the identification of literature with 'words on the page', and the suspicion of 'post-Gutenburg forms'. Though drama is older than books, not all modern academic writers accept that 'text' is anything other than print, and resist the suggestion that to strip a play of the accidentals of performance produces not the pure, essential work, but one text among many. Obviously there are practical problems in academic criticism of performance, but those are not the only reasons for the relative lack of interest in Harrison's active collaboration with musicians, designers, actors, and directors. Peter Levi writes that Harrison's 'contribution to the legitimate theatre, and the verse technique in which I am interested, end more or less with *The Oresteia*' and the 'long musical distraction began with *Bow Down* (1977) and *The Bartered Bride* (1978)'.[44] Outside semiotic analysis of theatre, academic criticism is bound to concentrate on words. Although a footnote may be sufficient to explain that Apollo's call 'Κανελλώ μου Ασπρουλα μου'[45] is the modern Greek equivalent of 'Daisy! Buttercup!' and that the 'mou' sound, which means 'my', became the lowing of the cows,[46] some effects and resonances cannot be so summarily reduced to words. Furthermore, the judges of the transient unrecorded, unrepeated performances which Harrison prefers are mostly theatre critics rather than academics. The latter like

---

43 Fiedler, 'Literature as an Institution', p. 80.
44 Peter Levi, 'Tony Harrison's Dramatic Verse', *Bloodaxe 1*, p. 163.
45 *Trackers*, Delphi text, p. 24.
46 My information about this comes not from a footnote to the play but from Oliver Taplin, 'Satyrs on the Borderline: *Trackers* in the Development of Tony Harrison's Theatre Work', in *Bloodaxe 1*, p. 460.

to have a text to study, and seem to turn their attention to plays some time after poems and novels.[47]

'One of the most evident strengths of [*School*]', for Ken Worpole, 'derives from the tension created between the classical literary form of the sonnet and the colloquial nature of the subject-matter [....] The familiar rhythms and patterns of rhyme make them immediately accessible to the ear and eye.'[48] But accessible to whom? Patterns of rhythm and rhyme are familiar only to those who have had a certain kind of education. He notes that

> [Harrison's] long introductions have come under fire from that literary critical tradition [...] which insists that every poem should be a self-contained, self-referential artefact or 'verbal icon' and that any outside references or contextualisation are not only extraneous but positively harmful. For that tradition there is no society, no history, just a succession of pure literary formations.

Poems which make obscure allusions ensure the necessity of a scholarly gloss or interpretation, and could be described as anti-popular, or alienating. The long introductions, however, in providing any necessary references, could be seen as an attempt to make the poems more accessible. According to Worpole, the sonnet form is easy, familiar, and 'a highly appropriate form in which to write about language and speech'. Because it derives from the Italian for little sound? Only to those who share this code, and it is not an idea put forward by Harrison. The form is not appropriate in any obvious way, nor is it particularly accessible, and Worpole's displaying of his knowledge of the etymology involved could alienate the 'common reader'. Ironically, an academic critic praises Harrison not for his masterly use of complex conventional metrics, but for his apparent mis-use of them: 'the verse-forms really have to flail around to hold together, and their ironic awareness of this, magnificent in *v*., is part of their meaning'.[49] Conversely, journalists writing for popular and non-academic newspapers assess Harrison's poetry as 'doggerel'[50] and 'shackled to relentless rhymes and rumty-tum rhythms, like a kind of politicised Pam Ayres'[51] – and a

---

47 A notable exception is Romana Huk. See note 18 above.
48 Worpole, 'Scholarship Boy', p. 68.
49 Eagleton, 'Antagonism', *Bloodaxe 1*, p. 349.
50 Butt, 'Disdain Versus Manners', *v*., p. 54.
51 Martyn Harris, 'To Show V or Not to Show V', *Daily Telegraph* (16 October 1987), reprinted in *v*., p. 48.

letter to *The Times* protesting against transmission of the film of *v*. says, 'art does not need the mass media. Art *is* for art's sake.'[52]

Whereas postmodernism typically displaces hierarchical distinction between popular and high culture, Harrison's poetry suggests a more complex attitude. In 'Bringing Up', another powerfully painful sonnet, a poet recollects his mother's reaction to his first publication; her tears, her hurt looks, and her cry: '*You weren't brought up to write such mucky books!*'[53] The dust-wrapper of *Loiners*, two horizontal panels in vivid red and yellow, is firmly undecorated, unfanciful, unpoetic, and suggestive of The Movement influence, but the distance it proclaims between itself and the poetic canon is only partly borne out by the contents.[54] The poems use straightforward, even demotic, language but also a wide range of references. There are many traces of the 'book-learning' to which characters in his poems react with awe or contempt: Copernicus, Gibbon, Spengler and Mommsen ('Thomas Campey and the Copernican System'); satyrs, Wyatt, Pascal ('Satyrae'); Conrad ('The Heart of Darkness'); Spanish history ('The Nuptial Torches'); Catullus, Yevtushenko, Kafka, Astraea ('The Curtain Catullus'); Chopin ('The Chopin Express'); Wordsworth ('The Excursion'); John Cleveland (*Newcastle*)[55] among others. Harrison is alert to the danger of his becoming 'the poet preserved beneath deep permaverse',[56] but perhaps a woman of Mrs Harrison's age and background was less likely to be upset by Tacitus and Copernicus than by profanity and descriptions of polymorphic sexuality.[57] Avoiding the academic, Harrison moves towards other forms of exclusivity. The suggestion in 'Bringing Up' that the book which so

---

52 S. Butterworth, *The Times* (24 October 1987), reprinted in *v*., p. 59.
53 *SP*, p. 166.
54 *Loiners* was the first hardback collection of Harrison's poetry. *Earthworks* (1964), the first collection, was a pamphlet, as was *Newcastle is Peru* (1969). *Aikin Mata* (1966), written in collaboration with James Simmons, was published in Nigeria.
55 At the time of *Newcastle's* composition, the source of its epigraph, 'News from Newcastle', was thought to be by John Cleveland, but the poem was later attributed to Thomas Winnard. See *Poems of John Cleveland*, eds Brian Morris and Eleanor Withrington (Oxford, 1967), p. xxxi.
56 'Art & Extinction 4: Killing Time', *SP*, p. 187.
57 Spencer argues that while Harrison develops an understanding of, or even 'comes round to', his father's position on a number of things, he makes no allowances for his mother's background, and seems to develop little sympathy for her political and moral standards. See *Poetry TH*, pp. 88–9.

upset his mother should be cremated with her: 'I'd've put my book in your stiff hand' – is evidence for the distinction he makes between the heart (in this case filial love), and the head (in this case writing: 'The Heartless Art'[58]). It might be an act of sacrifice for the narrator, and no transgression of religious mores, since he insists that he has none, but for his father (who, as he was concerned that his wife's wedding ring should remain in place, clearly did have strong feelings on the subject[59]) the notion of the 'mucky' words' ashes mingling with those of his wife might have been deeply repellent. Neither his father's feelings nor those which he might impute to his mother prevent the narrator from carrying out his idea, however. What holds him back is the thought that 'The undertaker would have thought me odd'.

Man of the people though he professes to be, Harrison also describes himself as a 'bard', a word with connotations of prophetic, taboo, apart.[60] Any suggestion of arrogance is, however, punctured by 'The Bonebard Ballads', where bards compose on demand for coppers, and belong to the 'ur-crappers'.[61] Though he is highly intelligent and educated, he writes anti-intellectual and anti-academic poetry – of a particular kind. Despite being half-ironic, Larkin's 'A Study of Reading Habits', in which he makes the famous remark, 'Books are a load of crap',[62] preserves a sense of distaste as much for the 'real' as for the vicarious life which the bookish boy finds in novels. A similar statement in Harrison's 'Working' has none of that cynicism.

> Patience Kershaw, bald hurryer, fourteen,
> this wordshift and inwit's a load of crap
> for dumping on a slagheap, I mean
> *th'art nobbut summat as wants raking up.*[63]

Perhaps because it is addressed to a victim, it conveys a sense of shame, rather as Larkin's address to the woman of 'Deceptions'

---

58 See *SP*, pp. 206–8.

59 See 'Timer', *SP*, p. 167.

60 *v.*, p. 7. Given the poem's model, this could be a reference to Thomas Gray's bard, who foresees the political fate of the English. See 'The Bard, A Pindaric Ode', *The New Oxford Book of Eighteenth-Century Verse*, ed. Roger Lonsdale (Oxford, 1984), pp. 361–5. See also Barrie Rutter, 'Observing the Juggler: An Actor's View', *Bloodaxe 1*, p. 419.

61 'The Bonebard Ballads 1: The Ballad of Babelabour', *SP*, p.102.

62 *The Whitsun Weddings* (London, 1964), p. 31.

63 *SP*, p. 124.

brings out an unusual compassion.[64] The encounter with the realities of Patience Kershaw's working life, it is suggested, make the stuff of the narrator's intellectual life seem trivial, and his word-juggling and versifying mere falsification, though in the next breath the narrator realises that only words can rake up Patience Kershaw from the slagheap of time.

Anti-intellectualism in poetry is not new, of course, and the anti-intellectual has usually been an intellectual. Often the expression of youth counter-culture, in carnival mode or more biliously, such 'low' poetry has been produced at least since the goliardic verses of the Schoolmen; only the extent of the exposure and critical attention accorded to its authors has changed. Unlike Larkin's poetry, which was anti-academic (though for 'an English tradition' located primarily in the nineteenth century), and nominally anti-intellectual, but hardly pro-populist, the newer anti-intellectual poetry is against mystificatory art, esoteric, culture and divisive education, and is likely to be aimed at the mass market. Editorial introductions to collections of this kind of poetry assert that the distinction between popular and high culture, has been blurred, and literary value problematised. The new poetry 'emphasises accessibility, democracy and responsiveness, humour and seriousness, and reaffirms the art's significance as public utterance'.[65] Geoff Hattersley's 'Frank O'Hara Five, Geoffrey Chaucer Nil' about sums up the approach as far the penultimate point, though how popular the 'New' and the 'New Generation' Poets are would be hard to say, even given a demographic break-down of the sales. If poetry briefly became 'the new Rock and Roll', as the Poetry Society claimed, it was, on the whole, a distinct species of poetry, youth-orientated, marketed and received as a separate genre from the established canon. Is this simply a result of the redrawing of a literary boundary, the inclusion within the genre of poetry of much that would once have been classified as verse, and an illustration of the impracticality of genre-definitions? If the concepts 'good', 'literary', or 'canonical' are functional but relational, then so, presumably, is 'popular'. The audience for the New Generation poets is not the same as that for living established poets such as Dunn, Mahon, or Harrison, but neither is it the same as that of popular fiction (for

---

64 *The Less Deceived* (Hessle, 1955), p. 37.
65 Hulse *et al.*, *New Poetry*, introduction, p. 16.

example, the science fiction and fantasy, romance, and graphic novels aimed at the youth market) or popular verse (for example, works by pop lyricists, rugby songs, and greetings-card verse). Thus some of the New Generation poets received as cold a shoulder from the literary press as the Beat Poets and the Mersey Poets in their time, but they were not ignored as outside the scope of literary critics in the way that a collection of contemporary pop lyrics might well be.

Haffenden assumes that Harrison wants to make his work as accessible as possible, and that writing plays will enable him to harness the traditions of popular theatre in the service of poetry.

> J. H. Did you turn to the theatre to make verse more accessible?
> T. H. Well, even with the most difficult thing I've done in the sense of accessibility, which is the *Oresteia*, the verse form I came up with tried to keep the maximum momentum with the maximum gravity.[66]

Music-hall and pantomime may be the theatre of uz, but modern drama tends not to be seen as accessible. The theatre is an exclusive space, 'not for the likes of us';[67] its social connotations, as well as the mechanisms of its staging, distance, if not alienate, sections of its potential audience.

'Serious versions of popular theatre have been very important',[68] for Harrison, and 'a sense of the theatricality of the pantomime, with its popular surface' has always been 'a touchstone' for him.

> If there are any specifically literary or cultural references in the sonnets of *Continuous*, one is Milton's sonnets [...] and another is the technique of the stand- up comedian. I went to music-hall all the time when I was a kid, and always admired that technique of setting something up and then taking it away, structuring the lines and being almost aggressively aware of line-endings and the rhythmical entity of each line.

This leads him to make an effective, if exclusive, conjunction of music-hall stand-up comedian and Demosthenes in 'Them & [uz]', where the catch-phrase 'aye-aye' is associated with the Greek 'αι αι', and the stammerer-become-orator with northern club-circuit eloquence. That almost aggressive awareness is also in the

---

66 'Interview', p. 238.
67 'As a working-class Labour voter remarked in my hearing "Theatre's not for the likes of us."' John Lucas, 'Speaking for England', *Bloodaxe 1*, p. 353.
68 'Interview', p. 237.

'switchback rhyme' which Harrison claims to have learned from songs of George Formby's such as 'Mr Wu':

> Once he sat down – those hot irons he didn't spot 'em
> He gave a yell – and cried 'Oh my – I've gone and scorched my
> ... singlet!'[69]

The device is used to good dramatic effect in *Misanthrope*:

> She's so envious, poor dear, she takes delight
> in doing me down to others out of spite.
> Prim and proper is she. O that's rich.
> She's stupid, rude ... in fact a perfect ... Dar-
> > Enter ARSINOE.
> -ling! I was worried for you. Here you are![70]

In 'The Rhubarbarians II', Harrison again quotes Formby:

> *One afternoon the Band Conductor up on his stand*
> *Somehow lost his baton it flew out of his hand*
> *So I jumped in his place and conducted the band*
> *With mi little stick of Blackpool Rock!*

– and invites us to

> Watch me on the rostrum wave my arms –
> mi little stick of Leeds-grown *tusky* draws
> galas of rhubarb from MET-set palms.[71]

Though this could be an acknowledgement of Harrison's debt to and affection for popular culture, it is used in a particularly intellectual way. Few of Harrison's readers will have a personal recollection of music-hall, which has moved from living tradition to theatrical history, and which was, anyway, not always a 'pure' vessel for popular culture.[72] While Formby did perform during Harrison's lifetime, the poet's experience of music-hall, as well as part of his sense of cultural inheritance, must be part of his literary inheritance.[73] This use of music-hall is typical of the way more remote history is

---

69 Quoted by Tony Harrison, 'Jane Eyre's Sister', p. 140.
70 *Misanthrope*, p. 37.
71 *SP*, p. 114.
72 See Michael Sidnell, *Dances of Death: The Group Theatre of London in the Thirties* (London, 1984), pp. 26–7.
73 Like T. S. Eliot, through poets of the 1890s such as Arthur Symonds and John Davidson. See Sidnell, *Dances of Death*, p. 17.

assimilated into Harrison's poetry in the way recent events are not. The first 'Rhubarbarians' poem is seamless: the Luddite riots are living history contiguous with the message of the speaking poet. In the second, Formby's song is an epigraph, and Harrison is only too aware that his father, for example, who understood and enjoyed Formby's songs ('The uke in the attic manhole once was yours!'), would be baffled by the poem. 'Sorry, dad, you won't get that quatrain.'

We should not assume that Harrison's borrowing from popular theatre is the product of a plan to reincorporate the masses into poetry, or to extend the reach of canonical literature beyond the usual canonic audience, any more than we should assume that all modernist writers were, like Geoffrey Grigson, reacting against mass values,[74] and producing verse 'rebarbative to the mass'.[75] Perhaps the acid test for poetic sympathy with, or exclusion of, the masses is the poet's attitude to the most popular medium. 'Intellectuals have opposed the spread of television just as vociferously as they condemned newspapers in the early part of the century. "I don't see how any civilised person can watch TV, far less own a set," pronounced W. H. Auden in 1972.'[76] (Though *Night Mail*, which Auden wrote for a GPO film, has been shown on English television.) That may be less true now than in the past, but, apart from Simon Armitage, few contemporary poets use television other than for broadcasts of readings or to discuss and publicise their poems.[77] Harrison writes for television, not just words to which images are set by a producer, but poems written with the possibilities and limitations of television film in mind. His reservations about it as a medium are not concerned with the status of its productions as high or low art, but with the function of such a production, the constraints it imposes. 'We might say that TV reaches such an amalgam [as the classical Greek theatre], but it is not present in the same space: TV viewers are not aware of each other attending, and therefore sharing not only the space and the light, but the illumination in the spiritual sense.'[78]

'Summoned by Bells' is rebarbative to the new consumerism,

---

74 Discussed in Valentine Cunningham, *British Writers of the Thirties* (Oxford, 1988), p. 275.

75 John Carey, *The Intellectuals and the Masses: Pride and Prejudice Among the Literary Intelligentsia, 1880–1939* (London, 1992), p. 17.

76 Quoted in Carey, *Intellectuals and the Masses*, p. 214.

77 See, for example, Simon Armitage, *Xanadu* (BBC TV, June 1992).

78 *Trackers*, introduction, p. xiv.

the love of possessions rather than art:

> I've had it wrecked, my rhythmic ear.
> by the new faith of the nation.[79]

The 'bloody bells' are not from church campaniles but from burglar alarms. Rather than summoning 'Come all to church good people',[80] they advertise the violation of the sacrosanct retreat of the modern town house, temple of possessions.

> Almost every day one goes
> and the new faith that it rings
> is vested in videos
> and the sacredness of things.

Television, here, is part of the process of retreat from the streets and the pubs to the locked doors of owner-occupied houses and into the private home entertainments of the nuclear families, but although the VCR is the emblem of this modern popular culture, the poem is not an attack upon working-class values. Harrison sees mammon-worship and the fracturing of a social life (exemplified by television versus theatre) as pervading the whole of society:

> The new calls to the nation:
> *Securi-curi-curi-cor!*
> *Join the flight against inflation!*
> Double-Chubb your door!

The irony of Harrison's pained dirge on the love of possessions and the closed family unit is that whilst composing a poem (presumably in his own house in Newcastle) on his peculiarly materialist themes, immersed in the supposedly rarefied pursuit of prosody and consequently deaf to the material world, he was burgled.

> What bothers me perhaps the most
> is I never heard the thief,
> being obsessively engrossed
> in rhymes of social grief.[81]

Adding insult to injury, the thief rejects the contents of the bag he steals:

---

79 *Gorgon*, p. 24.
80 A. E. Housman, 'Bredon Hill', *A Shropshire Lad* (1896) (London, 1927) XXI, p. 29.
81 *Gorgon*, p. 25.

Poems! Poems! All by me!
He dropped the lot and ran
(and who would buy hot poetry
from a poor illiterate man?)

Harrison perhaps sacrifices fictional plausibility for poetic correspondence. He uses the abandoning of the books to index consumer
society's contempt for poetry, yet if the thief were 'illiterate', he
would not be 'deeply pissed' that the books were poetry, because he
would presumably be unaware of the fact, as he would be unaware
that one of them was 'an Ezra Pound / *Cantos* manuscript', yet
Harrison seems to suggest that the thief could read the name, but
associated it with nothing of value. He thus makes 'illiterate' mean
'lacking literary competence', or 'ignorant of canonical literary
texts', and reinforces the suggestion that he has absorbed
middle-class stereotypes (burglars are working-class, poor, illiterate
– or non-literary – and male). There may be an acknowledgement of
this in his suggestion that he 'used' the thief:

I got my books, he went scot-free,
no summons, gaol or fines.
I used him for such poetry
this alarm leaves in these lines

on 'a botched civilisation'
E. P. helped to rebotch
where bells toll for a nation
that's one great Neighbourhood Watch.

As Adorno remarked: 'the further development of the aesthetic
debate [. . .] depends essentially on a true accounting of the relationship of the intellectuals to the working-class'.[82] The attic
Tarzan hears both the call of the street gang and of '*De Bello
Gallico* and lexicon', but his disconnection from both is summed
up in the line '*Ah, bloody can't ah've gorra Latin prose*'.[83] The
history of this line itself illustrates an interesting slippage of implication. In the next selection from the (continuing) sonnet sequence,
the 'School of Eloquence', *Continuous*, it appears as '*Ah bloody
can't ah've gorra Latin prose*'[84] – the deletion of the comma

---

82 Adorno to Benjamin, in Taylor *et al.*, ed., *Aesthetics and Politics*, p. 125.
83 'Me Tarzan', *School*, p. 15 (SP, p. 116). *De Bello Gallico* is Julius Caesar's
    history of his campaigns in Gaul.
84 p. 13.

removing any sense of self dramatisation (as in 'Ah! Bloody can't
...' or 'Ah ... (sigh) bloody can't ...'), and suggesting the stac-
cato, impatient, said-it-before-and-don't-like-it reply, carefully
devoid of emphasis, the boy might have made, since working-class
male youth culture does not encourage a too-skilled or subtle use
of language. But line 16 – 'like patriarchal Sissy-bleeding-ro's' in
School – becomes: 'like patriarchal Cissy-bleeding-ro's' in *Continuous*,[85] perhaps emphasising the working-class insult more than
the classical scholar.

Rylance's intellectual but non-academic loner seems to belong to
an urban (if non-capital), cosmopolitan setting, but for Robert
Crawford there is a pervasive provincialism in Harrison's work
which, surprisingly, locates him in the modernist tradition.[86]
Although '[a] cursory account of Modernism stresses its cosmopolitanism and internationalism, presenting it as a facet of "high"
metropolitan culture [...] there is also another, equally important,
side of Modernism that is demotic and crucially "provincial"'.[87] I
would wholeheartedly agree with Monroe K. Spears that the thought
of 'seriously undertaking to define any literary term is a depressing
one, and modernism has special difficulties',[88] and, whilst not
according Harrison's stated intentions any privileged status, I would
acknowledge that he does avoid 'the self-indulgences of obscurity
and some of the audience-dodging evasions of much modernism'.[89]
The provinces in which Crawford is most interested are Scotland and
the north of England, both of which, he believes, significantly influenced the development of English literature in the eighteenth and
nineteenth centuries. He finds a 'northwards movement of the imagination, spurred by Ossian, Burns and Scott', given 'impetus by
Wordsworth and the Lake Poets' and bearing fruit in the work of the
Brontës. The 'confident northern novelist' was 'able to articulate a
cultural identity to which the supposedly smooth southerner was a
stranger', he suggests. It seems to me that the imaginary north was

---

85 It remains 'Cissy' in both editions of SP, and the same spelling is used in
   'Painkillers II', *Ten Sonnets from 'The School of Eloquence'*, p. 4, and *SP*,
   p. 170 (not included in *SP*, first edn).
86 See Robert Crawford, *Devolving English Literature* (Oxford, 1992), chapter 5,
   pp. 216–70.
87 *Devolving English Literature*, pp. 218–19.
88 *Dionysus and the City: Modernism in Twentieth-Century Poetry* (New York,
   1970), p. 3.
89 'Facing Up', *Bloodaxe 1*, p. 442.

more significant than the northern novelist; a mythical Other cherished by non-northern artists of the picturesque and the Gothick as a strange wilderness containing wild, rugged beauty, untamed nature and rude natives, as in, for example, *Wuthering Heights*, and the sense of dangerous possibility which had been landscaped out of the manicured south, as in, for example, *Dracula*. The use of a town other than London as a novelistic microcosm was not, of course, restricted to the far north. Milton is said to be based upon Manchester; Middlemarch is a Warwickshire town; Cranford is in the Midlands. The subscription novel, the circulating library and the triple-decker novel enabled the novel of provincial life to be read beyond the compass of the metropolitan printing presses and publishers; they were part of the process by which the provincial margins were drawn into the centre, and the country gradually homogenised. Reading novels of nineteenth-century provincial life, we are struck not so much by the differences between the societies depicted as by their similarity. In its daily round, provincial middle-class life in Hampshire described by Jane Austen is very like provincial middle-class life in Kent or Warwickshire as described by George Eliot.[90] The north, then, came to represent both the mysterious other of wild nature and the undesirable, but necessary, other of industry; the matter of fantasy and of repression. Arnold's Hellenic spirit of 'sweetness and light' was associated with an idealised, Mediterranean south, while the north, despite its Hebraic virtues of industry and energy, was associated with hell.[91] But how north is north? Philip Dodd points out that north and south are in a differential opposition, which

> isn't to deny that there are some places in England more northern (yet more southern than others), but to argue that the relationship between actual places and people and their representation in writing, film and the visual arts is a complex one [....] 'the North' is not so much a category as a relationship – defined in terms of its difference from the norm of 'the South'. For example, the 'Southern Novel' is neither a critical nor marketing term in the way the 'Northern Novel' is.[92]

---

90 This is not to suggest that the novels were homogeneous: for example, *North and South* enters the sphere of industry, and the concerns of its main characters touch and are touched by working people, while in, for example, *Pride and Prejudice* (1813) the origin of characters' fortune in trade is usually obscured by them.

91 See John Lucas, *Romantic to Modern Literature* (Brighton, 1982), pp. 24–5.

92 Dodd, 'Lowryscapes', *Critical Quarterly*, 32, no. 2 pp. 17–18.

Crawford asserts that 'the culminating voice of the Victorian novel is not metropolitan but resolutely provincial. It is as important for Hardy to demonstrate that the full panoply of Greek tragedy can be played out in provincial Wessex as it is for Joyce to revoice the *Odyssey* in Dublin.'[93] The location of the 'culminating voice' is informed by hindsight, of course. The pastoral and the provincial may now be taken as characteristic voices of the nineteenth century because, before Dickens and the sentimental/reformist novel became popular, nineteenth-century novelists who have since become canonical worked in those modes, but nineteenth- century readers had access to a thriving tradition of metropolitan fiction, the early nineteenth-century *roman à clef*, and the novels of Disraeli, for example. The distinction which Crawford makes a matter of geography seems to be more a matter of class. Before Dickens made sweeps and pickpockets fashionable, matter was provided for the metropolitan novel, whether scandal, satire or romance, by the mythologised *beau monde* living in town houses during the season and on country estates out of it; taking metropolitan culture with them. Small-town provincial fiction centred upon the lives of the main market for prose fiction, the provincial middle classes, with the local land-owning family flitting between town and visits, often a felt absence.

The working and lower middle classes of the metropolis are given little more than walk-on and crowd-scene parts until they become objects of pity in Dickens and amusement in Weedon Grossmith,[94] their lifestyles and behaviour becoming legitimate subjects as topical issues, as John Carey points out, in *Robert Thorne: The Story of a London Clerk*.[95] Perhaps Crawford means that the middle and lower classes are always provincial, wherever they live, while metropolitanism resides in an attitude and lifestyle – aristocratic, intellectual, avant-garde or otherwise elitist. For Arnold, 'the provincial is the opposite of urbane', and he 'thinks of "the provinces" as "wanting the culture of the capital"', Lucas remarks.[96] 'In literature as in so much else, the relationship of

---

93 Crawford, *Devolving English Literature*, p. 217.
94 This is to generalise, of course, as there have been poor heroes since Piers Plowman, and perhaps before, but the newer genre did not immediately take to them.
95 Shaun F. Bullock, *Robert Thorne: The Story of a London Clerk* (1907), discussed in Carey, *Intellectuals and the Masses*, pp. 60–2.
96 *Romantic to Modern Literature*, pp. 18–19.

"North" and "South" is one of unequal power'.[97] The distinction is not necessarily between urban and bucolic, metropolitan and provincial or parochial, however, but may be between privileged and estranged or dispossessed.

> To ignore the voice of the provincial in nineteenth-century writing in England is to distort and oversimplify the development of that century's literature. There are hidden currents between these provincial voices and their twentieth-century inheritors which have yet to be fully explored.[98]

For Crawford, Harrison, provincial by birth and, to an extent, affiliation, is one of these inheritors. Despite his alienation from the working-class Leeds of the 1940s and 1950s, the grown-up Harrison does have strong ties with groups and symbolic centres, things 'to belong to'. His allegiance to Yorkshire persists from the time he played cricket with a white rose cut out of an old flour sack on his cap, to his reflection, in America, that he would rather 'croak' there.[99] Why should a well travelled and cosmopolitan man keep such a parochial allegiance? One significance of the rural north is that, like the rural south-west, it is emblematic of an undissociated, pre-lapsarian past so imbued with pantheistic magic that the inflections of even its nonsense language are potent. An example is 'the old Northern shepherds' spell':

> a spell any child could learn to say,
> a charm any child could chant to keep
> the darkness, the demons, the devil at bay [...]
> *Yan, Tan, Tethera*[100]

To be a working-class boy at an independent school, and a working-class northerner among southern literati, marginalised Harrison, but it also made him different, marked. Leeds (and, later, Newcastle) has been the other of Harrison's cultural environment as Ireland has been for some Irish writers. 'Ireland being a small

---

97 Dodd, 'Lowryscapes', p. 18.
98 Crawford, *Devolving English Literature*, p. 217.
99 'Cypress & Cedar', *SP*, p. 234. A wonderful example of Harrison's compression of signification, with its association of death, the inarticulate sound which marks the end of articulation, and that which enables articulation: 'with few exceptions, speech sounds are produced by the audible interference with expiratory breath from the lungs'. R. H. Robins, *General Linguistics: An Introductory Survey* (London, 1971), p. 88.
100 *Yan Tan Tethera, TW*, p. 303.

country, the Irishman can trade upon the glamour of minorities', Louis MacNeice reflects, remarking that for proof one need only 'inspect the behaviour of Irish children at English schools. Yeats was no exception when he went to school in London.'[101] According to MacNeice, an Englishman 'cannot make capital in the same way out of being English. England is far too over-populated and too complex.' Yorkshire, however, is perhaps not. If 'the south' is substituted for 'England', and 'northern working-class' for 'Irish', Harrison could partake of MacNeice's 'glamour of minorities', characterised by 'the effects of loneliness [...] the clannish obsession with one's family; the combinations of an anarchist individualism with puritanical taboos and inhibitions; the half-envious contempt for England [...] a sentimental attitude to Irish history [...]; an identification of Ireland with the spirit and of England with crass materialism'.

The sense of a place, for Seamus Heaney, makes us dwellers, namers, lovers, makers of homes, and searchers for histories. Lucas finds that it also 'refers us to matters that the language of the Academy, the culture of the centre, will not help us to define'.[102] For Lucas, '*that* language, *that* culture, are likely to thwart or impoverish any attempt at a fit utterance of such matters. This is what Hardy recognised when he jotted down in a Notebook of 1880 his conviction that "Arnold is wrong about provincialism.... A certain provincialism of feeling is invaluable. It is of the essence of individuality".' Lucas continues, 'and, I will add, of community'. It is this sense of place – Harrison's sense of possessing and being displaced from the 'place' of Leeds in the late 1930s to 1950s – which creates the dualism of insider/outsider in his poetry.

Leeds and Yorkshire provided the social and cultural circumstances necessary for Harrison's development into the poet he is, but perhaps because it is a county of wild beauty and industrial decay, poor weather and poverty, a strong sense of selfhood and strongly marked dialects, Yorkshire also resembles an extension of the Harrison persona, a huge site of contradictions. The north 'is not an uncolonised or innocent space but [...] dense with contradictory meanings'.[103] Harrison's Rhubarbarians, as Crawford notes, are within the tradition of the savage north; his Newcastle is a site of

---

101 MacNeice, *Poetry of W. B. Yeats*, p. 52.
102 Lucas, *Romantic to Modern Literature*, p. 27.
103 Dodd, 'Lowryscapes', p. 18.

primal blackness and raw emotion, untamed response and uncivilised manners, but it is also Peru – to the majority an unfilled blank, but explored and known to the cosmopolitan minority. The African references in Harrison's work align it not only with oppression and marginalisation, but also with the experience of the traveller, the polyglot and the wide-minded. Harrison's work is both more provincial and more cosmopolitan than that of the London–Oxbridge writers against whom Crawford's Modernists react. His homing instincts are to the provincial cities of Leeds and Newcastle, sites of urban decay, oppressed labour, low wages, and a low status for culture, but the locations of his immediate subjects are as likely to be Mozambique, Washington, Florida, or the biggest Apple, New York, making London–Oxbridge look very provincial by comparison. For Philip Dodd, the north is 'all past, has no future', but it is 'not only somewhere in the past, it is also in the dominant version inhabited by a particular group, the working class', and it is to this dominant version that many of Harrison's poems belong. Which 'is not to say that one could not construct a "middle-class" northern tradition [. . .] only that it hasn't gained the ideological prominence the working-class northern "tradition" has'.[104]

Harrison's translation-adaptation of medieval mystery plays into modern northern dialect could be seen as parallel to Pound's following one of the 'more arcane high-cultural pursuits (studying Icelandic literature), with a view to producing something with a primitive edge to it'.[105] Harrison's characters, however, are typically the product of an urban civilisation, either the beneficiaries of leisured culture or the workers whose labour makes it possible.[106] Their savagery is in linguistic violence and futile anger. They are not outside civilisation and/or imperialism, but are its victims.

For Crawford, the 'striking thing about the Modernists is that their most characteristic effects are gained by combining the materials on the outer edges – slang, foreign, dialectal' as a sort of collage. Their language

> is not the language of English gentlemen, nor is it meant to be. If

---

104 Dodd, 'Lowryscapes', pp. 18–19.
105 Crawford, *Devolving English Literature*, p. 219.
106 With possible exceptions in *Bow Down* and *Yan Tan Tethera*, though in the former characters represent rich versus poor, court versus country.

Modernism's cosmopolitanism can be seen as partly the result of 'provincial' concerns, then so is its use of the demotic. In this use, it brought back to the centre of high art those provincial improprieties which the teachers of Rhetoric and Belles Lettres and their successors had tried to banish. It is this demotic aspect of Modernism which constitutes one of the movement's most important legacies.[107]

Modernism uses demotic not as its first language but as one among a number of registers which will be foregrounded against the 'natural voice' of the poem, so modernist poetry will not necessarily be intelligible to native speakers of that demotic. Crawford asserts that because the movement drew 'so strongly on both anthropology and dialect', and aimed 'to outflank the Anglocentricity of established Englishness through a combination of the demotic and multicultural', it was 'an essentially provincial phenomenon', and as such 'placed various powerful stimuli at the disposal of a number of writers whom we can characterize not simply as provincials, but as "barbarians"'. The language of Eliot, Pound, and other Modernists may not be that of English gentlemen, but neither is it that of the English masses. Far from making the margins central, or opening the genres and canons of English literature to non-gentlemen, this was, in John Carey's view, a deliberately exclusive movement. The 'spread of literacy to the "masses" impelled intellectuals in the early twentieth century to produce a mode of culture (modernism) that the masses could not enjoy'.[108] For Fredric Jameson, modernist art depended upon the distinction between high and mass culture:

> its Utopian function consisting at least in part in the securing of a realm of authentic experience over against the surrounding environment of philistinism, of schlock and kitsch, of commodification and of Reader's Digest culture. Indeed, it can be argued that the emergence of high modernism is itself contemporaneous with the first great expansion of a recognizable mass culture (Zola may be taken as the marker for the last coexistence of the art novel and the bestseller to be within a single text.)[109]

Modernism, then, may produce demotic, but it is not democratic.[110]

---

107 Crawford, *Devolving Literature*, pp. 269–70.
108 Carey, *Intellectuals and the Masses*, p. 214.
109 Fredric Jameson, 'The Politics of Theory: Ideological Positions in the Postmodernism Debate', *New German Critique,* 33 (fall 1984), reprinted in David Lodge, ed., *Modern Criticism and Theory* (London, 1988), p. 382.
110 Though perhaps James Joyce could be seen as a democratic, if difficult, modernist.

Harrison, like Eliot, is a professional outsider; the difference is that Eliot's conservatism led him to attack industrial, secular, consumerist society, while the tensions in Harrison's poetic persona lead him to both denunciation and embrace. Rather than an excluded barbarian, the modernist writer was at the top of a carefully constructed meritocracy for which outsiderliness, difference from the herd (whether by blood and breeding or intellect), was a necessary condition. Eliot is 'the Great Modern who has been miraculously transformed into our Only Ancient; mentor and yardstick'.[111] Such writers were not strictly provincial because they bore no allegiance to indigenous local traditions and were only temporarily and conditionally in conflict with a national culture.

> Modernism, as Raymond Williams has argued, is among other things a running battle between a new mode of rootless, cosmopolitan consciousness and the older, more parochial national traditions from which this consciousness has defiantly broken loose [....] The deracinated fate of the modernist exiles and emigrés is a material condition for the emergence of a newly formalizing, universalizing thought, one which having spurned the ambiguous comforts of a motherland can now cast a bleak analytic eye, from its 'transcendental' vantage-point in some polyglot metropolis, on all such specific histories, discerning the hidden global logics by which they are governed.[112]

Joyce, Pound, and Eliot, Eagleton suggests, roam 'across a whole span of cultures in euphoric, melancholic liberation from the Oedipal constraints of a mother tongue'. The modernist metropolis 'is the cultural node of a now thoroughly global capitalist system, and is in the process of both relinquishing and reinterpreting from a distance the national enclaves within which capitalist production has traditionally flourished'. Harrison uses Yevtushenko as an epigraph: 'Frontiers oppress me ... I want to wander as much as I like ... to talk, even in a broken language, with everybody.'[113] Elsewhere, however, his work recognises the notion of the 'mother land'. Conversely, though Harrison makes innumerable references and appeals to 'the nation', his handling of national and cultural allegiances is ambivalent. *Banquet* expresses fear and contempt of extremism, including nationalism, yet he usually associates the

---

111 Jonathan Raban, *The Society of the Poem* (London, 1971), p. 10. Also see pp. 11ff.
112 Terry Eagleton, *Ideology of the Aesthetic* (Oxford, 1990), pp. 320–1.
113 'The Curtain Catullus', *SP*, p. 52.

notion of a global culture, or anything 'global', with disaster:

> Since Hiroshima what we've done
> paradoxically's to make the whole earth one.
> We all look down the barrel of the same cocked gun.
> One target, in one united fate
> nuked together in some hyperstate.[114]

Though Harrison watches the patriotism of the returning Geordies in 'The Act' with detached interest,[115] he does not appear to reflect ironically on his relationship with his own homeland, the north, which figures in his shorter poems as an object which is evocative, nostalgic, painful, and always just lost – both a construct and a centre:

> it is not that [... the] modernising, cosmopolitan North is any more the essential 'North' than the one constructed and 'preserved' in the works [...] discussed. But [...] why is this 'other' North absent? [...] the Lowryscape North has to be preserved in order that 'We' can speak on its behalf, lament 'Our' separation, and speak of its settled virtues.[116]

It may be significant that many of Harrison's 'hearth and home' poems were produced when he was living in Florida. As a visiting alien in a new social and cultural nexus, he could become 'continuous' with the recollected north once more.

Larkin's resolute provincialism and low diction are enough for Crawford to bracket this most anti- of anti-modernists with the 'provincial savages' of modernism, but I would suggest that, unlike Harrison's, Larkin's colloquialism is always spoken with a sneer, even when it describes his own history. The modern working- and lower-middle-class world is, for Larkin, peopled by sub-human stock types, doing the pools, listening to the 'jabbering set';[117] painted from a gaudy palette, upholstered in vulgar, ersatz materials:

> In parodies of fashion, heels and veils, [....]
> The fathers with broad belts under their suits
> And seamy foreheads; mothers loud and fat;
> An uncle shouting smut; and then the perms,
> The nylon gloves and jewellery substitutes[118]

---

114 *Chorus*, p. 49.
115 *Gorgon*, pp. 19–21.
116 Dodd, 'Lowryscapes', p. 27.
117 Philip Larkin, 'Mr Bleaney', *The Whitsun Weddings* (London, 1964), p. 10.
118 Philip Larkin, 'The Whitsun Weddings', *Whitsun Weddings*, pp. 21–2.

Larkin is anything but egalitarian. His resemblance to modernist poets is in his venting of spleen upon 'a Bleaney-world to which the poetic personae feels superior'.[119]

The declared intent to 'occupy [their] lousy leasehold Poetry' may be tantamount to Crawford's provincial poets' 'outflanking' and appropriation of metropolitan culture, but the classification of Harrison as a modernist barbarian could be an over-simplification. He is called 'barbarian' by his teacher in 'Them & [uz]', and t'mob are treated as barbarians by their overseers in 'The Rhubarbarians I'. They do not choose the title, it is a term of scorn.[120] Though Harrison appropriates the name through theatrical and local associations in 'The Rhubarbarians II', it still represents the outcast, not the self-proclaimed outsider. Despite the threat in 'Them & [uz]', the barbarian is not a revolutionary; he begins by wanting in. Crawford describes Harrison's aim as 'forthrightly to "occupy your lousy lease-hold Poetry" without betrayal or compromise'.[121] The planned takeover required mastery of the rules, and, as Harrison assimilated them, 'Poetry' could be said to have assimilated him. One kind of occupation became the other kind, enforcing betrayal, or at least compromise, as some 'School of Eloquence' poems describe. They also describe Harrison's desire to re-establish a personal and group identity as well-defined as T. W.'s. Thus, rather than the simple concept of the barbarian, tension between the drive to be an insider and the drive to be an outsider provides much of the impetus for his poetry.

Another useful and revealing way of looking at Harrison's poetry is provided by Romana Huk in her account of the 'Leeds Renaissance' of the 1950s and 1960s. Huk describes the work of Merle Brown on two of the poets whom she includes in the 'Leeds School', Geoffrey Hill and Jon Silkin, as 'a starting point for understanding the ways in which conflicting drives toward commitment to, and re-examination of, stances have in some measure shaped the work of these poets'.[122] The title of Brown's book, *Double Lyric*, Huk explains, refers to poems which 'defy traditional assumptions that poetry is generically monologic and unified', inwardly focused, isolated from political

---

119 David Lodge, *The Modes of Modern Writing* (London, 1971), p. 219.
120 See also his use of 'ur ur ur' paralleling the Greek use of 'bar-bar' (or 'baa-baa') in 'The Ballad of Babelabour', *SP*, pp. 102–3.
121 Crawford, *Devolving English Literature*, p. 282.
122 Huk, 'Leeds Renaissance', pp. 78–9.

activity. 'Attesting to the fact that all subjects are, unavoidably socially constructed, such lyrics display an inner divisiveness so strong that unified utterance becomes *dialogic*, dramatic, even "polycentric" when the poet mediating between voices steps back to implicate his/her own role in their construction.' This effect is 'akin to diversification, dialogue and debate in response to destabilisation in the political, only here the sphere is the poem which cannot be closed upon any one central voice within the poet'. Quoting a *Poetry and Audience* review by Geoffrey Hill of Jon Silkin's *The Re-ordering of the Stones* (1961), Huk describes the effect as 'a curious amalgam of the forthright and tentative', and she attributes at least part of their shaping to the influence of Harrison. 'None of the Leeds poets', she believes, 'demonstrates a greater attraction to and affinity for the dramatic and dialogic modes than Tony Harrison.' She cites *v.* as

> one of the clearest examples of such poetry, with its explosion of mono-logic form by means of inner debate, decentring of positions, and analysis of his own stance as a poet [...] though his work communi-cates as readily and rhythmically [as Shakespeare's], this happens by sheer force and avoidance of impeding allusions and *despite* the fact that he confounds clear roles and trips up clear stances by crowding working-class voices into established metres, effecting a kind of dialogue in close quarters between ghosts of the possessors and the occupying dispossessed.[123]

The shifting perspectives and subject-positions of *Loiners*, as well as the more obvious geographical shifts, for example, 'the complicated, polycentric sequence that follows its subject [...] into another land-scape [...] where they suddenly become the "possessors" [...] among another group of "natives"', demonstrate, for Huk, the perfecting of this choral technique.

> Harrison, linked unmistakably to both the 'PWD [Public Works Department] Man' [...] and the 'White Queen', professor, poet and Victoria's representative and carrier of imperialistic power and disease, circles round and back from the scene to the north of England again, constantly shifting his vantage points along the way, until we meet him again at last in 'Ghosts' through his own newly pluralised perspec-tive.[124]

---

123 Huk, 'Leeds Renaissance', pp. 79–80.
124 Huk, 'Leeds Renaissance', p. 80.

That 'linked unmistakably' is slightly troubling. Bakhtin's remarks on the dialogic nature of discourse and the polyphonic possibilities of the novel form seem to have been appropriated on the one hand as a revamped term for 'negative capability', that is, the nominal suppression of the writer's own personality in the service of his or her supposed entering of others', and on the other hand as a description of writing which is a chorale for many voices, all of them recognisably aspects of the writer. If a dominant strongly defined personality is recognisable through 'masks' of the PWD man and the rest, the sequence is of the latter kind. Todorov warns of the 'embarrassing multiplicity of meanings' with which a term such as 'dialogical' is loaded,[125] and perhaps in Harrison's work we should distinguish between types of intertextuality, forms of heteroglossia,[126] in particular the dialogue between the I and the other, and the discourses within the I which divide it into a set of others. Behind dialogical utterances must stand distinct 'authors', even if there is one writer, whose presence the utterances ostend.[127] If Harrison's poetry is an expression of the decentred subject, it should not present characters such as the PWD man or the White Queen as ventriloqual of the poet, or masks to be donned and doffed at will, or 'linked' to the artist any more, or any less, than the character Tony Harrison is linked to him.

Huk finds that it is 'the book's rejection of any simple stance toward the problem – any assignment of blame, any side to be taken – that gives it its authentically polycentric identity'.[128] In this reading, then, *Loiners* is not politically prescriptive, yet nor is it impartial. It is not only through 'the great and beneficial force of humour' that Harrison makes his resistance.[129] The carnival voice may be important in his work, but neither 'low' diction and 'vulgarity' nor humour are present in everything he writes. Sometimes the attempted subversion is by rhetorical persuasion and not by the 'slippery moments full of "heteroglossia" [...] and destabilising fun' which Huk describes.

125 See Tzvetan Todorov, *Mikhail Bakhtin: The Dialogical Principle* (Minneapolis, 1984), p. 60.
126 As M. M. Bakhtin does in 'Discourse in the Novel'. See *The Dialogic Imagination*, pp. 91–130.
127 See M. M. Baktin, *Problems of Doestoyevsky's Poetics*, trans Caryl Emerson (Manchester, 1984).
128 Huk, 'Leeds Renaissance', p. 81.
129 Konrad Lorenz quoted by Harrison in his notes for the catalogue *72 Drawings by Jiří Jirásek* (Newcastle-upon-Tyne, 1969), p. 8, quoted by Huk, 'Leeds Renaissance', p. 81.

There is not much humour in *Blasphemers' Banquet*, nor does carnival play a part in *Gorgon*, though *Cold Coming* was named with, and uses, mordant, tasteless humour as one of its most powerful signifying devices.[130] To what extent, then, does Harrison's style embody 'that subversive moment in evolving social history when language, in figurative enactment of emergent political upheaval, renews itself and overturns the barriers of traditional genre forms to become dialogised, permeated with laughter, irony, humour, elements of self-parody, and finally [...] a semantic open-endedness, living contact with unfinished, still-evolving contemporary reality'?[131] The ending of 'Ghosts' is not a resolution, 'the perspective of the poet' is 'more like an anti-position than a position' and, as Huk says, 'the point of such polycentric poems is that they are never "done", they can't resolve for us in a stance we would believe or want. The centre not only does not but *should* not hold.'[132] Yet if Harrison's poetry is polycentric, unresolved and positionless, how will it make 'truth emerge' through humour? What truck would it have with the resolution of reaching an absolute such as 'truth'?

A Bakhtinian approach to Harrison's work contradicts the conclusions of writers such as Woodcock and Dunn. Rather than a reflected lyric 'I' of thinly (if at all) disguised autobiography, it reveals a decentred subject which produces not just a chorus of many voices but an infinitely slippery identity. Helga Geyer-Ryan uses poems by Harrison (as well as Brecht's 'Questions from a Worker who Reads') 'to show how the principle of social and ideological dialogization, which for Bakhtin is a formative element of prose style only, becomes a central artistic device in poetry too'.[133] She describes Harrison's poetry as a transposition of 'the scandal of phonologically-based social differentiation in the spoken language' on to the medium of writing, an attempt to 'find the voices which have been silenced in the process of monopolization and monologization of speech perpetrated by the social powers that be'. Not only the language of the poems, but the poet himself is (socially) dialogised. The 'proletarian Harrison [...] in the course of a policy

---

130 See *Cold Coming*, pp. 9–10.
131 Bahtin, *Dialogic Imagination*, p. 7.
132 Huk, 'Leeds Renaissance', p. 83.
133 Helga Geyer-Ryan, 'Heteroglossia in the Poetry of Bertolt Brecht and Tony Harrison' (hereafter 'Heteroglossia'), in Willie van Peer, ed., *Taming of the Text: Explorations in Language, Literature and Culture* (London, 1988), p. 200.

of school reform expands his linguistic and cultural competence to such an extent that he becomes a writer'. For this kind of poet, something 'negatively termed "falling between two classes", "leaving" or even "betraying one's class" turns out to be the advantage of social polyphony. Only by constructing social polyphony is it possible to recognize and represent the losses of monologic speech'.[134] This process is one of dialectisation in both senses:

> On the one hand, it is the relativization of a monopolistic dominant language. By holding it up to the mirror of another, underprivileged language, it is made to take on an equal status as a dialect itself, one language among many. But dialectic also means that the two languages do not stand in opposition to one another in an antagonist configuration, but rather stand together as evidence of the fact that the whole wealth of experience of a socially diversified society can be conveyed in polyphony. Only in that way is the *status quo* of culturally, politically and linguistically established patterns brought in tension and movement.

This tension and movement is achieved by a refusal of both the universalist and the particularist position. 'Whether the universalists propagate the extension of the dominant sociolect to all as an element of reform, or whether the particularists see the purity of local varieties of speech as a potential form of resistance, the arguments remain within the bounds of monological exclusivity. It is precisely this which Brecht's and Harrison's polyphonic poetic procedures fight against.' Randomisation, fragmentation, and unexpected juxtaposition are tools which we might expect Harrison to use to resist monological exclusivity, but if his poetry 'does away with a theory which says that class politics should be dug in along the demarcation lines between linguistic spheres' and 'forces open' those preserves 'as a means of extending reality for all speakers', then in what sense is this achieved by the 'poetic fusion of discourses'? Just as things made strange by the poetic image can be normalised, so cross-cultural and sociolectal juxtapositions, once subsumed into a poetic, become acceptable. Once these 'border crossings' are no longer marked 'deviant', they cease to 'fight' in Geyer-Ryan's sense. A sense of 'fusion' is to be avoided; the various discourses must preserve their separateness from one another and their otherness from the privileged poetic discourse and the domi-

---

134 Geyer-Ryan, 'Heteroglossia', p. 201. Geyer-Ryan does not ask whether the process is possible in reverse, i.e. whether a native RP speaker can learn a proletarian dialect and thus examine the losses of monologic speech.

nant sociolect; they must remain 'pragmatic linguistic fields, the identities of which are institutionalized and safeguarded by exclusion and
the creation of a positive hierarchy';[135] yet they must be appropriated
into poetry and made to function as a system of equivalents. The poem
must be a mosaic whose tesserae do not too readily blur into a harmonious picture. How?

By referring to Harrison's continual rearrangement of linguistic
areas 'from poem to poem to form new sociolinguistic patch-works
and pastiches [to] embrace all the discourses which have been
invested with power and domination', Geyer-Ryan perhaps implies
that the success of the enterprise she imputes to his work depends
upon its always changing the mixture, finding new polyphonies.
That is, she treats Harrison's *oeuvre* as the 'whole utterance' in
which dialogical discourse can be found. This would suggest that we
should not judge the work's success on the evidence of one or even
several poems, but need to examine the kaleidoscope of the whole
canon – if we can establish what that is.

While poems such as 'The Bonebard Ballads' triptych contain
obvious tensions between sociolects, in which sense are poems such
as 'Timers' or 'Pain-Killers' dialogic? What is the status of poems
such as *Fire-Gap* and 'Cypress & Cedar'? Did Harrison abandon
polyphony and heteroglossia, for the time being, with the 'School of
Eloquence' and 'Art & Extinction' poems, and turn to a more traditional poetic for the 'American' poems? Or could the later poems
function as the background which will foreground the earlier, and,
possibly, those yet to come? Is the voice and the discourse of the
later poems monadic, or could they be described as either pastiche or
patch-work?

In Chapter 2, I suggested that Harrison's italicisation of the
printed representation of working-class speech, and his restricting of
it to external dialogue (including that of his own earlier avatar) is
dialogic only in the narrower sense, which is not that form described
by Bakhtin as a characteristic trait of the novel, and for which he
regarded authorial intention to be essential.[136] Just as the Leeds
dialect has a different function from Harrison's more recent idiolect,
so the other 'voices' in his work are not always accorded parity of
status. In 'Illuminations', for example, he opens with the voice of a

135 Geyer-Ryan, 'Heteroglossia', p. 200.
136 Bakhtin, *Dialogic Imagination*, p. 358.

narrator in the present relating an anecdote of his past to implicit but anonymous and invisible auditors or readers:

> The two machines on Blackpool's Central Pier
> *The Long Drop* and *The Haunted House* gave me
> my thrills the holiday that post-war year
> but my father watched me spend impatiently[137]

The following line, divided from this first stanza by a line space, represents direct speech from the past, that of Harrison's father, and is distinguished from the narrative voice by italicisation:

> *Another tanner's worth, but then no more!*

Then the narrator, still imaginatively inhabiting the past, turns to address the recollected speaker:

> But I sneaked back the moment that you napped.

Reminding his father of how he 'snapped' at the child Tony, Harrison uses the same convention to represent indirect speech as he did for direct:

> *Bugger the machines! Breathe God's fresh air!*

The third stanza moves from a narration of the past within which the present narrator is invisible: 'I sulked all week', a story still being told to the poet's father (who had died in 1980): 'and wouldn't hold your hand' to a narration happening 'now', told with hindsight:

> I'd never heard you mention God, or swear,
> and it took me until now to understand.

In the closing lines the narrator is in the present tense, but he continues to address his father, not as a ghost haunting the present (he is not 'here') but as an historical trace:

> I see now all the piled old pence turned green,
> enough to hang the murderer all year
> and stare at millions of ghosts in the machine –
>
> The penny dropped in time! Wish you were here!

'Illuminations' could be described as a dialogue between the present and the past. To be dialogic, however, a poem requires a divided voice which can participate in the exchange of dialectic, but

---

137 'Illuminations I', *SP*, p. 146.

which does not give the sense that the sum of its parts constitutes a reconstitutable undivided whole. Each element must have a different 'conceptual horizon'.[138] In the process of literary creation, the mutual illumination of a native language and a foreign language [if it occurs in the work] underscores and objectifies the "conception of the world" facet of both languages, as well as their internal form, and their respective systems of values.'[139] The difference between the dialogised utterances resides not only in syntax or morphology but in conception of the world. Thus the introduction of a foreign term into a poem would not necessarily be dialogic, nor would the use of native dialect within a poem composed largely in the 'standard' language be dialogical if the two forms of discourse did not represent different systems of perceptions. Bakhtinian dialogism, I suggest, requires conflict rather than mere co-existence of different discourses within a text. The languages of the two distinct speaking subjects in 'Illuminations', Harrison and his father, are the expressions of different outlooks, different worlds, but, in Bakhtin's sense, they are presented in a different degree. Mr Harry Harrison could be said to be depicted as a 'full presence' in the poem, as his words are represented as explicit dialogue. That dialogue is, however, also shown to be transmitted through the memory of the young to the grown-up Tony Harrison.

It could be argued that it is Bakhtin's second degree or hybrid. The boy did not understand the outlook of his father because they do not share the same history, even though they do, to an extent, share a dialect. The man, who no longer shares that dialect (exclusively of others), believes that he does understand his father's 'conceptual system'. When the penny has dropped and the man wishes the father 'were here', he closes that dialogism[140] by ending the dialectic, but he thus also implicitly leaves open the third degree, in which 'the other's discourse receives no material corroboration and yet is

---

138 Thus poetic tropes such as metaphor are not dialogic, for 'one language, one conceptual hoizon, is sufficient to them all: there is no need of heteroglot social contexts. What is more, the very movement of the poetic symbol (for example the unfolding of a metaphor) presumes precisely this unity of language, an unmediated correspondence with its object'. Bakhtin, *Dialogic Imagination*, p. 297.
139 M. M. Bakhtin, 'Iz predystorii romannogo slova', *Voprosy literatury i ésteki* (Moscow, 1975), p. 427, quoted in translation by Todorov, *Bakhtin: The Dialogical Principle*, p. 61.
140 Though obviously not the dialogical orientation which is a characteristic of all discourse. See Bakhtin, *Dialogic Imagination*, p. 92.

summoned forth: it is because it is held available in the collective memory of a given social group'[141] – because the shared social discourse of working-class Leeds, of family life, is present in the adult Tony Harrison, and its world-view is still other than his own.

The narrative 'I' of 'Fire-eater' consumes the 'tongues of fire' of his father and uncle, but their evocation or projection from past to present is not a dialogical process but one of amalgamation; they are drawn into the always-present of the poem in order to serve that present.[142] Thus the poem's imagery is of knotted strings, handkerchiefs, scarves, and flags, 'One continuous string', but the 'Fire-eater' is singular: Harrison – not his father and uncle.[143]

For Bakhtin, the novel, not poetry, was the genre of dialogism, because 'The language of the poet is *his own* language; he is wholly immersed in it, and inseparable from it [....] Every word must express in unmediated and direct fashion the poet's design; there must be no distance between the poet and his discourse'.[144] whereas the prose writer 'does not speak in a given language, from which he distances himself to a greater or lesser degree, but he speaks *through* language, as it were, a language that has gained in thickness, become objectivized, and moved away from his mouth'.[145] The dialogue of Harrison's plays is not necessarily dialogical, though within a dramatic character's speeches there may be dialogical utterances. The exchange between the inspector and Lysistrata in *Chorus* represents the interaction (and failure to gain common ground) of two distinct perspectives, two discourses, as does the dialogue between the satyrs and Kyllene in *Trackers*. Bakhtin, however, makes a further distinction between the dialogic novelistic language and that of other genres. The former 'does not merely represent: it is itself an object of representation. Novelistic discourse is always self-critical, and therein lies the difference between the novel and all the "direct" genres – the epic, the lyric and drama in the strict

---

141 Todorov, Bakhtin: *The Dialogical Principle*, p. 73.

142 'Fire-eater', *SP*, p. 168.

143 Textual variations in the poem may reflect a distance between the respective sociolects of poet and and an early editor. The version in *Continuous*, p. 46, has 'inwards' at l. 3, while *SP* has 'innards'. (This could, of course, be a straightforward typo, as the substitution of 'embarassed' for 'embarrassed' at l. 7 of 'Bringing Up', *Continuous*, p. 44.)

144 Bakhtin, *Dialogic Imagination*, pp. 98–109.

145 Bakhtin, *Dialogic Imagination*, p. 112.

sense'.[146] Harrison's poetry does not offer the reader an unmediated communion with its subject-matter. The poet does not camouflage either his own presence or that of the language which places interference between, whilst it creates the distinction between, subject and object. In this, and in his reflecting upon his own poetic, Harrison resembles Brecht. Geyer-Ryan finds that the 'heteroglot attitude to language in Brecht and even more so in Harrison [...] draws its energy from their own linguistic experiences'.[147] Although linguistic schism is both the catalyst of personal division and the product and symptom of underlying social schism, Harrison's heterogeneity is not only linguistic. A personality or series of personalities is also dramatised as a site of conflicts and tensions which are not directly related to class and language. A Bakhtinian analysis of Harrison's work would need to differ from one of Brecht's because – as well as dialogising his poetic voice, and presenting the reader with a most slippery subject[ivity] in contemplation of the themes of the poems – a dialogised identity, an ostension of a self, is the object of that contemplation. Since readers have felt able to reconstruct and discuss the personality of the poet as revealed by his poetry, presumably there is a distinct dominant personality for them to apprehend, and the utterances of this 'I' generally have a different status from any other.

Harrison's poems, then, have been subjected to a number of different kinds of interpretation and categorisation. Equally varied has been the evaluation of their literary merit, particularly by writers producing the kind of normative criticism which sets as a given that the poems are intended to be political (in senses defined to a greater or lesser degree), and which then criticises them for failing to be so. It is to that kind of criticism that the next chapter turns.

---

146 Bakhtin, 'Iz predystorii romannogo slova', p. 66.
147 Geyer-Ryan, 'Heteroglossia', p. 207.

CHAPTER 5

Poetry and truth: readings of Harrison's class war

'*It's not poetry we need in this class war.*

v.

Harrison's poetry has been accused of not being political enough as often as it has been accused of bringing politics into the inappropriate medium of art. The very critics who complain that Harrison writes as though he were the only person ever to be alienated from his class by education seem also to expect him to write like a stereotypical working-class, left-wing intellectual; committed to the party line and a festering grudge. The 'v' aspect of Harrison's writing, its oppositional and sometimes antagonistic nature, seems to produce the expectation that it will be, if not radical, at least pro-active. As Trotsky wrote, 'quarrels about "pure art" and about art with a tendency took place between the liberals and the "populists". They do not become us.'[1]

A speech written for Albert Finney to give at the inauguration of the National Theatre's Olivier stage, but never delivered, is dismissed by Luke Spencer as 'off-the-peg-doggerel' symptomatic of the absence of a radical stance in Harrison's work:

> And so between Big Ben and Wren's great dome
> The National Theatre has made its home.
> This (one of London's choicest) Thames-side site,
> between St Paul's and Parliament's just right.
> Somewhere between devotion and debate
> a nation's drama animates the state.[2]

Finney, Spencer infers, was too embarrassed by the thudding metre and 'theatrical back-slapping' to deliver the speech, but perhaps the

---

1 Leon Trotsky, 'Literature and Revolution', in Paul N. Siegel, ed., *Leon Trotsky on Literature and Art* (New York, 1970), p. 30.
2 'Prologue', *Critical Quarterly*, 28, no. 3 (autumn 1986), pp. 69-70, quoted by Spencer, *Poetry TH*, p. 20.

lines' monotonous form was a thin smoke-screen over a swiftly apparent irony. The social institutions, church and government, 'devotion and debate', echo *'rege et lege'* in *Big H*, reminding us that the National Theatre is not free from institutional pressure and constraint.[3] The line 'A folly? No! No concrete Xanadu' is surely ironic, and the laconic 'the nation's committed its resources to',[4] given Harrison's feelings about the concentration of wealth and resources in the southern cities, may not be congratulatory.

More feeding hands were bitten when the National's *Trackers* transformed satyrs into the contemporary inhabitants of London's cardboard city. The invitation extended to the audience to feel both responsible and guilty could be seen as exploitative not only of them but also of the homeless, and hypocritical, given that Harrison and the rest of the company would, presumably, return to their respective homes, and not cardboard city. This could be provocation in the cause of making a point and a protest.[5] Through Spenser's reading, however, it could seem to be less [uz] against 'them' than the iconoclastic individual making a 'v'-sign at authority.

Spencer quotes from a *Stand* editorial, 'The Grudge', in which Douglas Dunn 'argued that the special predicament of a working-class writer like himself is that "His work is ... directed at an audience who do not receive it; instead, it is received by an audience of those he is against"'. For Dunn, the best way of negotiating that dilemma, is '"commitment ... the idea under which a working-class poet can organise the sundry circumstances which belong to him and which cohere in the form of beliefs about the world"'.[6] Spencer sees the poet's vision of a classless society as fostering a grudge whose purity must be kept intact 'to prevent the dilution and assimilation of the working class poet's emancipatory project'. Cited as poets with successful grudges are Dunn and Harrison, who 'by learning to make creative use of their grudge [...] have proved to be the most successful of working-class poets'.

Grudge is presented as a powerful motive force in Harrison's work:

---

3 See, for example, Harrison's comments on the rejection of his *Lysistrata* (later incorporated into *Chorus*) in 'Facing Up', *Bloodaxe 1*, p. 449, and p. 454 note 3.

4 'Prologue', *Poetry TH*, p. 20.

5 As Oliver Taplin suggests in 'Satyrs on the Borderline: *Trackers* in the Development of Tony Harrison's Theatre Work', in *Bloodaxe 1*, p. 464.

6 *Poetry TH*, p. 6.

My bloodgrudge should boost you back into action.
Bloodgrudge is a goad to upholders of bloodright.[7]

– and 'retrospective aggro' is described as a source of that work.[8] Aggression and aggressive acts do provide both the dramatic impetus of many of the plays, and an underlying motif of the 'School of Eloquence' sonnets, but we should be wary of seeing in these the poet's own, 'real' or 'sincere' grudges. Spencer goes on to relate the creative use of 'grudge' to 'supplying the kind of social perspective (or "art of the real") demanded by [Eric] Homberger',[9] but the suggestion that the essence of poetry is resentment, an overflowing personal response – poetic *furor* – does seem curiously old-fashioned. What is the 'art of the real'? Being Scots did not prevent Dunn from writing about working-class Hull.[10] To divide poetry into grittily realist working-class efforts spun from real experience of oppression, and whimsical fancies spun out of the sugary strands of leisured classes' aesthetic appreciation, is as unfair to Shelley as it is to Harrison. *Stand* has no monopoly on committed individuals.

Rather than pursuing the 'political', perhaps we should look for the 'social' poetry which Homberger opposes to entrenched inwardness.[11] While some modern English poetry produces antagonism, an enraged reaction does not necessarily indicate either a radical or social perspective. As Spencer points out, Jon Silkin's *Stand* anthology merely highlighted the lack of a radical perspective among English writers.[12] For Spencer, at the time of the anthology's publication, 'the two most popular substitutes for a social perspective in this country were either Philip Larkin's disdainful digs at the welfare state or Ted Hughes's anti-humanitarian primitivism'.[13] If '*v.* is the most outstanding social poem of the last twenty-five years', is it because the poem is 'about our times in a way no other poem has achieved'?[14] The matter of *v.* is the emotional reaction, from melancholy to rage and back again – of one individual (albeit one with a complex identity) to the horrors he observes in Thatcher's Britain.

---

7   *Oresteia, TW*, p. 267.
8   See Wilmer, *Poets Talking*, p. 101.
9   *Poetry TH*, p. 6.
10 See Douglas Dunn, *Terry Street* (London, 1969).
11 Discussed in *Poetry TH*, pp. 4–6.
12 Jon Silkin, *Poetry of the Committed Individual: A Stand Anthology* (London, 1973).
13 *Poetry TH*, p. 5.
14 Martin Booth, *Tribune,* quoted on *SP*, back cover.

The poet brutalised by social ills is at its centre, not the agencies and forces which created those ills. As for effectivity – although Neil Astley 'couldn't claim that a few thousand copies of a poetry book could do much to challenge [...] complacent assumptions, even if it was – as *Tribune* said – "the most outstanding social poem of the past 25 years"', he does suggest that only the poem's limited circulation restricted its effectiveness. 'Thanks to the publicity, generated initially by the tabloid press', however, 'the poem reached an audience of several million'.[15] The consequence of that exposure is impossible to quantify, of course. Again, it seems that distinctions between personal, introspective or emotional, and social or political poetry are neither clear-cut nor absolute.[16]

'Society, class, language, and the extinction of species and of language [...] seem to be the chief areas of concern', John Haffenden noted when he interviewed Harrison in 1983, but wondered 'to what extent what you are actually dealing with is a personal, psychological issue, and [...] you appropriate an historical-social resentment in order to give a larger authority to that issue?'[17] Harrison replied that he saw the two as intimately related. The intimacies of the private life, he suggested, 'are a kind of earthing area for the lightning of history and of political struggles', while 'people who [...] find culture more comfortable if it is ahistorical and apolitical' separate those issues. Much of Harrison's poetry does take its matter from personal as well as national and class history, and certain poems, 'Flood', for example, are offered as (superficially) more or less fictionalised autobiography. Eight years after the Haffenden interview, however, Harrison affirmed that he wrote on political themes, 'both in a narrow sense and also in a broader sense'.[18] Blake Morrison concurs, finding that:

> Harrison's poems about his parents are more than simple elegies, [...] to praise them for being 'moving' (as most reviewers and critics have done) is to emasculate them of their hard political edge [....] The poem ['Book Ends'], like many of Harrison's, is an elegy, but it shows that the elegy need not be an apolitical form.[19]

15 Astley, 'The Riff-raff Takes Over', *v.*, p. 36.
16 Eagleton makes the distinction in the reviews quoted above, and John Lucas assumes that Harrison's poetry has a political agenda. See 'Speaking for England?', *Bloodaxe 1*, pp. 351–61.
17 'Interview', *Bloodaxe 1*, pp. 230–1.
18 Wilmer, *Poets Talking*, p. 99.
19 Blake Morrison, 'The Filial Art', in *Bloodaxe 1*, p. 55.

Morrison traces resemblances between 'Book Ends' and Larkin's 'Reference Back':

> where a similar emotional and cultural gap opens up between parent and child [....] But the difference between the poems is instructive. The pain in Larkin's is the illusion that mother and son could have preserved the more intimate relationship they had when he was a child, that 'by acting differently we could have kept it so' [....] Harrison's is a more blaming poem [...] the son 'a scholar', the father 'worn out on poor pay', they have been forced apart not by the passing of time but by a system which assimilates bright working-class boys into the middle class.

The poem is not 'merely' moving and, presumably, in order to be a successful poem it must have more than purely personal application. Harrison does describe the gap which 'opens up between parent and child' as 'cultural' as well as 'emotional', but is his making a cultural referent from his personal experience indicative of a hard political edge? In asserting the grittily particular against the non-specific poetic universal, does Harrison blunt any political edge? Political oppression and division are dominant motifs of the 'School of Eloquence' sequence, as war is the dominant motif of *Gorgon*, even though the surface subject matter is often intimate, but to what extent does Harrison look beyond the particular and personal instance, the effect of the oppression, to its determinants? It has been suggested that in *v.*, '[Harrison's] thoughts are really about himself, not about them [his parents and the desecrated grave]'.[20] Harrison's poetic voice is inflected by political and social struggle, yet, in taking the intimate as its subject, and foregrounding the personal, it perhaps invites just such a reading. On the other hand, Harrison claims to have tried to bring the energy of drama into poetry in the way Donne is said to have brought the energy of drama into the love lyric,[21] and it could be argued that his dialectical sonnets bring to the lyric the robust particularity of the dramatic/narrative verse.

What is political poetry? Is effectivity in opposition to affectivity? As Yeats and Auden demonstrate, that poetry has an effect at all – that it can *do* anything – is open to debate.[22] It could be said that

---

20 May, 'A Note on the Poem', *v.*, p. 65.
21 'Conversation', p. 45.
22 See, for example, W. H. Auden, 'In Memory of W. B. Yeats', *Collected Shorter Poems* (London, 1969), p. 141.

Harrison's *v.* 'achieved' nothing tangible. After the deluge, according to the IBA, the 'flood of public protest expected was not realised'.[23] After transmission they received four letters of complaint (two from MPs) and two of congratulation. Sales of the new edition of *v.* 'with press articles' were, if not outstanding, reasonable, as were those of the second edition of *SP*, which included *v.* as well as other new poems. How many of those who knew or discovered that the poem ever was a book, however (almost none of the newspapers mentioned it), or who were directed to either of the editions by Channel 4, found the poet they expected? Did *v.* make new 'poetry supporters'? The film was seen by millions, of course. It won the Royal Television Society's Best Original Programme Award, which is a recognition of something, but if it opened television to demotic English, subsequent debates on swearing show that it was not by much; if it expanded the register of poetry, it was no more than others had done before; if it made poetry for the people, it did not make poetry on pages and in stanzas, rather than in streets and rap, recognisable as for the likes of uz. Presumably, then, 'political poetry' can only be defined as a relative term.

Eagleton finds that since the nineteenth century it has been in a differential relation to poetic tropes: 'in post Romantic England, the aesthetic and the institutional, the sensuous and the social, were reconstituted as polar opposites'.[24] It would be a crude exaggeration to say that the Romantic aesthetic generated a literary apartheid which put feeling, imagination, spirituality, and the sublime into the woolly fold of 'true' or 'high' poetry, whose proper vehicles were metaphor and imagery, while consigning to the goats polemic, propaganda and politics, for which the ballad and other low or unuplifting forms were felt to be adequate, but, as Eagleton points out, after 'the works of Blake and Shelley, myth and symbol in English literature becomes increasingly a preserve of the political right, and "political poetry" an effective oxymoron'.[25] Harrison himself located the last period during which canonical poetry could comfortably be appropriated for political propaganda, in his analysis of eighteenth-century translations of *The Aeneid*, a work which has

23 'Public Response to *v.*', extract from the IBA's case-study 'Why Did We Broadcast *v.*?', *v.*, p. 73.
24 Eagleton, 'Gaze of the Gorgon', p. 53.
25 Eagleton, *Ideology of the Aesthetic*, p. 61.

been made to bear both Royalist and Republican interpretations.[26] 'High' poetry has never been by definition an inappropriate medium for all political messages, of course, but it has been made to sit ill with left-wing radicalism.

'The choice is between being pained primarily by oppression, and being pained primarily by division and disunity – the difference, roughly, between radical and liberal.'[27] Read as a threnody for a united Britain, *v.* is not radical. Nor if it is read as a poet's melancholy introspection in a graveyard. The Gulf War poems do not examine the economic determinants of war, and their use of myth may seem to resort to some familiar mystifications. Though he does not restate a radical agenda for social revolution with each new poem, Harrison is neither reactionary nor hide-bound. 'What we expect from a Harrison is a radical rather than a liberal perspective,' Eagleton asserts, 'since we aren't likely to get it from ninety percent of his literary colleagues.'[28]

Harrison's poem 'Dichtung und Wahrheit' ('Poetry and truth'), though supportive of the 'fluent propagandist' of the Mozambique freedom fighters, Frelimo, Marcelina Dos Santos, is a powerful statement against the usual consequence of radicalism as a political *modus operandi* – violence. The poem begins by depicting Dos Santos in heroic light. He speaks 'the cloven tongues of four colonial powers':

> and swears in each the war will soon be won.
> He speaks of 'pen & sword', quotes Mao's phrase
> about 'all power' the moment his guests gaze
> on the 14-18 bronze with Maxim gun.[29]

Then the narrative voice pleads:

> Dulciloquist Dos Santos, swear to them
> whose languages you'll never learn to speak
> that tongues of fire at a 1000 rpm
> is not the final eloquence you seek.

---

26 See T. W. Harrison, 'English Virgil: The Aeneid in the XVIII Century', *Philologica Pragensia*, X (1967), pp. 1–11, 80–91.

27 Eagleton, 'Antagonisms', p. 348.

28 Eagleton, 'Gaze of the Gorgon', p. 54.

29 Though Harrison italicises most foreign words in his poetry, and occasionally uses Gothic script, the German title of this poem is printed in Roman. See *SP*, p. 181.

Spondaic or dactylic those machines
and their dry scansions mean that truths get lost,

and a *pravda* empty as its magazines
is Kalashnikov PK's flash Pentecost.

If Harrison's poetry depicts machine-gun tongues of fire as leading to nothing but apocalypse, a fruitless Pentecost, it does not commend the tongues of fire of dulciloquy and poetic eloquence as capable of bringing redemption. Again and again the poems deplore war and the death of language, eloquence, life, but they are not agendas for a better way. Rather, 'truths get lost', perhaps, in the movement from oppositions and conjunctions based on historical and social specifics (Mozambique freedom fighters and government) to those which are linguistic or conceptual (the links between machine-gun fire, tongues of fire, the Pentecost, *Pravda*, and the pun on 'magazines'). Similarly, the solidity of specification in the historical and personal anecdotes is not matched by descriptions of the politics of the present or a detailed manifesto for the future. There is a tendency to start from Brecht's 'bad old days' rather than the (possibly) good new ones.

Michael Schmidt finds that 'Class conflict in his poems has a rather 1930s feel about it', and suggests that 'the poet who wishes to get direct purchase on his present political world faces the perennial problem of dating or dated allusion [....] a problem Donald Davie identifies'.[30] If time, as Davie suggests, makes political fact and historical tragedy 'quite strictly fabulous', perhaps Harrison's record of class oppression is similarly robbed of verisimilitude. Perhaps: 'what for them [Harrison's father and uncles, and all his Rhubarbarians] were agonies' indeed 'for us / Are high-brow thrillers'.[31] The detail which Davie cites as making a poem 'more remote than Ithaca or Rome' – 'abandoned workings' – has an echo in *v.*, which suggests, perhaps, that if reference back to historical occasions or particulars inevitably puts a poem at a remove from its readers, then those particulars can become relevant again.

Eagleton concedes that 'there is something to be said' for the idea that poetry is about 'the inward, the interpersonal, the fleeting

---

30 Michael Schmidt, *Reading Modern Poetry* (London, 1989), pp. 25–6.
31 Donald Davie, 'Remembering the 'Thirties', *Collected Poems* (Manchester, 1990), p. 34.

intuition and stray tender detail, the frail aperçu or metaphysical frisson', because, perhaps, poetry can

> salvage that which a rationalist system discards as so much waste product; and to restore the integrity of experience, in a period when human subjectivity itself is increasingly processed and regulated, is in its own mild way a social protest.[32]

By this account, much of Harrison's poetry is mild social protest, but it is not only the relative strength of the protest which counts in determining the poem's function. Social comment in English poetry has tended to be confined to descriptions of suffering and complaints about the observable phenomena of injustice, rather than their deeper determinants.

> War poets are supposed to write about what it feels like to be gassed, not about the structure of monopoly capital; yet to suppress the latter is to collude with the dangerous myth that war is just some inexplicable orgy of collective unreason, in the characteristic style of the liberal humanist.

Far from advocating an Eliotesque detachment and suppression of personality, Eagleton praises Harrison's 'fury', and describes 'A Cold Coming' as 'stunningly powerful', but adds: 'there are moments when this oblique, implicit style of politics will no longer serve, and one of them was known as the Gulf War'. It is, however, difficult to achieve a radical perspective when the subject is war:

> since that abstraction already displaces historical specificity – and so the possibility of understanding – to moral lament. Here as in *The Waste Land* it is as though all wars are one war; and it is a short step from that conflation (not that Harrison explicitly takes it) to original sin, the darkness of the human heart, the beast beneath the skin and other such convenient mystifications of material greed and ideological contention.[33]

In a sense, 'material greed' and 'ideological contention' are no more historically specific and no less generalised and abstract than 'original sin' and 'the darkness of the human heart'. The latter are, however, *convenient* mystifications; obscurantisms with particular political effects. The function served in *Gorgon* by Harrison's taking 'this terrifying creature of legend who turns men into stone as a

---

32 Eagleton, 'Gaze of the Gorgon', p. 53.
33 Eagleton, 'Gaze of the Gorgon', p. 54.

metaphor for what the Kaiser unearthed into our century' and describing 'her long shadow still cast across its closing years'[34] is not that of obscuration for political ends, though perhaps the reducibility of the most apparent message of one poem in the collection, 'The Pomegranates of Patmos', to lapel button slogans (roughly, 'Make Love Not War') does obscure radical political content.

An unsigned editorial from the period when Harrison edited *Poetry and Audience* endorses the distinction between historical specificity and mythic mystification. The author condemns writers whose poetry becomes 'Poesy', and in whose work 'human beings become Humanity, and real life, as it does in many rejected contributions [to the magazine], finds apotheosis in the Springs of Helicon and Parnassian Streams'. Equally deplored, however, are the poets of 'Social Realism', who are recommended, instead of submitting verse to *Poetry and Audience*, to 'join a welfare organisation and be practical' or, 'if their Blank Despair is so full of Horror and Torture', to 'kill themselves'.[35] The more mature Harrison took neither course after visiting Bosnia. The poems he submitted to the *Guardian* neither turn the perpetrators and victims of the fighting into poetic abstractions nor excise the details of their reality. 'The Cycles of Donji Vakuf' does not contain a direct-address appeal for the end of the war, or indeed of War, nor the characteristic Harrison image of apocalyptic fire. In some ways, it is a return to the mode of the earlier sonnets which look at war from the micro rather than macro level: local, immediate, personal; conveying a message largely by conglomerations of things. The things in 'A Close One' are displaced and out of context; the debris of both air raids and bereavement; vividly evoking a time of disconnection and disorientation, of a darkness spasmodically lit by images which, for the child in the Blitz, have both great and enigmatic significance.[36]

---

34 *Gorgon*, preface, p. 58.
35 Unsigned editorial, *Poetry and Audience*, 7, no. 1, pp. 1–2. No date appears on the cover, but as the magazine was at that time produced weekly during term, and vol. 7, no. 2 is dated 23 October 1959, the likely publication date of this issue was 16 October 1959.
36 Rick Rylance discussed Harrison's use of objects to convey the sense of unity and disunity in 'Tony Harrison and Community', an illuminating but as yet unpublished talk given at the Oxford University Department for Continuing Education, June 1997.

Hawsers. Dirigibles. Searchlight. *Messerschmitts.*
Half let go. Half rake dark nowt to find . . .

Day old bereavement debris of a blitz
there's been no shelter from, no *all clear* whined.

Our cellar 'refuge room' made anti-gas.
Damp sand that smelled of graves not Morecambe Bay.
Air Raid Precautions out of *Kensitas.*
A Victory jig-saw on Fry's Cocoa tray.
Sandwiches. Snakes & Ladders. Thermos flask [. . . .]

my Redhill container, my long-handled hoe.[37]

The objects in 'The Cycles of Donji Vakuf', other than the literal
and metaphorical weapons of destruction (Kalashnikov and scythe)
are more systematically displaced in that they have been looted. The
shifting ownership of cow, goat, bicycle, and mandolin, and the
mirror-image gladness and sorrow of their winners and losers
reflects the see-saw, pointless nature of the war, as well as the poet's
ethnically (if not ethically) neutral approach to it. The child's
perspective is again important, though here the viewpoint is dual,
and the two children imaginary.

This time it's the Bosnian Muslims' turn
to cleanse a taken town, to loot and burn.
Donji Vakuf fell last night at 11 [. . . .]
A goat whose udder seems about to burst
squirts out her milk to quench a victor's thirst
which others quench with beer, as a cow,
who's no idea she's a Muslim's now,
sprays a triumphal arch of piss across
the path of her new happy Bosnian boss [. . . .]
When he's balanced his booty, he makes off,
for a moment forgetting his Kalashnikov,
which he slings with all his looted load
on to his shoulder and trudges down the road,
where a solitary reaper passes by,
scythe on his shoulder [. . . .]
And tonight some small boy will be glad
he's got the present of a bike from soldier dad,
who braved the Serb artillery and fire
to bring back a scuffed red bike with one flat tyre.

---

37 'A Close One', *SP*, p. 160.

And, among the thousands fleeing north, another,
with all his gladness gutted, with his mother,
knowing the nightmare they are cycling in,
will miss the music of his mandolin.[38]

This is both specific and impersonal. It doesn't attribute war to Universals of Human Nature or cry over the Human Condition, but neither is it, in Eagleton's sense, radical, and it will thus probably receive the same kind of criticism as *v.* and *Banquet*. Bruce Woodcock, for example, suggests that the poetic forms he chooses 'invite him [Harrison] into an easy verse-making', but that 'because of the grand gestures invited by the tragic sense of the human condition, it could be argued that Harrison loses the political and satirical bite Shelley sustains in his broadside'.[39]

Dunn suggests that the twentieth-century modification of the lyric strain has entailed the marriage of a prosaic materialism to lyric subjectivity and emotion. He describes the lyricism of Harrison's work (as well as that of Larkin, MacCaig, and Heaney) as

> drawn from an ability to engage with the materials of ordinary life, and then absorb them, not necessarily to transcend them, or adjust ordinariness to the mysterious or the irrational; instead, although very different from each other in convictions, backgrounds and styles, and in nationality, they prove that poetry begins in reality as well as in the imagination that apprehends it.[40]

Harrison is very much the poet of 'what can be seen, heard, felt, smelled and touched, as well as the conclusions that can be drawn from them'. Things in his poems are used in varying degrees of subtlety, from the self-conscious objective correlative of the Eccles cake,[41] and the choc-ice,[42] to the resonances of Mrs Florrie Harrison's wedding ring on Harrison's palm,[43] and the striking humorous incongruity of the perished red-rubber douche.[44] Harrison's work is also, as Dunn writes, 'a poetry of subjective

---

38 'The Cycles of Donji Vakuf', *Guardian* (15 September 1995).
39 Bruce Woodcock, 'Classical Vandalism: Tony Harrison's Invective', *Critical Quarterly*, 32, no. 2 (summer 1990), p. 63.
40 Douglas Dunn, 'Importantly Live: Tony Harrison's Lyricism', *Bloodaxe 1*, p. 254.
41 'Currants' I and II, *SP*, pp. 151–2.
42 'Continuous', *SP*, p. 143.
43 'Timer', *SP*, p. 167.
44 'Schwiegermutterlieder', *SP*, pp. 50–1.

dilemmas and dramas', but do the 'intuitive procedures of lyric poetry' render that subjectivity 'impersonal and therefore acceptable to the reader'? For Dunn, Harrison's poetry 'can engage with history and politics directly' and be 'oppositional to orthodox social expectations',[45] yet Dunn attributes the strength of the poem he is considering ('Long Distance') to its authenticity and unbridled emotion.

> Harrison runs the risk of narrating his own behaviour and his private thoughts; he wagers on their authenticity with himself and what used to be known as the Muse. The gesture is extreme and candid, and made possible by a refusal to surrender to reticence. Instead, he places all his tact at the service of how effectively he can make his poem. Nothing else matters to him, or to any poet who recognises that it is in these heightened moments of writing where he or she lives at his or her most important.[46]

The conclusion that the power of 'Long Distance' to move and exhilarate comes from Harrison's 'refusal to surrender to reticence' is followed by a reference to 'an aesthetic as severe and as classically informed as Harrison's [which] introduces its own special restraint on lyricism'. Dunn might have said that part of the strength of Harrison's writing is the tension between powerful emotions, self-autopsies, and formal constraints, but he felt it necessary to write in terms of irresistible impulses and the poetic vocation. Admittedly, Dunn is addressing 'lyricism' in this article, but, judging from the other pieces collected in *Bloodaxe 1*, he does tend to treat Harrison as a predominantly lyric poet.[47] Thus 'all' of Harrison's 'tact' is 'at the service of how effective he can make his poem' and 'Nothing else matters' because 'these heightened moments' of intuition transcend everyday life. It seems to be difficult to write about lyric poetry without producing such remarks, partly because the genre seems indelibly associated with metaphoric, imagistic modes and inscribed with concepts of transcendent, mystical inspiration:

> the term 'image' or (poetic) 'imagination' continues to labour under the burden of aesthetic mysticism left by its romantic past [...] while the

---

45 Dunn, 'Importantly Live', p. 254.
46 Dunn, 'Importantly Live', p. 256.
47 'Formal Strategies in Tony Harrison's Poetry', pp. 129–32, and 'Acute Accent: *Continuous*', pp. 212–15.

poetic 'image' may be acknowledged as a symbol or vehicle of truth, the implication always is that this truth is never due to any organic or effective presence in it of intellect or rational discourse or ideas.[48]

Though Eagleton reminds Harrison that 'the solace and unity *v.* finally seeks in sexual relationship isn't abstractable from the destiny of nations',[49] 'Durham' suggests that Harrison already knows:

> You complain
> that the machinery of sudden death,
> Fascism, the hot bad breath
> of Powers down small countries' necks
> shouldn't interfere with sex.
>
> They *are* sex, love, we must include
> all these in love's beatitude.[50]

An early poem describes a house, a room, a lover, as a bulwark of peace against the outer world:

> Outside the storm drew tide and land,
> And with the land, the promised seed.
> The house she had, but not the need
>   Her house would keep without
>   where winds impede
>
> The struggling winds and strangle trees.
> (Outside there may be storm and flood;
> Within, this wind should blow us good;
>   There should be light and calm [....]
>
> Again. 'Was that a shot I heard?')
> Love is no luxury in war.[51]

In another poem not included in *SP*, sex defies politics – in so far as 'politics' is equated with geo-political division. In their shared sleeper, an American and Russian are not representatives of opposing powers, but constitute:

> Neutrality! Brave cocks and cunts
> belong to no barbed continents.[52]

---

48 Galvano Della Volpe, *Critique of Taste* (London, 1991), p. 15.
49 Eagleton, 'Antagonisms', p. 350.
50 'Durham', *SP*, p. 70.
51 'The Promised Land', *Earthworks*, pp. 8–9.
52 'The Chopin Express', *Loiners*, pp. 69–70.

This is in its way a political act. Though they don't 'belong', the lovers are metonyms for their respective continents:

> Look, I spurt
> my seed into her Russian dirt
> The whole globe or the Bering Straits
> divide the Soviets from the States.
> They didn't then.

The smoke-screen of its half-comic, earthy language notwithstanding, the conceit is surely more Romantic than metaphysical. The consummation is expanded to global proportion, this union depicted as healing of political division:

> I felt the broken world all come
> together then, and all between
> a conshie and a commie bum.

The climax of the poem is made the description, from the inside, of the narrator's sexual climax, which itself relieves his global anxieties:

> Relieve my tension. I can't come.
> The world's a crematorium.

The centre of the poem, then, is not politics but, again, personal experience:

> Hold me! Hold me! Eyes screwed tight
> against the sizzling of the light.
> I'm coming! Count-down! 3-2-1-
> Zero! Earth! Moon! Sun!
> The Constellations!

Thus it is made to seem almost as though the division or unity of the world depends upon the intensity of the narrator's orgasm. Does the poem fail in not being political or radical enough? Does it matter? It's wonderfully paced, funny, audacious, and moving. It *is* about personal experience, but surely that is the point; its perspective is subjective, the subjective experience of orgasm which *can* seem to make the Earth (moon, stars, sun) move, and the subjective experience of lovers which *can* seem like a union of two hemispheres. The usual divisions did not apply 'then'.

In *v*., Harrison shakes off thoughts of the miners' strike, unemployment, urban blight, and class division, and turns

Home, home to my woman as the red
darkens from a fresh blood to a dried.
Home, home to my woman, home to bed
where opposites seem sometimes unified.[53]

Home to a hearth whose flames are in Harrison's work opposed to
the fire of apocalyptic war. The 'sometimes' seems significant.
Sexual love is the mainstay which takes over when the child breaks
away or is wrenched from the continuous [uz] of blood and class
bonds.

The ones we choose to love become our anchor
when the hawser of the blood-tie's hacked or frays.[54]

As 'Durham' shows, however, love does not preclude, any more
than it replaces or defeats, politics. The lovers' meetings seem to
constitute a private refuge from the public ill:

Bad weather and the public mess
drive us to private tenderness

But Harrison doesn't leave it there. He suggests that lovers might be
a communal cure as well as a mutual refuge, through a kind of inoc-
ulation, but he does not allow himself to indulge in a romantic
fantasy of all-conquering love. He does not assert, but wonders:

if together we,
alone two hours, can ever be
love's anti-bodies in the sick,
sick body politic.

With this characteristic undercutting, Harrison refuses to take up 'a
position' on politics or radicals, to preach soap-box certainties.

'Durham' and 'The Chopin Express' seem to reinforce Jerome
McGann's assertion that a preoccupation with personal relationships,
or sex, is far from asocial, and the 'sexual event [...] is, as the poets
have always known, a model of the textual condition'.[55] For
McGann, sex connects. 'The climactic marriage of our persons is
most completely experienced as a total body sensation almost mystical in its intensity as in its meaning. In those moments we realise (in
both senses of the word) that to be human is to be involved with

53 v., p. 26.
54 v., p. 31.
55 Jerome McGann, *The Textual Condition* (Princeton, 1991), p. 3.

another and ultimately with many others.' He reminds us that both the practice and the study of human culture comprise a network of symbolic exchanges, two manifestations of which are sexual and textual acts, and these symbolic exchanges 'always involve material negotiations', and even 'in their most complex and advanced forms – when negotiations are carried out as textual events – the intercourse that is being human is materially executed: as spoken texts or scripted forms'. While this analogy seems fair, it breaks down in its equating of the extended network behind (as well as before and after) text with a network of related acts of sex.

> Beyond that great and strange experience of immediacy the sexual event organizes a vast network of related acts of intercourse at the personal as well as more extended social levels: courtship rituals, domestic economies, political exchanges, and so forth. All of these activities take multiple particular forms. Love, even romantic love, is a social event [....] As such, love is and has ever been one of the great scenes of textuality.

McGann's belief that the 'elective affinities between love and textuality exist because love and text are two of our most fundamental social acts' makes Harrison's textual/sexual acts not a refuge from the social but the social itself. 'They *are* sex, love.' This comes about because 'to participate in these exchanges is to have entered into the textual condition'. Behind a sexual act, however, is a symbolic and anthropological network at a level of abstraction greater than the networks (of production, reiteration and inter-textuality) which link textual acts. The sexual act may be altruistic on the part of both lovers, and forge strong bonds between them, but the climax as described by Harrison is both an inward-turning – a separatist act of self-absorption – and a dissolution, a release from bonds of social or self consciousness:

When I come
I'm out of the sandbagged nets and soar away
into release and *my* Thanksgiving Day.[56]

v. could be described as a dramatised narrative, an ideal vehicle for the Bakhtinian polyphony of voices in Harrison's 'I' (for example the skinhead as avant-garde street artist/social commentator/lager

---

56 'Giving Thanks', *SP*, p. 200.

lout/victim/aspect of Harrison), but, despite the direct speech and dramatic (in the sense of tempestuous) dialogue, the poem's mood is elegiac. Elegies, coming after the fact, cannot by definition prevent or cure the specific ill, though they can warn against recurrence. Alastair Fowler argues that, although an emphasis on feeling and expressiveness in the eighteenth and nineteenth centuries made lyric the paradigm of poetry, it was the modulation of lyric by elegy which resulted in the modern perception of lyric as an interior voice, a 'passionate meditation'.[57] Lindley agrees, citing Coleridge's description of the elegiac mode as the characteristic voice of the Romantic passionate meditation. 'Elegy is the form of poetry natural to the reflective mind. It *may* treat of any subject, but it must treat of no subject for *itself*, but always and exclusively with reference to the poet himself.'[58]

Harrison's saving graces of humour and self-mockery prevent his self-reflexiveness from becoming mere self-excoriation or introspection, but one of the many paradoxes in his work is the coupling of energetic language with an apparent resignation to the inevitability of his poetry's being bracketed within this elegiac tradition, exposed to 'social indifference, self-destructiveness, time, nothingness – the whole fatuity of the belief that writing poetry will *do* anything'.[59] Is Harrison's essentially an elegiac voice? Is the force of his poetry dependent upon its passion; and its social effectiveness, if any, dependent upon the reader's identification with the poet's emotional response? Does *v.* really have a hard edge? For Woodcock, Harrison's ability to engage with local and international politics is compromised by his mastery of form. 'Harrison extends the range of the poem's reflection on contemporary violence to include images of Ulster and the Gulf, but with an almost gratuitous ease. It is as if the formal facility of his verse writing invites him to package his meditations in too easy a form.'[60] Can a poet be too good, too metrically assured? Perhaps the metrical infelicities which Lucas finds in Harrison's work are a defence against such an accusation.[61] Harrison's metrical felicity does not lie in Swinburnean cadences or inappropriate lyric 'music', but in strong, flexible,

57 Alastair Fowler, *Kinds of Literature* (Oxford, 1982), p. 207.
58 S. T. Coleridge, *Table Talk*, quoted in David Lindley, *Lyric* (London, 1985), pp. 68–9.
59 Harrison, quoted in 'Introduction', p. 14.
60 Woodcock, 'Classical Vandalism', p. 62.
61 See Lucas, 'Speaking for England?', p. 359.

varied lines. Occasionally, as in *Misanthrope*, the couplets' regular-
ity, combined with some adventurous rhyming, can distract the
audience from the meaning, as they wonder how Harrison is going
to pull it off this time, but that only adds to the comic effect.

Can grudge and a political agenda shine through elegiac
miasma? Woodcock suggests not. 'Instead of being a badly needed
"Mask of Anarchy" for the 1980s, *v.* finally has more in common
with Wordsworth's "Immortality" ode, its rancour gagged by the
elegiac strain and by a tendency to grand gestures.'[62] I would
suggest that a more productive way of reading *v.* is not as 'personal'
elegy, a lament for a lost loved one – not even for the parents at
whose grave the dramatic action takes place – but as (at least in part)
an extended epitaph (a comunity's as well as an individual's).[63] Its
subject is a past time, its form 'the historical epitaph, the meditation
over a vanished past which has the same relation to the ruin [or the
worked-out mine] that the individual epitaph has to the gravestone.[64]
The inscribing of such an epitaph is a declaration of the 'death' of
working industrial England, and, in its way, a political act. Is the
poem's political effectiveness undermined by its veering away from
historical epigraph toward the elegy of exile (Harrison's exclusion
from the 'united', organic extended family of working-class Leeds),
and thus towards the exile himself?

Equating the lyric genre with elegy, Fussell notes that although
the 'squalor of the contemporary urban scene is often adverted to
[and ...] social and erotic disappointments are dwelt upon [...] the
mutability theme [...] seems now virtually defunct'. That is, 'as
defunct as what can seem its corollary, significant rhyme and
metre'.[65] The 'rigid poetic forms' of 'mutability laments', Fussell
argues, 'tension and technical irony – they provide a fixed element
as an ironic counterface to the verbal argument of the poem'.[66]
(What, then, is their function in dramatic and narrative poetry?) He
suggests that readers 'whose idea of "poetry" derives in part from

---

62 Woodcock, 'Classical Vandalism', p. 62.
63 Like his hero Keats, Harrison plans his own epitaph, an ambivalent inscription
    which does not include the poet's name. While he does not predict that his
    'name' or fame, or verse will be 'writ in water', he does foresee pilgrims bring-
    ing water or solvent to obliterate other inscriptions from his stone. See *v.*, pp.
    32–3.
64 Northrop Frye, *Anatomy of Criticism* (Princeton, 1957), p. 97.
65 Paul Fussell, *Poetic Forms and the Lyric Subject* (London, 1992), pp. 24–5.
66 Fussell, *Poetic Forms*, p. 8.

the earlier lyric contemporary practice in both America and Britain will seem to have concluded that current poetry is ignorable, except as filler now and then in weekly periodicals',[67] but finds this attitude most prevalent in America. He sees evidence of Rhoda Koenig's 'all-American rejection of the tragic sense', which 'seems one of the things implied by the failure of the lyric subject to take up residence in the New World'. Thus, the 'technique of unrhymed and loosely structured verse can now be seen to be one powerful bulwark against that tragic sense', and '"poetic closure" and the firmness of stanza form have been seen by contemporary American critics such as Marjorie Perloff as offensively British, which means offensively retrograde, emblems of political error'.[68] This would, perhaps, explain the (relative) lack of success of Harrison's personal, non-dramatic poetry in America (though, of course, his opera libretti have enjoyed considerable popularity), but how accurate is it as a description of the contemporary reception of poetry? Few of the 'New' or 'New Generation' British poets use strict metrical and stanza forms, but, for example, neither Heaney nor Derek Mahon has abandoned metre as a signifying system. Perhaps Koenig's rejection of the tragic sense is a rejection of elegy's tendency to move from the particular grief or regret to meditation upon universal mutability, in which case she would probably concur with Woodcock's finding in *Banquet* an 'upstaging of political and even cultural anger' by 'the ponderous themes of Time and Death'.[69]

Entrenched in political error or not, the 'most admired and advanced poets of the twentieth century are chiefly those who have mastered the elusive, meditative, resonant, centripetal word-magic of the emancipated lyrical rhythm'.[70] As, for example, *The New Poetry* demonstrates, lyric is not the only popular form of contemporary poetry, and, as Shakespeare and Simon Armitage demonstrate, dramatic verse, verse dialogue, and verse narration, as well as full-blown verse plays, can still be both canonical and popular. The different forms do, however, appear to perform different functions, and to set up different expectations in their readers or audiences. Frye found that the lyric is 'an internal mimesis of sound and

67 Fussell, *Poetic Forms*, p. 28.
68 Fussell, *Poetic Forms*, p. 27.
69 Woodcock, 'Classical Vandalism', p. 63.
70 Frye, *Anatomy*, p. 273.

imagery, and stands opposite the external mimesis, or outward representation of sound and imagery, which is drama'.[71] While, to an extent, the free (or rather more free) verse narrative poem has replaced lyric as the norm of modern verse, this division, to an extent, still exists.

The different treatments of the subject of war in Harrison's lyric and dramatic poetry may illustrate the imposition of different treatments of subject matter by these different genres. In the plays, speeches which oppose war are largely given to women characters, while in the non-dramatic poetry they are spoken by the poet's narrative 'I'. While the women lament the pity of War, or describe battles which are either fictional or so ancient as to be equally remote from reality, Harrison's 'I' describes historical events within living memory (though of course, the peace camp women in *Chorus* do talk about nuclear missiles and modern US bases). It's interesting that the speech in *Labourers* linking a battle between the ancient Athenians and Persians with the recent fighting in eastern Europe is given to 'Tony Harrison / The Spirit of Phrynichos'.[72] The plays are for communal consumption, while the war poems in which the 'I' appears are short, or in short sections, and are for consumption in private or at public readings by the ostended author / subject. Harrison's 'I' is the ostension of a recognisable, living person, while the female characters are at several removes – taken from myth in *Big H*, from a play within a play in *Chorus,* from the remote past in *The Oresteia*. The rhetoric of female characters in *Chorus* and *Square Rounds* can sometimes seem stilted or mannered. The plays' pantomime humour and stylised effects make them interestingly textured and universally applicable to an audience conversant with the conventions of modern anti-realist drama, but it also makes them less accessible for the putative audience represented by the base guards who watch the women's *Lysistrata*. Similarly, that the women's 'sense of nuclear extinction makes them feel responsible for the past and future' and 'gives the play a sense of movement from modern Britain to ancient Greece [and World War I] and back again'[73] may reinforce the message that 'all wars are one war'. Of course, theatre never is realistic: 'theatrical semiosis invariably [...]

---

71 Frye, *Anatomy*, p. 250.
72 *Labourers*, pp. 143–5. Phrynichos was the ancient Greek playwright who, most unusually, wrote about contemporary events, in *The Capture of Miletus*.
73 *Chorus*, cover copy.

connotes itself. That is, the general connotative marker "theatricality" attaches to the entire performance [...] and to its every element [...] permitting the audience to "bracket off" what is presented to them from normal social praxis',[74] but this very willingness on the part of the audience to suspend referential signification in favour of connotation and ostension can dilute the political import of a play. A problem facing the dramatist of a story which has a specific agenda is illustrated by the Inspector's reaction to the long speech which Lysistrata carefully couches in his own and the guards' terms of reference, painstakingly delineating the economic consequences of war:

> OK then, no more references to anything Greek!
> The money represented by the wire fence
> could be used on education if men had any sense.
> The millions of pounds in your barbed wire barricade
> could go on education here, or for Third World Aid.
> [....]
> Those destructive systems waste enormous wealth
> better spent on Housing, Education, Health.
> [....]
> We protest against those billions that are poured
> into payloads the nation can't afford.
> Cash that's needed to house, feed, clothe, heal, teach.
>
> INSPECTOR
> Just open the bloody gate. Forget the Budget Speech.[75]

Harrison's 'I' uses vernacular. The Common women do use profanity and slang but the 'I' uses more obviously demotic language, with more breaks and elisions and far more cultural and biographical references which tie the poems to an historical moment and an increasingly well-known personality with which the reader can identify. Lysistrata is in danger of becoming Woman, as the young girl at the end of *Chorus* becomes Peace.[76]

Does Harrison's use of mythology, via Classical Greek drama or directly, entail the displacement of the determinants of war and other suffering by convenient mystifications? Eagleton describes the 'dramatic re-entry into European culture' of mythological thought in

---

74 Keir Elam, *The Semiosis of Theatre and Drama* (London, 1987), p. 12.
75 *Chorus*, p. 47.
76 *Chorus*, stage direction, p. 49.

the late nineteenth and early twentieth centuries coinciding with the point of capitalism's 'gradual mutation into "higher" corporate forms' and with 'a radical shift in the whole category of the subject – a rethinking which involves Ferdinand de Saussure as much as Wyndham Lewis, Freud and Martin Heidegger as well as D. H. Lawrence and Virginia Woolf'.[77] He suggests that when 'a laissez-faire economy' moves into 'more systematic modes' there is 'something peculiarly apposite about the rebirth of myth – itself, as Lévi-Strauss has taught us, a highly organized "rational" system – as an imaginative means of deciphering this new social experience'. For Eagleton:

> it is really no longer possible to pretend, given the transition from market to monopoly capitalism, that the old vigorously individualist ego, the self-determining subject of classical liberal thought, is any longer an adequate model for the subject's new experience of itself under these altered social conditions. The modern subject, much like the mythological one, is less the sharply individuated source of its own actions than an obedient function of some deeper controlling structure, which now appears more and more to do its thinking and acting for it. [...Thus] this period witnesses a turning away [...] from the traditional philosophy of the subject of Kant, Hegel and the younger Marx, troubledly conscious as it is of the individual as constituted to its roots by forces and processes utterly opaque to everyday consciousness.[78]

The effect of these implacable powers, whether they are named 'Language or Being, Capital or the Unconscious, Tradition or the *élan vital*, Archetypes or the Destiny of the West', is to 'open up a well-nigh unspannable gulf between the waking life of the old befeathered ego and the true determinants of its identity, which are always covert and inscrutable'. In examining his own personality as at least in part a product of determinants neither covert nor inscrutable (the scholarship system, Classical education), Harrison would seem to resist this mystification of the subject, but what about his depiction of the world which that subject inhabits? Eagleton continues to argue that, given that the subject is accordingly 'fractured and dismantled, the objective world it confronts is now quite impossible to grasp as the product of the subject's own activity'. Above and beyond the individual is 'a self-regulative system which

---

77 Eagleton, *Ideology of the Aesthetic*, p. 316.
78 Eagleton, *Ideology of the Aesthetic*, pp. 316–17.

appears on the one hand thoroughly rationalized, eminently logical in its minutest operations, yet on the other hand blankly indifferent of the rational projects of human subjects'. Thus the world appears as an 'autonomous, self-determining artefact' which 'takes on all the appearances of a second nature, erasing its own source in human practice so as to seem as self-evidently given and immobilized as those rocks, trees and mountains which are the stuff of mythology'. No one suggests that writers 'believe in' or try to convince their readers of the existence of divinities, nature-spirits or the other raw material of mythology, but the prevalence of mythologising beyond the 'modernist' and into the 'post-modern' must be significant. Harrison responds to Macneile Dixon's observation that the muses were unique because 'in honour of these, unlike other divinities, no blood was spilt', by saying that 'the Muses have to inspire work in a world where the many other "divinities", the personifications and the ideologies, continually have the blood of victims spilled and holocausts created'.[79] He also writes of the power of mythological allegory to 'make the real and imagined interdependent as we of this fifth age bear in our memory all responsibility now for the struggles and aspirations of the past, of all ages, not only fifth-century Athens'.[80] Does this support the claim that the 'allegorical signifier shares in a sense in the frozen world of myth, whose compulsive repetitions foreshadow Benjamin's [...] image of an historicism for which all time is homogeneous'?[81] A passage from *Chorus* perhaps does:

> So Greece is Greenham, Greenham Greece,
> [....]
> Not just all places, all human ages too
> are dependent on the likes of us and you.[82]

The National Theatre text of *Trackers*, by transforming the satyrs/hooligans of the Delphi text into satyrs/hooligans/homeless, and setting up parallels between the satyrs discarded by Apollo and robbed of the lyre, high culture and the respect accorded 'real' human beings, and the inhabitants of the South Bank's cardboard city, uncovers no more than allegory beneath allegory, and is no

---

79 'Facing Up', *Bloodaxe 1*, p. 435.
80 'Facing Up', *Bloodaxe 1*, p. 449.
81 Eagleton, *Ideology of the Aesthetic*, p. 327.
82 *Chorus*, p. 49.

more radical than the Apollo v. Silenus, lyre v. ghetto-blasters, Kyllene (high Victorian poetic diction, Apollonian art) v. the satyrs (vernacular speech, profanity, football fans) oppositions. Homelessness, the play could lead us to infer, is attributable to a contemporary Apollo, a convenient mystification which enables Harrison to avoid considering the deeper economic determinants of homelessness. There is, however, no reason to assume that if the play had been as tied to historical specifics as *v.* it would have escaped the criticism levelled at that play, for example: 'powerful as *v.* is, it is very much of its moment [...] those ungainly passages to which I have alluded are what make it a poem of the 1980s in a manner which may in the end prove limiting'.[83]

Rather than categorising Harrison's allegories and associations as a hangover from modernist technique, and a form mass-produced by the system of monopoly capitalism, it might be worthwhile to look in more detail at the model for his use of myth, Classical Greek drama, whose own manipulation of gods, heroes, and their interaction is not as simple as, perhaps, it might seem. The figures of the Olympic gods do personify abstractions and universals, an 'integral and immutable part of human nature, of the natural world, or of the physical cosmos' and 'as such they had an inherent rightness, and an unquestionable beauty'.[84] The gods could be used to laud approved or condemn outlawed behaviour, but their presence did not preclude the use of historical reference in the plays, nor did they necessarily function as convenient mystifications, masking the social and economic determinants of the wars between the city states and surrounding nations by reference to divine intervention and the inexplicable, or to universals of the human condition.

The 'gods' of psychological and behavioural types are neither invincible nor above criticism.[85] Dionysus, for example, is neither wholly admirable nor infallible, but as complex a character as the humans in *The Bacchae*, which itself is not a condemnation of either Dionysus or his religion.

> The 'worship' which Greek gods required was not adoration, nor gratitude, nor even unreserved approval; and was thus quite unlike what

---

83 Lucas, 'Speaking for England?', p. 361.
84 Philip Vellacott, trans., Euripides: *The Bacchae and Other Plays* (London, 1973) (hereafter *Bacchae*), introduction, p. 31.
85 See, for example, Ion's criticism and reproach of Apollo: in, Euripides, Ion, Vellacott, *Bacchae*, pp. 85–6.

'worship' means in a Christian context. It was simply a recognition that they existed [....] *The Bacchae* is – among other things – a demonstration that the consequences of refusing 'worship' in this sense to Dionysus are disastrous, since such refusal is a denial of undeniable fact.[86]

We should not, of course, assume that Classical Greek audiences were always or completely orthodox. Euripides's time, Vellacott argued, saw 'the progressive loss of faith in any agency external to man himself which man might look to, either for aid in confronting the dangers of life, or for guidance in solving moral problems'. We are reminded that 'the modern world has derived its traditional code of behaviour even more specifically from divine injunction than did ancient Greece; and today's irrational search for credible sources of guidance suggests parallels with that addiction to imported religions which made *The Bacchae* a topical piece'.[87] Euripides shows an awareness of the desire for extra-human agency:

> The gods,
> I know, are treacherous allies; yet, when misery
> Drives to despair, it seems in some way suitable
> To call on gods[88]

His plays also depict the extrapolation from this which blames the gods for perfectly explicable human actions. Hecabe's ironic speech in *The Women of Troy* uses a laughable example to depict the ridiculousness of the extremity of this 'don't-blame-me-it's-fate-and-the-gods'-will' attitude, and thus casts a sceptical eye upon the process of myth-making:

> I don't believe
> Gods to be capable of such folly, as that Hera
> Should bargain away Argos to barbarians,
> Or virgin Pallas see her Athens subjected
> To Troy. Why should they indulge in such frivolity
> As travelling to Mount Ida for a beauty-match?
> What reason could the goddess Hera have for being
> So anxious about beauty? Did she want to get
> A husband of higher rank than Zeus? Or was Athene,
> Who begged her father for perpetual maidenhood,
> Disdaining love – now husband-hunting among the gods?[89]

---

86 Vellacott, *Bacchae*, introduction, pp. 30–1.
87 Vellacott, *Bacchae*, introduction, p. 10.
88 Euripides, *Women of Troy*, in Vellacott, *Bacchae*, p. 106.
89 Euripides, *Women of Troy*, in Vellacott, *Bacchae*, pp. 121–2.

153

In other words: by all means talk of personifications; use the conventional symbols; but don't blind yourself to your own and others' motives by blaming them; don't start *believing* in them.

> To cloak your own guilt, you dress up the gods as fools;
> But only fools would listen to you. And Aphrodite,
> You say – what could be more absurd? – went with my son
> To Menelaus' palace! Could she not have brought
> You, and your town of Amyclae, from Peloponnese
> To Ilion, without stirring from her seat in heaven?
>   No; Paris was an extremely handsome man – one look,
> And your appetite became your Aphrodite

Though balance is vital in that neither rationality nor impulse, obedience to convention nor anarchy, shall prevail, and that balance is kept by law, it was realised that laws were not immutable – right and wrong could shift. Thus Hecabe says:

> It is a good man's duty to uphold the right,
> And always, everywhere, to punish wickedness.

The chorus remark:

> Strange how in human life opposites coincide;
> How love and hate change with the laws men recognize,
> Which can turn bitter foes to friends, old friends to foes.[90]

As Taplin reminds us, 'Most cultures have their expressions of fatalism; they are one of our chief sources of solace in the face of the pointless waste of ill fortune: "che sera, sera", "God's will be done"', and, 'like most cultures, for a pattern or purpose behind catastrophe they [the ancient Greeks] looked to superhuman forces, personal or impersonal'. This tendency, however, 'does not, within the compass of a drama, preclude the free will of the characters or their responsibility', most of the time, 'they are presented as free agents working out their own destinies'.[91]

More significant than the extent to which dramatic characters are shown as puppets of the gods, in this context, is the extent to which what happens to them is shown as the consequence of 'the darkness in the human heart', 'man's inhumanity to man', and other

---

90 Euripides, *Hecabe*, trans. Philip Vellacott, in *Euripides: Medea/Hecabe/Electra/Heracles* (London, 1963) (hereafter *Medea et al.*), p. 88.
91 Taplin, *Greek Tragedy in Action*, p. 165.

mystificatory references to human nature. Euripides, presenting the Trojan Wars as historical fact, shows their origins as economic and political; the desire for wealth and land, not as the result of the gods' whims or universal evil. Born just before the battles of Salamis (480 BC) and Plataea (479 BC), living through the period in which security enabled Athens to nurture artistic and intellectual development, and surviving into the Peloponnesian War (from 431 BC), Euripides was in a good position to observe war's determinants and consequences. While *The Women of Troy*[92] and *Helen* do not make specific reference to the acts which led to war between Athens and Sparta, Vellacott attributes to Euripides an intent to make *The Women of Troy* a timely reminder to the Athenians of their ill-advised action in sacking the island of Melos (an old ally of Sparta which had sued for neutral status), and thus support the Peace Party in their opposition to the forthcoming Greek expedition to Sicily, whose alliance would prolong the war.[93] *Helen* dramatises the futility of blaming war upon inexplicable phenomena, irrational passions or supernatural phantoms, and turns the device to its own purpose, whilst reminding us that economic and other determinants of war are not always available to our understanding, either at the time or with hindsight. The poet's

> condemnation of the futile war which Athens repeatedly refused to end is most powerfully conveyed by his use of the contrived tale, invented by Stesichorus a few generations earlier, that Paris went off to Troy with a phantom Helen, while Helen herself spent seventeen years in Egypt. By accepting this tale as true, he shows the greatest war in ancient history as a disastrous error from beginning to end, all its crimes and agonies a purposeless performance, its heroes puppets, its achievements nothing. It was nineteen years since Athens first went to war with Sparta; if her motives were clear then, and her purposes intelligible, in 412 only a phantom was left, and reason and motive had yielded to helpless paranoia[94]

While the working through of ancient curses and blood-grudges in plays such as the *Oresteia* could be taken as confirming Eagleton's

---

92 The references above to '*The Trojan Women*' follow Tony Harrison's. Here, '*The Women of Troy*' refers to Philip Vellacott's usage in his translation of the play.
93 Vellacott, *Bacchae*, introduction, p. 17.
94 Vellacott, *Bacchae*, introduction, p. 28.

suggestion that myth describes every continent piece of experience as the manipulated product of underlying sub-structures, they could also be calls for the breaking of such apparent cycles: demonstrations of the consequences of our becoming stuck in a certain mind-set or code of behaviour. The human is not shown to be entirely subordinate to divine will in Greek drama, nor the course of human life predestined.

Woodcock finds a failure of politicisation which he attributes to Harrison's use of Classical dramatic models.

> The timeless verities of existence elegantly elaborated in his [Harrison's] beloved classics can over-ride the historical actualities of society in a writer who feels himself an individual who can't belong, however deep his compassion and understanding. Harrison's snarling invectives against death are genuine. His snarling invectives against an unjust and unequal society have a more problematic status.[95]

If we accept that existence is not a drama of the clash of human will and divine power and whim, but of social structures, then texts which use myth allegorically could be said to be static and dealing in mystification rather than engaging with history dialectically. The structures of myth are not binding, however, nor their cycles inescapable. No characters in Harrison's poetry blame their mistakes or malevolence on *ate* (temporary insanity or irrationality sent by the gods). Harrison does not usually borrow anonymous, atavistic myths of the collective imagination which present themselves as timeless universals concerning humanity – mystifications – but rather tends to appropriate later workings of myth by Classical dramatists, seeing *The Trojan Women* or *Lysistrata* as the products of historical individuals, as well as embodiments of a particular kind of 'civilised' and enlightened outlook which can serve as lesson and example to a time when 'the book-burners are abroad again'.[96] His history is contained in memory, and thus in language, spoken or written.

> Remember, if you can, that with man goes the mind
> that might have made sense of the Hist'ry of Mankind.
> It's a simple thing to grasp: when we're all dead
> there'll be no further pages to be read [...]
> If we're destroyed then we
> take with us Athens 411 BC.

---

95 Woodcock, 'Classical Vandalism', p. 64.
96 'Facing Up', *Bloodaxe 1*, p. 449.

The world till now up to the last minute
and every creature who was ever in it
go when we go, everything men did or thought
never to be remembered, absolutely nought.
No war memorials with the names of dead on
because memory won't survive your Armageddon.
so Lysistrata! (   )[97] – it's one name.
Since 1945 past and present are the same.

In its mixture of historical specifics (both modern and ancient) and mythology, *Chorus* could be seen as avoiding the frozen world of compulsive repetition. The play could be read as a fusion of the two uses of mythological archetypes described by MacNeice, who found that the Greek tragedians 'had taken modern themes and disguised them in mythology', but that with 'Ibsen it is almost the other way round: he takes the archetypes and disguises them in Here and Now'.[98] Nor is the mythology which Harrison appropriates for his non-dramatic poetry homogenising. The snake in *Fire-Gap*, for example, may represent the closed circle of eternity, but, unlike Yeats, Harrison does not extrapolate from circles to cycles, to recurring patterns of life, to mystical supra-human cycles of the universe.

Harrison pays tribute to the scholarship and insights of Oliver Taplin, and, while there is no reason to suppose that their readings of Greek drama are identical, I would suggest that Taplin's assertions about tragedy are useful in a reading of Harrison's work.[99] Taplin claims that 'it *is* the action which takes place *on* stage which is important, and is part of what the play is about: the action off-stage is only of interest from a simple-minded preconception of what constitutes action; it only counts the huge violent events of narrative history – battles, riots, miracles'.[100] Thus, 'the stuff of tragedy is the individual response to such events; not the blood, but the tears', and it is 'the life-sized actions of this personal dimension which are the dramatist's concerns, and which he puts on stage'. Not only famine and revolution would occur off-stage, then, but also their underlying determinants. This drama, like lyric, is concerned

---

97 In Chorus, p. 50, an asterisk indicates a footnote: 'This parenthesis should be the name of the actress playing the role of Lysistrata'. In 'Facing Up', *Bloodaxe 1*, p. 450, Harrison, quoting from an almost identical draft of the play, writes that he hoped to see Glenda Jackson in the role.
98 MacNeice, *Poetry of W. B. Yeats*, p. 36.
99 See 'Facing Up', *Bloodaxe 1*, pp. 429, 432, 433, and 441.
100 Taplin, *Greek Tragedy in Action*, p. 161.

more with reaction than (grand) action.

Harrison insists that his work is not an exercise in antiquarianism but quite the reverse, part of his quest for 'a public poetry'.[101] Thus, 'my obsessive concern with Greek drama isn't about antique reproduction, but part of a search for a new theatricality'. This new theatricality does not depend upon novel devices. Neither the disruption of temporality nor the introduction of characters from earlier periods into a modern context are new ideas.[102] He qualifies the statement. The concern with Greek drama is 'also a way of expressing dissatisfaction with the current theatre where I want to work as a *poet*'. This does not mean 'going "back to civilisation", a going "back to the Greeks", a reactionary cry I sometimes hear at the Delphi drama meetings, but "forward to the Greeks", or "forward *with* the Greeks"'.[103] In combining (for example) Greek myth, English ideas about Indian religions, and Victorian mores (in *Phaedra*) Harrison creates an intertextuality which evades Bakhtin's typology of the myth as at the opposite end of 'the intertextual continuum' to the novel, because myth 'implies a transparency of language, a coincidence of words and things' while 'the novel starts out with plurality of languages, discourses and voices and the inevitable awareness of language'.[104] Myth is an 'absolute fusion of discourse and concrete ideological meaning is [...] one of the basic constitutive features of myth, determining, on the one hand, the development of mythological representations, and on the other determining the specific apprehension of linguistic forms, significations, and stylistic combinations'.[105]

What does the evolution of a work such as *Phaedra*, from archaic Greek myth to collected and transcribed myth, to Euripides's *Hippolytus*, to Seneca's play, to Racine's adaptation of that play, to Harrison's version, tell us about this process? It could be seen as a series of attempts to translate the past into the present, but also as attempts to translate the present into the past, to rewrite the culture of 'now' on the model of the culture of 'then'. That Harrison's is not an entirely reactionary art is, however, indicated by the translation of his *Misanthrope* into French. Elements other than those to be

---

101 *Bloodaxe 1*, preface, p. 9.
102 See, for example, Caryl Churchill, *Top Girls* (London, 1982).
103 'Facing Up', *Bloodaxe 1*, pp. 440–1.
104 Todorov, *Bakhtin: The Dialogical Principle*, p. 66.
105 Bakhtin, 'Discourse in the Novel', Holquist, *Dialogic Imagination*, p. 180.

found in Molière's *Misanthrope* must be present in Harrison's, or their existence in French together would be redundant. In his use of the myth of Minos and Pasiphaë in *Phaedra*, Harrison is not merely invoking a convenient mystification, because the cause of the tragedy is grounded in the historical moment, in British cultural and gender imperialism. A review of Harrison's *Misanthrope* found it 'encrusted with gems of modern reference, from foundation cream to Charles de Gaulle, that shine and glitter'. These were 'flashes of contemporary life which illuminate, and seem perfectly consonant with the philosophy of an alien society and a vanished time'.[106] Another critic suggested that 'had he lived in the eighteenth century, Tony Harrison could have made a good living as a dramatist and a satirist'.[107] Similarly, *Phaedra* is offered as an emblematic work with the resonance and universality of Greek myth, in a modern register:

> T.H. The British in India thought of themselves as representatives of reason against disorder, in the way that Theseus was originally conceived in classical mythology. The residences the British built in the middle of the jungle seem to have been an emblem for classical culture [. . . .] 'La Fille de Minos et de Pasiphaé' is a terrific line, but you have to know who Minos and Pasiphaë were [. . . .] There had to be an equivalent with real ramifications which we still feel today [. . . .]
> J.H. In one way you translated the myth into politics.[108]

Harrison allies himself with Dryden's position on translation and adaptation: '"I hope the additions will seem not stuck into Molière, but growing out of him"', adding: 'no more intrusive, that is, than the sackbut, psaltery, and dulcimer the Jacobean translators of the Bible introduced into the court of Nebuchadnezzar, or the Perigord pies and Tokay that the anonymous translator of 1819 introduced into his version of *Le Misanthrope*'.[109] This is not just a matter of giving anachronisms the appearance of homogeneity, but of making an entirely distinct work which is neither layered strata of old and new, nor a bedrock of old with new elements grafted on. The comments on Dryden are particularly interesting in the light of Woodcock's comments (discussed above) on the 'timeless' quality of

---

106 Harold Hobson, *Sunday Times* (25 February 1973), reprinted in *Bloodaxe 1*, p. 155.
107 Peter Levi, 'Tony Harrison's Dramatic Verse', *Bloodaxe 1*, p. 161
108 'Interview', *Bloodaxe 1*, p. 240.
109 'Jane Eyre's Sister', *Bloodaxe 1*, p. 139.

Harrison's 'beloved classics', as Harrison himself traces the development of 'political specialisation' of translations of Virgil's *Aeneid* from that of Gavin Douglas (1513) to Dryden's, noting that the 'hidden general truths and sentences become specific moral and political lessons for seventeenth-century England', a 'sharpening of focus' which 'can be quite clearly demonstrated in two separate translations of the *Aeneid* produced by the indefatigable John Ogilby' (1649 and 1654).[110]

According to Harrison, translation plays a special part in the life of an 'embattled culture in which the normal aspirations of a writer's work are blocked by censorship'.[111] To an oppressed culture

> the works of the past are continually read as if they were written yesterday. They have to skirt that very narrow line between censorship and subversion, and I found it a lesson for my own work as a translator. Their [the Czech people's] translations have a very strong regard for the past, for the original author, but they also bristle with a sense of the present.[112]

He seems to be suggesting that translation and adaptation can provide allegories and satire which will slip through the net of official scrutiny, canonic policing, moral watchdogs, or other censors, whilst affording a rich sub-text to the acute audience. Though contemporary literature in England may be subject to less stringent censorship than that of Czechoslovakia during the time Harrison was there, it could be regarded as 'embattled', and brutality and murder are acceptable in performances of 'classics' such as *King Lear*, but cause for complaint in the more recent *The Romans in Britain*.[113] To what extent, however, does contemporary English drama need to camouflage its political points, and do Harrison's translation/adaptations avoid censorship otherwise exercised over his original dramatic work?

Harrison describes himself as keeping the social function of Greek drama in mind in his adaptation. The introduction to *Trackers* underlines the poet's affinity with the circular dancing-space of Greek drama, and his association of the *orchestra* with the scorched circle left on a Leeds street the morning after the VJ night celebrations: 'I learned to relate our celebratory fire, with the white-hot coals from domestic

---

110 T. W. Harrison, 'Dryden's Aeneid', in Bruce King, ed., *Dryden's Mind and Art*, p. 143.
111 'Interview', p. 236.
112 'Interview', p. 237.
113 Howard Brenton, *The Romans in Britain* (London, 1981).

sofas, to that terrible form of fire that brought about the "VJ" when unleashed on Hiroshima and Nagasaki in August 1945.'[114] The space of the circle contained celebration and terror; celebrant and sufferer. Things 'just as "dark"' as bombings 'occurred in this *orchestra* of Dionysus but it was lit by the sun and was surrounded by a community as bonded in their watching as we had been by our celebratory blaze'. The theatre itself contributed to this bonding:

> Greek drama [...] was staged in the common light of day. A shared space and a shared light [...] not only did the audience *see* the actors and chorus but the actors and chorus *saw* the audience [....] that 'obvious reciprocity', that Harbage found between actors and audience in Shakespeare's theatre, was created.[115]

Printed poetry, of course, makes possible no such reciprocal gaze, though lyric offers the illusion of one-to-one communing. Modern drama, the 'divided art' of the darkened auditorium, is 'perpetuating divided audiences, divided societies'. Harrison notes that a contemporary survey had shown 'that modern theatre audiences are composed of élite and privileged *sectors* of our society'.[116] He cannot recreate the conditions which enabled the Athenian theatre to be an amalgam of society, nor make his kind of poetry into radical expositions of the socio-economic determinants of the divisions within ours.

If history is over-ridden by poetry in certain of Harrison's lines, others acknowledge poetry's ineffectiveness in the face of – and its inability to contain (the wholeness of the Greek dramatic imagination notwithstanding) – some of the horrors of history. In the middle of one of the longer 'American' poems, which have been hailed as indicating a new 'harmony' or 'relaxing' in Harrison's work,[117] come the lines:

> a century of history on this earth
> between John Keats's death and my own birth –
> years like an open crater, gory, grim,
> with bloody bubbles leering at the rim;
> a thing no bigger than an urn explodes
> and ravishes all silence, and all odes[118]

---

114 *Trackers*, introduction, p. vii.
115 *Trackers*, introduction, p. viii.
116 *Trackers*, introduction, p. xiii
117 See, for example, 'Introduction', p. 22.
118 *Kumquat*, p. 182.

This brings to mind MacNeice's remark: 'As soon as I heard on the wireless of the outbreak of war, Galway became unreal. And Yeats and his poetry became unreal also.'[119] In a sense, Harrison depicts the very act of writing poetry, of articulation, as political. Although he refers to his poetry as political, he does not claim that it offers a radical perspective on the underlying determinants of social injustice, nor that it can change anything. Describing his *Misanthrope*, he writes that 'it involves a person who is splenetic in his outbursts against society and yet cannot see his way towards changing it, and that seemed to me a very contemporary dilemma'.[120]

---

119 MacNeice, *Poetry of W. B. Yeats,* p. 2.
120 'Interview', p. 237.

CHAPTER 6

αι αι; aye-aye; I, I: Harrison's protagonists

All I'm sure of is I'm not your sort!
Medea: A Sex-War Opera

The collection of essays published to celebrate Harrison's sixtieth birthday was called *Loiner* in part because a Loiner is a native of Leeds, as Harrison is, and in part to bring to mind the wonderful poems in Harrison's 1970 collection *The Loiners*, which are often overlooked in favour of the 'School of Eloquence' sequence and the 'American' poems. The title also, however, marked one of the book's subjects, Harrison's protagonists (including the character 'Tony Harrison') – his Loiners. As well as 'loins', the word suggests 'loner', significantly leaving a separate 'I'.

> Harrison's Loiners resemble the *metoikoi* of Greek city-states (residents without the rights of natives); characters divided from one another, and within [....] Their sense of self is strong, however divided, but they are dispossessed from the very things which, for most people, constitute the sense of self: origin; family; language; culture; rights. Whether citizens of Leeds, expats, nameless travellers, or the narrative 'I', they are internal aliens within insecure communities clotted together by conformity against the threat of outside; often with strong affiliations, but at home nowhere. A Loiner may be dispossessed by politics, economics, or other intrinsic forces, but the resultant change which alienates him from his roots is internal.[1]

Loiners are not heroes. They are not idealised or laden with sentimentality, though there is compassion as well as humour. Articulate Loiners speak for themselves, often in monologues veering between self-loathing, bitterness, and comic relish for their misdeeds. The PWD (Public Works Division) man is an articulate Loiner owing much to music-hall turns and, perhaps, to the comic devils and Herods of Mumming and Mystery plays, and vaunting

---

1   TH: *Loiner*, introduction, p. 19.

163

villains in the style of Shakespeare's Richard III. He boasts and
gloats of his exploitation of impoverished black women, and is
nauseatingly self-congratulatory about paying them in silver rather
than coppers, but he has his own kind of morality, condemning the
police Inspector who tried to force a woman, and despising both
British hypocrisy and the life-in-death of retirement in England. The
long (almost in poulter's measure) lines in iambic couplets give the
zestful raconteur a jauntiness which is as engaging as his homely
similes for the exotically beautiful Fulani women 'like polished
Whitby jet' and 'like Rowntrees coffee creams'.[2] Also engaging are
his shifts of tone from gleefully boastful to frankly practical.

> I'll bet you're bloody jealous, you codgers in UK,
> Waiting for your hearses while I'm having it away
> With girls like black Bathshebas who sell their milky curds
> At kerbside markets out of done-up-fancy gourds [....]
> No Boy Scout's fleapit dreams
> Of bedding Brigitte Bardot could ever better these.
> One shy kiss from this lot has me shaking at the knees.
> It's not that they're casual, they're just glad of the lifts
> I give them between markets and in gratitude give gifts
> Like sips of fresh cow-juice off a calabash spoon.
> But I'm subject to diarrhoea, so I'd just as soon [....]

When he contemplates his death, and remembered Leeds ceases to
evoke 'sporting smoky Yorkshire'[3] and a dreaded retirement, or 'a
sense of dismal pride' in the products of its manufactures outlasting
the 'rains and harmattan' of Africa,[4] he achieves a kind of pathos:

> As kids when we came croppers, there were always some old
>   dears
> Who'd come and pick us up and wipe off blood and tears,
> And who'd always use the same daft words as they tried to
>   console,
> Pointing to cobble, path or flagstone: *Look at the hole*
> *You've made falling.* I want a voice with that soft tone,
> Disembodied Yorkshire like my mother's on the phone,
> As the cook puts down some flowers and the smallboy scrapes the
>   spade,
> To speak as my epitaph: *Look at the hole he's made.*[5]

2 'The Songs of the PWD Man I', *SP*, p. 41.
3 'The Songs of the PWD Man I', *SP*, p. 43.
4 'The Death of the PWD Man I', *SP*, p. 45.
5 'The Songs of the PWD Man II', *SP*, p. 44.

Inarticulate Loiners are simply portrayed in a context which says it all. Poems such as 'Ginger's Friday', 'The Pocket Wars of Peanuts Joe', and 'Allotments'[6] combine the grotesque or sordid with the all-too familiar and mundane, producing repugnance and sympathy by turns. The effect of 'Ginger's Friday' is in the detail. It's a battery of impressions; powerfully evocative smells, sounds, sights, or textures which trigger associations familiar enough to seem like memories. The scent of strawberries, rather than incense, candles, and flowers, wafting up the aisle of a church is powerful because it's unexpected. The sounds coming from behind the grille of a confessional are powerful because their source is concealed. The sight of the conjugal coupling is powerful because forbidden. The shadows and sounds of the darkening park are powerful because mysterious, and invested with imagined terrors. The shouted *Aves* and *Paternosters* are powerful because they evoke childhood fear and its futile talismans. When Ginger reaches home, and 'Daley's and his father's broad black belts' crack in the kitchen, whether we have been, or could sympathise with, a Catholic boy, a *voyeur*, a scared child, or none of the above, most of us, I think, cringe away and glue our backsides to the chair.

Whilst not a Loiner, Commodus is the apotheosis of the Harrison baddie, and, like many of the others, is in part the creation of the high culture whose exponents look away from the violence he wreaks. He recollects sitting in the arena as a child, next to his father who, dictating his Stoic *Meditations*, averted his gaze from the bloodshed which Commodus relished.

> I was on his right. He spoke above my head,
> so I had to listen to every word he said,
> except when at those moments the crowd's roars
> drowned out the stoic apothegms and saws.
> Since then, no matter how many beasts I've slain,
> those boring banalities bombard my brain.[7]

Commodus and Marcus Aurelius, father and son, tyrant and philosopher, Caesar and Caesar, are both, in their different ways, culpable; opposites and twins. Several of Harrison's protagonists have a dark twin.[8] This is a 'real' opposite in *Bow Down*, whose twin sisters are

---

6 *SP*, pp. 15, 16–17, 18–19.
7 *Kaisers*, p. 101.
8 Called 'my bright twin' in 'The Pomegranates of Patmos', *Gorgon*, p. 28.

literally fair and dark, and in *Yan Tan Tethera*, which has two sets of twin sons. In *Aikin Mata*, *Medea* and *Chorus*, the two genders become one another's twin, opposed in both covert and outright conflict. In *Square Rounds*, the leading female part, Clara, is an archetypal loving wife or mam who wishes to live in harmony with man and nature, while her husband, another Harrison music-hall baddie, harnesses the power of nature through science for ends which are anything but harmonious or peaceable.

FRITZ HABER

With my elegant invention I put to sleep
the unsuspecting enemy entrenched at Ypres.
As my silky releases hissed and swirled
for the first time ever in the history of the world
I have to confess that I felt rather proud
of the simple device of my suffocating cloud.
The Prospero of poisons, the Faustus of the front
bringing mental magic to modern armament.[9]

Elsewhere, the opposite is an *alter ego*, a psychic projection, a return of the repressed, or an unnameable, amorphous, 'monster from the deep', as in *Phaedra*:

The lower self comes creeping up from its lair
out of the dismal swamps of God-knows-where.[10]

The Big H has teachers/Herods; *Trackers* has Apollo/Silenus (and Apollo/Grenfell, Silenus/Hunt); *Oresteia* has the Olympic gods/ Eumenides; *v.* has poet/skinhead. These pairings are not between 'self' and 'other'; they are not symmetrically divided and diametrically opposed. Nor are they just complex personalities; they are truly divided, in that the parts barely communicate with one another, and offer no possibility of integration. Forced to acknowledge his identity with the dark avatar, when the skinhead 'aerosolled his name. And it was mine', the poet narrator is so shocked that his interior dialogue momentarily stops, and in the absence of his voice we hear 'The boy footballers bawl *Here Comes the Bride*' before his thoughts cohere again, and he says,

---

9 *Square Rounds*, pp. 48–9.
10 *Phaedra*, p. 35. Huk raises this point in 'Tony Harrison's Verse Drama', in Acheson, *British and Irish Drama*, p. 212.

αι αι; aye-aye; I, I

One half of me's alive but one half died
when the skin half sprayed my name among the dead.[11]

There is a dialogue between the two in *v.*, indeed much of the poem is concerned with the efforts of one half to bring about unity:

Half versus half, the enemies within
the heart that can't be whole till they unite.

Neither fusion nor even mutual understanding is achieved, however, and the two aspects go their own ways, with a brief off-stage cry[12] reminding us that not even '30 years of bleak Leeds weather' will 'erode the UNITED binding [them] together'. Perhaps Thomas Theophilus is an typical Harrison persona[13] not because he is a half-caste, but because, as his first name suggests, he has a twin, the monster which rises from the Governor's Residency – a communal sink of iniquity – an embodiment of the repressed desires of the Governor, his wife, and the rest of their court. Perhaps, however, Thomas is more important in 'as much as he embodies the two conflicting selves of his father'.[14] The Governor is a better model for the Harrison persona because he is a Persephone figure, spending half of the year in the 'light' of civilisation, and half in the 'darkness' of the primitive. Or so he represents it, glossing over his part in burglary, rape, and murder.[15] As Burleigh makes clear, however, though the Governor expresses fear and contempt for *négritude*, the darkness is within His Excellency; in his dealings with people 'who live without *our* discipline',[16] it is he who brings the savagery and perversity.

One knows his nature [....]
his 'scholar's' passion for the primitive [....]
let's say 'researching' some strange marriage rite!
Leading some new unfortunate astray![17]

---

11 *v.*, p. 23.
12 'Wanker!', *v.*, p. 31.
13 Harrison identifies himself with the dualistic hermaphrodite African cult deity Shango, who is associated with St Barbara and St John. See 'Shango the Shaky Fairy', *London Magazine*, new series, 10, no. 1 (April 1970), reprinted in *Bloodaxe 1*, pp. 88–103.
14 *Phaedra*, preface, p. xxiii.
15 *Phaedra*, p. 33.
16 *Phaedra*, p. 39.
17 *Phaedra*, pp. 1–2.

He, practising Victorian sexual (and other) double standards, survives to end the play. His wife (as the child of Minos, an emblem of strict judgement, and Pasiphaë, an emblem of sexual transgression, as much a half-breed as her step-son) is torn apart by her internal division, and kills herself.

If the respective fates of the Governor and his wife remind us that in Harrison's poetry halves are rarely in perfect equilibrium, he reminds us that binary distinctions such as barbarian and civilised (wo)man are constructs. 'Assailed as the British felt on all side by an irrational India with its dark sensual gods and "primitive" customs, they created in their imagination defensive roles for themselves as the inheritors of rational civilisation.'[18] Harrison declares himself to be an inheritor of rational civilisation by constructing the literary equivalent of 'residencies and public buildings in classical style', but, by voicing sensuality and 'darkness' – death, despair – within those edifices, he equally claims the identity of the barbarian. This half-caste or twin is aware of the fruitlessness of either the civilised or the barbarian caste's 'attempting to realize in external marble what they felt unable to realize internally in their far from securely stable minds'.

Although Harrison insists '[uz] [uz] [uz]',[19] and expresses a longing to restore the 'continuous' of 'our Tony'[20] and the family, geographical, or social group, it is 'my name' and '[my] own voice' which are loudest; not 'we', but 'I'. The starting point of many of the 'School of Eloquence' poems is, crucially, the loss of membership of a group ('Me Tarzan', 'Confessional Poetry') or a 'sense of place', or a pairing ('Isolation', 'Cremation'). 'Them & [uz]' may be a defiant declaration of affiliation to the group whose standard is Leeds dialect, but the poem is told as an old story. Leeds Grammar School, Shakespeare classes, persecution, are another country, and the scholarship boy is dead. Harrison refused to join [ʌs], but dropping 'T. W.' did not restore 'our Tony' to assimilation with [uz]. 'I'm *Tony* Harrison no longer you!' refutes class-migrant T. W., but the emphasis could also be 'I'm *Tony Harrison* no longer [one of] you!' Personal as well as social dispossession produces the dialectic of certain poems, and their creative momentum:

---

18 *Phaedra*, preface, p. xxiii.
19 'Them & [uz] II', *SP*, p. 123.
20 'Bye-Byes', *SP*, p. 163.

αι αι; aye-aye; I, I

> Their aggro towards me, my need of them's
> what keeps my would-be mobile tongue still tied –
>
> aggression, struggle, loss, blank printer's ems
> by which all   eloquence   gets justified.[21]

Just as the oppositions which Harrison articulates are significant, so are those which he does not. For example, we are shown the antagonism between father and son, a working-class older and an aspiring younger generation; Harry Harrison v Tony Harrison; Florrie Harrison v Tony Harrison; Tony Harrison v the ignorance, puritanism, intolerance, extremism, and cowed fear of authority he finds in working-class Leeds; but not the v of divorce, except, fleetingly, in *v.*:

> These Vs are all the versuses of life
> From LEEDS v. DERBY, Black/White
> and (as I've known to my cost) man v. wife[22]

Nor do we 'see' the lover whose departure makes 'the gate creak on the hinges',[23] and leaves Harrison 'flu-wracked and forsaken', with a thermos flask of grog to make him forget

> when waking, drenched and half delirious, why
> the shape beside me's mine roughed out in sweat.[24]

We see only the effect of her absence.

If the physical absence of the narrator's wife from 'Ghosts' precludes stock synecdochal description – high heels, swing coat, or lipstick-stained cigarette – neither is she a rounded character-study. Her existence is only that of a series of relations to Harrison: a third of the nymph/mother/crone causing him grief; a woman he has laid in the past and whose ghostly presence he lays in the poem. Even the images which describe her miscarriage (a recollection rather than part of the present of the poem): red splashes, blood in spurts 'like piss', blenching, bleeding, are detailed but not intimate and particu-

---

21 'Self Justification', *SP*, p. 172.
22 *v.*, p.11.
23 'Two into One 1: The Beast with Two Backs', *Guardian* (12 January 1994). At the time of writing, 'The Beast with Two Backs' and 'Grog' are the most recent additions, after a considerable gap, to the 'School of Eloquence' sequence and, unlike most of the poems of the sequence, are concerned with the same subject matter as their structural model, the Meredithian sonnet of *Modern Love* (1862).
24 'Two into One 2: Grog', *Guardian* (12 January 1994).

lar. She screams: 'insisting that I read [...] a bit of *Pride &
Prejudice*'.[25]

Discontinuity in his relationships foregrounds Harrison as an
artist, observer, outsider – a man alone and between. Also, a man
divided and dualistic, sometimes duelling. The position of the life-
affirming sensualist (first) narrator of 'The Pomegranates of Patmos'
is endowed with more sympathy than that of his brother, Prochorus,
a misanthropic misery who, having 'this weird sect' run by 'a batty
old bugger called John', prophesies the apocalypse. For the narrator,
the fruit of the title is 'a gem-packed pomegranate / best subjected to
kisses and suction', while, for his brother, its seed stands for 'the
sperm of the Future flame-lit from Hell':

> an orb of embryos still to be born,
> a globe of sperm globules that redden
> not with the glow of the Aegean dawn
> but the fires of his God's Armageddon.
>
> My orb of nibbleable rubies
> packed deliciously side by side
> his roes of doom-destined babies
> carmine with God's cosmocide.[26]

The device of the first narrator's following a pair of lovers walking
arm-in-arm to a taverna, by a beach, and sowing in their brains 'a
pop poemegranatey ditty',[27] whose six verses and seven refrains are
then transferred to the voice of the familiar Harrison poetic 'I',
ensures that we associate the love-making, life-loving latter with the
first brother:

> To hell with St John's
> life-loathing vision
> when I feel in my jeans
> your fingers go fishing.[28]

After reading the poem, however, we might recollect that elsewhere
in the collection, especially in the title poem and 'A Cold Coming',
the apocalyptic prophet is the first-person narrator.

---

25 'Ghosts', *SP*, p. 72. Compare 'Schwiegermutterlieder', where the wife is
   depicted as half of 'Mother and daughter German refugees', and the breast (but
   not belly) on which her mother's real violets are displayed. *SP*, pp. 50–1.
26 'The Pomegranates of Patmos', *Gorgon*, p. 30.
27 'The Pomegranates of Patmos', *Gorgon*, p. 33.
28 'The Pomegranates of Patmos', *Gorgon*, p. 34.

Harrison's dramatisation of the tensions within the poetic persona 'Tony Harrison' is described by his some time producer, Richard Eyre:

> The man is the work. It is not so much that it is autobiographical (though much of it of course is) but that the content invariably dramatises the ambivalences at the heart of his character and attempts to reconcile them. Tony does not deal in the familiar English modes of ellipsis and reticence, but in an unremittingly direct address that is at times almost unnerving. Those opposing valencies that he invokes in *v.* are not a poet's conceits but are the syntax of his daily life. Heart/brain, soul/body, male/female, family, freedom, class, culture, this is the divided territory in which he searches for harmony and despairs at its elusiveness.[29]

The creative use of the attempt at reconciliation and the search for harmony in Harrison's work depends upon their not being successful; he poetry is not so much reaching out to grasp a distant reconciliation or harmony as reaching into space, indexing the want of (desire for) harmony and reconciliation and the want (absence) of them. It is crucial for the drama of the poetry and for the *dramatis personae* of the poet's character that they are not attainable except in brief or illusory moments. The 'opposing valencies' that are the 'syntax' of the poet's (narrated) daily life, dramatised in so many poems, are not just the large concerns of gender, class, culture, and nation, but the contrarieties of personality. The narrative I is as ambiguous as the other Loiners. In 'The Heartless Art', the narrator, addressing a dying friend, says:

> I'll show you to distract you from the pain
> you feel, except when napping, all the time
> because you won't take drugs that dull the brain,
> a bit about my metre, line and rhyme.[30]

But instead of being the recipient of a poetry lesson, the friend becomes the subject of a poem, and a gift to poetry.

> I've often heard my fellow poets (or those
> who write in metres something like my own
> with rhyme and rhythm, not in chopped-up prose

---

29 Richard Eyre, 'Such Men are Dangerous', first published in *v.*, revised and enlarged version, *Bloodaxe 1*, p. 363.
30 'The Heartless Art', *SP*, p. 207.

and brood on man's mortality) bemoan
the insufficiency of rhymes for death –

We learn that the poet has 'stored away' the potential rhyme for his friend's name since they first met, and now:

Knowing you crawled on hands and knees to prime
our water pump, I'll expiate one debt
by finally revealing that stored rhyme
that has the same relentlessness as death
and comes to every one of us in time
and comes to you this April full moon, SETH!

The horrific inappropriateness of those full caps, that exclamation mark, is stunning. It suggests a beaming comedian gesturing for a cymbal-crash to reinforce his punchline. Stanzas one and two had drawn the narrator in heroic mode:

protecting delicate plants; taking part in communal rituals of husbandry; milking the day of its last drop because it will be the last day of his friend; pitting his vigour against the fast-coming dark, the looming abyss, significantly filling a hole (which had been cleared by Seth). Stanzas three to five exhibit his sensitivity to his friend's pride and pain. The appalling sixth stanza reveals anti-heroic traits, not the intellect which enables the 'I' to calculate the effect of a rhyme and make matter of a dying friend – that characteristic is offset by its coexistence with the evident tenderness and respect for that friend – but the self-congratulation and self-centredness of the artist absorbed in his art. The direct address and slow pace leads up to that comma, which foregrounds the final name like a punch-line – boom-boom! – a capitalized, depersonalized, objectified signifier: SETH! (pause for laughter/ applause).[31]

We perhaps remember Silenus's excuse for Apollo's heartlessness:

he was a poet and he'd probably follow,
when it came to the crunch, the laws of Apollo.[32]

The heartless art of poetry demands a sacrifice of all reticence. The outdoors man of the opening stanzas is shown to be as polyvalent as the PWD Man, the White Queen, and the other Loiners.

Is Harrison Christopher Caudwell's 'bourgeois poet', who sees himself as 'an individualist striving to realise what is most *essentially*

---

31   TH: *Loiner*, introduction, p. 25.
32   *Trackers*, p. 135.

himself by an expansive outward movement of the energy of his heart, by a release of internal forces which outward forms are crippling'?[33] Caudwell goes on to describe this as 'the bourgeois dream, the dream of one man alone producing the phenomena of the world'. In this dream the man alone is 'Faust, Hamlet, Robinson Crusoe, Satan and Prufrock'. Though Caudwell is read with many reservations, the image of the solipsistic poet as the anguished site of creative energies divorced from the material, social world seems to persist. Each of the characters he mentions is a loner who represents one half, or embodies both halves, of an unending dialectic. Harrison depicts himself as Faust ('I'll burn my books'[34]), and education as the Mephistophelian broomstick which wafted him out of his native sphere, but perhaps Hamlet is the closer analogy. Though Harrison substitutes 'books books'[35] for Hamlet's 'words words', both are at a remove; from the everyday they observe, from others; preoccupied by hag-ridden introspection. But not blinded or indifferent; there's nothing fey or otherworldly about these scholar/contemplatives-cum-men of action; each projects a very strong sense of his self. Harrison articulates a strong sense of himself as body, and the identity of his poetic 'I' is partly that body and its location in communities and places, but it is also an essence whose boundaries evade the body's, so that the 'I' is sometimes inside looking out, and sometimes outside looking in.

> My fingerprints still lined with coal
> send cold shudders through my soul.
> Each whorl, my love-, my long life-life,
> mine, inalienably mine,
> lead off my body as they press
> onwards into nothingness.
> I see my grimy fingers smudge
> everything they feel or touch.[36]

Dramatising the divisions in Harrison's character and experience, as well as in his view of the world, his poetry seems to portray a displaced psyche in search of completion. The prizes and privileges brought to him by the scholarship system, like the magical gifts of fairy-tales, had two faces. 'I had a very loving upbringing; without

---

33 Christopher Caudwell, *Illusion and Reality: A Study of the Sources of Poetry*, (London, 1946), p. 60.
34 'Aqua Mortis', *SP*, p. 137.
35 'Book Ends I'.
36 *Newcastle*, *SP*, p. 67.

question a very loving, rooted upbringing. Education and poetry came in to disrupt that loving group, and I've been trying to create new wholes out of that disruption ever since.'[37] Imagery in longer poems such as *Newcastle* and *v.* seems to describe half of a Platonic soul desperately seeking its completing counterpart to be

> curled in a circle, sucking its own tail,
> the formed continuum of female/male[38]

Lying down without his woman, Harrison sees 'life circling life like the Eddystone' but 'dizzy, drunk, alone', his circle is not made 'just'; it has neither 'sense nor centre, nor circumference'.[39] The sexual unions described are climactic and fulfilling; shadows of the ultimate consummation; but after them the couple divide again, the poet pours back into the confines of his skin, and takes up his solitary pursuit. The '*working* marriage [...] a blend of masculine and feminine',[40] and the reconciliation of opposites, unification, is finally described in the later poems, particularly 'Cypress & Cedar', where the stinking cypress and the sweet cedar blend:

> My love, as prone as I am to despair,
> I think the world of night's best born in pairs,
> one half we'll call the female, one the male,
> though neither essence need, in love, prevail.
> We sit here in distinctly scented chairs
> you, love, in the cedar, me the cypress chair.
>
> Though tomorrow night I might well sit in yours
> and you in mine, the blended scent's the same [....]
>
> I'll have my coffin made of cedar wood
> to balance the smell like cypress from inside
> and hope the smoke of both blends in the sky,
>
> as both scents from our porch chairs do tonight.[41]

The blending is not permanent, however. 'The Beast with Two Backs' contains another 'twin', a ghost-image.[42] The shape beside the poet is his own, 'roughed out in sweat' on the sheet, as though to

---

37 'Interview', p. 246.
38 'The Lords of Life', *SP*, p. 213.
39 *Newcastle*, p. 64.
40 *v.*, p. 22.
41 'Cypress & Cedar', *SP*, pp. 233–4.
42 'The Beast With Two Backs', *Guardian* (12 January 1994).

compensate for the absence of the other, presumably a lover, who has left; the narrator's feverish mind has projected another self. The figure of lover and/or wife appears in many poems, often in contexts which gloss her as Eve to the poet's Adam (*Kumquat*, 'Following Pine'); sweetness and light to his bile and darkness ('Cypress & Cedar'). These characters do not, however, seem to me to be representations of the Platonic *anima*, and they do not complement or complete the poet any more than other poetic personae. The lover offers the poet respite from the polyvalency and tension, and refuge, but is both less and more than his 'other half', in being a distinct character endowed with only some of his characteristics, which is why their unity, indeed their union, is temporary and conditional, and no permanent solution to or consolation for the things the poet encounters outside the beds in Newcastle, Durham, Prague, Leningrad, and elsewhere.

It is not, perhaps, surprising that Harrison, having had a painful personal experience of social upheaval, should seek a peaceful continuum, or that he should turn poetry, the agency of the disruption, into the agent of unity. The solace and reconciliation he seeks in sexual love never do produce unification in Platonic fusion.

> The head and heart
> are neither of them too much good apart
> and peace comes in the moments when they're blended[43]

But, as much of it is dedicated to showing us, this poetry comes not from peaceful union but from embattled division. The only full, if temporary, communion is between past and present selves. Though the scent of cypress and cedar mingle inextricably and the man and woman share their porch in communing silence, where *alter egos* skinhead/poet are ontologically equivalent in *v.*, the 'you' of 'Cypress & Cedar' has a quite different status in the dedication of *SP*. She is only a part of the whole, the product and not the producer: '... son io poeta, / essa la poesia'[44] (reminiscent of 'Man Does, Woman Is'?[45]). The poetic personality is always the focus. We should, perhaps, be wary of making too much of Harrison's habit of portraying women by piecemeal images of anatomical parts. The 'I' of 'Allotments' is not sketched in any more detail than the

---

43   'Cypress & Cedar', *SP*, p. 233.
44   Dedication, *SP*, p. 5.
45   Robert Graves, *Collected Poems*, p. 260.

partners he takes to the cemetery and the abattoir. If the girls are represented by rumpled jumper, nylons, a bum embossed with an epitaph, the young 'I' is also clammy mackintosh and winter vest, and, visually, no more solid or complete an image. The difference is that the young woman is described only in terms of her clothes and body, while we are given an insight into the narrator's thoughts and feelings. He 'felt'

> Street bonfires blazing for the end of war
> V.E. and J. burn us like lights, but saw
> Lush prairies for a tumble, wide corrals,
> A Loiner's Elysium[46]

The lover in 'Pomegranates of Patmos' is an agent of the narrator's gratification; a human equivalent of the pomegranates and figs he enjoys. Even the woman in the 'American' poems is more emblem than persona. She is 'my wife', the naked Eve in the garden, the occupant of the other, sweet-smelling chair. This in part, of course, ensures that we are not distracted from the central character, the narrative I, but it's also a blessed reticence. The reduction of the women to common denominators 'Wife! Mouth! Breasts! Thigh!'[47] suggests that Harrison, unlike some of his contemporaries, does not assume that his readers will be automatically fascinated by the minutiae of anything or one associated with him.

The ambiguous Lo[i]ner 'Tony Harrison', then, is central to Harrison's writing. How does that colour readings of the poems? Harrison's narrative 'I' is all too often identified with the 'real' Tony Harrison; is the establishing of his public persona a reflection of particular marketing strategies, or an effect of the poems themselves, and the kinds of readings they prompt?

Spencer's description of Ted Hughes's work as a substitute for social poetry, in opposition to Harrison's, which is the real thing,[48] seems odd, as Harrison's writing is far more personal than that of Hughes in the sense that Harrison's poetic 'I' appears in or is the subject of many of his poems, while Hughes is almost entirely absent from his. As Peter Forbes says:

> In Hughes the drama is in nature: 'The wind flung a magpie away and a

---

46   'Allotments', *SP*, p. 19.
47   'The Heart of Darkness', *SP*, p. 39.
48   *Poetry TH*, p. 5.

black- / backed gull bent like an iron bar slowly.' In Harrison nature
and the self mingle but there's always a strong sense of the man sensing
himself sensing nature.[49]

Forbes is writing of the narrative and lyric verse, and what he says
is less true of the plays, but even they, because they mostly enact the
same themes and introspective dialectic as the non-dramatic pieces,
and because their *dramatis personae* are not the three-dimensional
characters of realist theatre, can seem to be narrated by a dominant
and familiar voice.

In the sonnets, the long, contemplative poems, and, sometimes,
even in the plays and films, extrinsic subject matter rarely
submerges a distinct and strong personality. Harrison fills the 'big
O' with the other 'big H' – Harrison. The circle of the dramatic
orchestra is a space cleared for his public poetry, a big O filled, to
an extent, with political and social concerns, but in the non-dramatic
poetry that O can contract to a spotlight on the poet himself. In
'Facing North', his act of poetic composition is described as the
luminous O of common light, itself illuminating.[50] The glow from an
overhead light in his writing room: 'my paper lantern nothing will
keep still' lets him 'make things happen in its O', and becomes the
'flooded orchestra'. When the lamp swings and the circle of light
shifts, it 'throws up images of planets hurled / still glowing, off their
courses' – a state of cosmic catastrophe. But 'long years of struggle'
help the poet to 'concentrate', 'weather out these feelings', and
restore cosmic equilibrium, so that he finds (presumably with relief)
'an Earth that still has men', and his own 'inkling [significantly a
little bit of ink?] of an inner peace'.

'Facing North', though it contrasts the bleak light and cold
winds of the English north with the liberating warmth of America, is
none the less affectionate and evocative. Like Auden's 'In Praise of
Limestone',[51] the poem evokes not just a landscape but a psychological terrain – Harrison's. The north-facing room with its orchestra of
light from the swaying paper shade is a solid repository of the poet's
feelings about love and writing. The poem is compelling partly
because by 1983, when it appeared in the *TLS*, or 1984, when it
appeared in *SP*, readers had had the opportunity to follow the life
history of a compelling character through *Loiners* and the 'School of

49 Forbes, 'Bald Eagles of Canaveral', p. 491.
50 'Facing North', *SP*, pp. 190–1.
51 W. H. Auden, 'In Praise of Limestone', *Collected Shorter Poems*, pp. 238–41.

Eloquence' sequence. 'The North', as we are reminded by the epigraph to this poem, 'begins inside'.[52]

Harrison's name, as 'Tony', 'our Tony', *'Tony* Harrison', or 'my name' appears frequently in his poetry, as do other appellations, usually associated with his art, or its debunking ('the lad who gets the alphas',[53] 'the "scholar" me',[54] 'poet',[55] 'bard',[56] *'Wanker'*[57]), and signifiers usually connecting him with his ancestors or parents ('her son', 'the son', 'your son'). Names generally are important in Harrison's work, as is the act of naming.[58] Brand names (Harp,[59] Camp,[60] *Shelltox,*[61] *Dettol* and *Od-o-ro-no,*[62] Dunlop sandals, *Raleigh,*[63] C*oca-cola*[64] and BUTOX[65]), otherwise undistinguished places (*Sunny Sunglow's* jam factory,[66] *The Moonshine* and *West End* clubs,[67] The Omar Khayyam restaurant[68]) slogans (*Dig for Victory, Band of Hope,*[69] GOD IS LOVE[70]), and signs (used, for example, in *Big H,* 'Divisions', and *Banquet)* are all relished, but personal names seem to be the most significant, especially his own. He asks why 'skins with spraycans' should not write their names, or signs, on walls and hoardings, when they are dwarfed by

52 Louis MacNeice, 'Epilogue for W. H. Auden', *Letters from Iceland* (London, 1937), p. 250.
53 'Classics Society', *SP,* p. 120.
54 'Book Ends I', *SP,* p. 126.
55 'Heredity', *SP,* p. 111, and elsewhere.
56 *v.,* p. 7, and elsewhere.
57 *v.,* pp. 20, 31, and elsewhere.
58 See, for example, 'Fire-eater', SP, p. 168. *A Maybe Day in Kazakhstan* (*Shadow*, pp. 19-27) is concerned with a country's name, and of the act of naming a country and its people. For Harrison's interest in the poet as nomenclator, see his review of several collections of Latin American poetry, 'New Worlds for Old', *London Magazine,* new series, 10, no. 6 (September 1970), pp. 81–4.
59 *v.,* p. 18.
60 'Old Soldiers', *SP,* p. 159.
61 'The White Queen 2: The Railroad Heroides II', *SP,* p. 27.
62 'The White Queen 4: Manica, I The Origin of the Beery Way', *SP,* p. 31
63 'The White Queen 5: *from* The Zeg-Zeg Postcards, X', *SP,* p. 36.
64 'The White Queen 5: *from* The Zeg-Zeg Postcards, XI', *SP,* p. 37.
65 'The White Queen 5: *from* The Zeg-Zeg Postcards, XIII', *SP,* p. 37.
66 'Ginger's Friday', *SP,* p. 15.
67 'The White Queen 1: Satyrae I', *SP,* p. 21.
68 Setting of *Banquet.* See *Banquet,* pp. 53, 64.
69 'Allotments', *SP,* p. 18.
70 'The Songs of the PWD Man II', *SP,* p. 43.

αι αι; aye-aye; I, I

The big blue star for booze, tobacco ads,
the magnet's monogram, the royal crest,
insignia in neon [....]

Letters of transparent tubes and gas
in Düsseldorf are blue and flash out KRUPP.
Arms are hoisted for the British ruling class
and clandestine, genteel aggro keeps them up.[71]

He enjoys pretending 'in fun' that the 'HARRISON on some Leeds building sites' blazons his own name which, he tells us, 'I've also seen on books, in Broadway lights'. He describes in detail his finding of old posters, programmes and scripts of his plays recycled for various purposes, or dumped, and is fascinated by traces of himself such as 'the fragmentary letters ON ... IS of my own name on what was once a poster for my version of *The Misanthrope*'.[72]

This centrality of the authorial persona(e) in writing which is ostensibly concerned with the discrete event, experience, or object is a characteristic which some of Harrison's poetry shares with much Movement verse.[73] The title of Robert Conquest's poem may suggest that it is 'about' some Arctic landscape 'Near Jakobselv'; D. J. Enright might lead us to expect a poem 'about' 'Baie des Anges, Nice', but, as Andrew Crozier observes, 'the poems are not discrete events in the sense that they correspond as such to their discrete occasions. They are discrete, rather, in the way they wrap around their author-subject.'[74] While titles of Harrison's such as *The Fire-Gap* and 'Y' might suggest a metaphoric rather than metonymic relation to the poems' subjects, and more abstract or removed matter, others ('The Morning After', 'Durham') suggest that they will be concerned with discrete events and objects. Any such expectation on the part of the reader is, however, undermined by the poem. Crozier suggests that, to an extent, 'a poetics of objects, sites and moments [such as the Movement's and, it could be argued, Harrison's] placed its exponents in the tradition of enfeebled Romanticism, the decadence of conventional poetic emotions', but

---

71   *v.*, pp. 15–16.
72   *Chorus*, introduction, p. viii.
73   Taken here to be represented by Robert Conquest's *New Lines* anthology (London, 1956) and to a lesser extent *New Lines 2* (London, 1963).
74   Andrew Crozier, 'Thrills and Frills: Poetry as Figures of Empirical Lyricism', in Alan Sinfield, ed., *Society and Literature 1945–1970* (New York, 1983), p. 206.

179

that 'at the same time they place themselves outside that tradition by earnestly demystifying its conventional occasions'.[75]

Like the Movement poets, Harrison often seems to approach the occasions of his writing with self-consciousness and irony, and it could be said of his work that 'the expressive discourse potential in the occasion [may be] found to reside less in the occasion itself than in its conventional status'. The long-distance telephone conversation and (projected) visit to a bereaved parent of 'Long Distance I' might be thought of as a conventional poetic occasion, as might the funeral of 'Blocks', but it is not qualities inherent in the occasions themselves which generate the matter or sentiments of the poem. The lonely old man is described with a ruthless lack of sentimentality, and his son in a determinedly unheroic light:

> Your bed's got two wrong sides. Your life's all grouse.
> I let your phone-call take its dismal course[76]

The 'occasion' of the poem does not proceed from a moment of pathos or communication during the transatlantic visit, but from the poet's finding a significant parallel in his father's past desire for sweet things, once supplied by his wife, and his own attempt to satisfy that desire, which is frustrated:

> *Them sweets you brought me, you can have 'em back.*
> *Ah'm diabetic now. Got all the facts.*

Desire for (sweet) food is associated with life, and rejection of food (and loss of the provider of that food) with the loss of desire to live, and with impending death:

> *Ah've allus liked things sweet! But now ah push*
> *food down mi throat! Ah'd sooner do wi'out.*

Significantly, the offered but rejected sweets are called '*Lifesavers*'. The irony of the poem is available to the reader only because of the privileged knowledge we are given, extrinsic to the occasion of the poem, but central to the character of the poetic 'I', that the sweets were

> only bought
> rushing through JFK as a last thought.

---

75 Crozier, 'Thrills and Frills', p. 105.
76 'Long Distance I', *SP*, p. 133.

αι αι; aye-aye; I, I

A poem dedicated to Teresa Stratas, but concerned with another singer, Jenny Lind, 'Loving Memory', similarly undermines a conventional visit to a revered (or, as it turns out, forgotten) grave,[77] and 'Poetry Lesson' *is* a lesson in poetry rather than a description of one.[78]

Harrison's poetry, then, can suggest, as John Holloway's does for Andrew Crozier, that the occasions of poems, 'however necessary they may be to poets, are not felt to be trustworthy', not 'full with a world of realized experience', but rather that his 'experience of them was wryly deficient'.[79] Deficient or, perhaps, over-determined. This kind of poem does not offer itself as the definitive experience or autonomous artefact, the well-wrought urn. In terms which could equally be applied to Harrison's work, Crozier writes of Movement poets:

> their occasions are treated with scepticism, and the texts distort and buckle as a consequence of inner tension. Traditional forms are invoked not so much for the freedom that they confer as for support. They define the space in which the self can act with poetic authority, while at the same time, in the absence of assurances provided by conventionally felt poetic experience, they secure the status of the text.[80]

Harrison is not a Movement poet, of course, though his earliest published poetry did appear around the time of the publication of *New Lines*. The characteristic which most clearly distinguishes his writing from the (professed) poetic of Conquest *et al.* is sentiment. Like the *Mavericks* poets, he resists Movement 'antagonism towards sensibility and sentiment', and has no 'fear [of] primary Dionysian excitement'.[81] Perhaps his work could fruitfully be read as incorporating both Movement insistence upon the here-and-now, and scorn of the pretentious and phoney, and a *Maverick* (or Keatsian) conveying of excitement in personal experience.

Readers' construction of poet from poetry could be the product of a habit of reading long reinforced by conventional criticism. As Antony Easthope says, this, 'for all its pluralism, generally retains

---

77 'Art & Extinction 2: Loving Memory', *SP*, p. 185.
78 'Poetry Lesson', *Gorgon*, p. 17.
79 Crozier, 'Thrills and Frills', p. 204.
80 Crozier, 'Thrills and Frills', p. 206.
81 Howard Sergeant and Dannie Abse, eds, *Mavericks* (London, 1957), introduction: 'Two Letters', first letter, p. 9.

the historical author as centre for its theoretical framework'.[82] For critics such as F. R. Leavis, Easthope suggests, the poet is 'conceived in terms of a self-consciousness fully present to itself and thus able to inspect its own experience, experience in which there is no hidden or unconscious quality [...] as source and author of his poetry, the poet is simply taken for granted'. If the effect described is not entirely attributable to the poet, nor is it wholly the product of critical or other reading. The process is reciprocal. Easthope argues that 'in the poetic tradition from the Renaissance on, the formal features of poetic language, especially rhyme and metre, were organised so as to draw attention from the poem to "the poet", to give the effect of an individual voice "really" speaking'.[83] (Presumably, he does not mean *all* post-Renaissance poetry.)

'Despite the powerful resistance of the reading public', Stead asserts that 'it is away from discourse and towards the Image that the most vigorous poetic minds have striven' in the early and middle parts of this century, in a reaction against 'the popular discursive of Victorian poetry'.[84] For Lindley, a form of personal poetry has returned to popularity after a period of unfashionability. 'Despite the efforts of various schools to blot out the "lyrical ego", the latter part of this century has seen its reintroduction, albeit in very different ways.'[85] Paul Fussell suggests that traditional lyric poetry has been a casualty of post-structuralist de-centring, which displaces conventional perspectives and assumptions upon which lyric depends.[86] One of these is the 'notion of a "correct" reading' which 'in its simplest form, is philosophically humanist, presupposing a shared essence that guarantees the possibility of perfect communication between writer and reader. But subjectivity is mobile and self-divided, composed and recomposed in ways it seldom chooses and often does not or cannot recognize'.[87] While these perspectives change the way we read lyric poetry, they have not done away with its production, and, indeed, provide a fruitful way of reading lyric poetry which recognises the divided subjectivities of writer and

---

82   Antony Easthope, *Poetry and Phantasy* (Cambridge, 1989), p. 3.
83   Easthope, *Poetry and Phantasy*, pp. 4–5.
84   C. K. Stead, *The New Poetic: Yeats to Eliot* (London, 1975), p. 191.
85   Lindley, *Lyric*, p. 81.
86   See Fussell, *Poetic Forms and the Lyric Subject*.
87   Francis Mulhern, *Marxist Literary Criticism* (London, 1992), p. 21.

reader, and articulates the problematic nature of communication.

Helga Geyer-Ryan describes the lyric voice as 'the dominant tradition in European poetry of the modern age', and 'the linguistic expression of one kind of idiosyncratic subjectivity which presents itself as an autonomous and absolute entity'.[88] She suggests that this voice 'points to the existence of a self in the world and, conversely, it represents the heterogeneous and centrifugal dynamics of the world as being focused and filtered, as they are, through the perspectives of a synthesizing and unifying linguistic agency'. The autonomous author or subject is not threatened by literary 'techniques of fragmentation', because behind them 'is still the ideological construct of a monadic subject'. Geyer-Ryan argues that 'as the idea of the subject is oriented towards monadic substantiality, so the idea of lyricism is oriented towards monological inwardness'. Thus the 'heteroglossia of the world, its plurality of discourses, is expected to reappear in lyrical poetry in that one authentic voice after its journey through the soul'.[89]

Taking the view that 'the death of the author' led to widespread casualties among readers, Lindley attributes the 'relief with which many readers come to the poetry of Philip Larkin or Seamus Heaney' to 'their affiliation to Hardy or to Wordsworth', in which he finds 'a relatively unproblematic recuperation of the[ir] lyric "I"'. He detects 'a representation of Larkin' (or at least of the public persona of Larkin) in 'The figure in "Church Going" who removes his cycle clips', and suggests that this figure's meditation upon and response to the church 'seems very traditional in its procedure'.[90] Like Larkin and Heaney, Harrison has become a (relatively) familiar figure. When television and the press play a large part in the formation of canons, and the poet, like the film actor or pop musician, is commodified, 'personal' poetry, which provides scope for biographical speculation, is, presumably, likely to become more popular. Eagleton describes this as a process of commodification and deprivatisation of the 'intimate sphere'.

> As bourgeois society develops into the modern epoch, the relations between public sphere, intimate sphere and state undergo significant changes. With the increasing 'stratification' of the public sphere, the

88 Geyer-Ryan, 'Heteroglossia', van Peer, *Taming of the Text*, p. 194.
89 Geyer-Ryan, 'Heteroglossia', p. 195.
90 Lindley, *Lyric*, p. 81.

'intimate' sphere becomes progressively marginalized; state education and social policy take over many of the functions previously reserved to the family, blurring the boundaries between 'public and private' and stripping the family of its social, productive roles. The 'intimate' sphere is in this sense deprivatized, pulled into public society – but only, in a notable historical irony, to be reprivatized as a unit of consumption. Private consumption and leisure, based upon the now shrunken space of the family, replace the forms of social discussion previously associated with the public sphere.[91]

Emphasising his ancestral roots, the extended family in Leeds, and the nuclear family of his maturity, in poetry, Harrison and the poetry industry turn them into units of consumption. He declares himself against the 'freehold withdrawal' of the monastic art of retreat and exclusion; deploring poetry which 'inevitably' depicts life as 'somewhat rude'; in which 'the "world's rude fingers" pry into the retreat';[92] and in his own work moves between the intimate and private. In poems such as 'Pomegranates of Patmos' we are forced voyeurs of his lover's fingers fishing in his jeans, while film poems such as *v.*, and single-performance plays such as *Kaisers* seek to restore poetry to performance in the common light, and the public sphere.

Harrison's work has been subject to the kind of processes that Trotter describes as afflicting Larkin and Betjeman, though there are clearly great differences between the public personalities of the three poets. Discussing the existence of readerships outside the academy, Trotter remarks:

Common Readers [...] have not altogether disappeared [....] Unfortunately, it has proved more and more difficult to attract the attention of those readers, and the very few poets who do manage to attract it (notably John Betjeman and Philip Larkin) have sometimes been put to strange antics; at least, they have been put to the cultivation of 'personality.[93]

When, in *England of the Mind*, Heaney turns to Larkin, Trotter

---

91 Terry Eagleton, *The Function of Criticism: From the* Spectator *to* Post-struc-turalism *(London, 1984), pp. 117–18.
92 See Harrison's review of poems by Clifford Dyment, P. J. Kavanagh, George Macbeth, Hugh MacDiarmid, and Donald Davie, 'Beating the Retreat', *London Magazine*, new series, 10, no. 8 (November 1970), pp. 91–2. The comments above refer to poems by Clifford Dyment.
93 Trotter, *The Making of the Reader*, p. 233.

notes that 'his argument alters for the first time from a preoccupation with tonal and mythic resource to a preoccupation with personality'. The personality seems important in part because it is *im*personal, a personification of a type.

> 'He [Larkin] *is* urban modern man, *the* insular Englishman [....]' At that an image familiar to every reader of his poems floats into view: an alert and fastidious observer whose anorexic wit has for so long needled the national decline, a will-have-been among has-beens. This image is the convention according to which each new poem will be read.

The choice of Heaney may be a little unfair. His concern (in, for example, 'The Main of Light') with what he sees as the visionary quality of some of Larkin's writing is perhaps bound to move from an interest in the vision to an interest in the visionary.[94] Trotter quotes Anthony Thwaite, however, who, also writing of Larkin, finds that, from *The Less Deceived* onwards, 'the personality is an achieved and consistent one, each poem restating or adding another facet to what has gone before'. Trotter adds:

> But the personality has also gained a certain currency outside the poems. It is customary for newspapers to pay some attention to poets who have just published a book or won a prize, but Larkin has on occasion been interviewed because he is Larkin [.... An article illustrated with a photograph of Larkin] is entitled 'A Voice for our Time' it is that voice, defined here in relation to social and political issues, which we look for behind the poems.

Tony Harrison's personality, perceived through the characters of his poems, would not be precisely consistent, but, as suggested above, the cumulative effect of encountering all those personae from *Loiners* on is to build up an image of a large, polyvalent, heterogeneous, dolphin-torn and gong-tormented, yet contradictorily coherent 'I'.

It has been suggested that the cult(ivation) of personality described by Trotter was shaped by modern habits of reading. Trotter finds that few readers who have made 'the element of compulsive contact' with a poet which Larkin describes as 'the only right reason for reading' seem reluctant to read poems by anyone else. In his opinion, 'it is as though the Common Reader cannot cope

---

94   See Seamus Heaney, 'The Main of Light', *The Government of the Tongue*.

with more than (say) three poets at once'.[95] The line of thinking
which associates the reading of literary texts with 'compulsive
contact' – communion with the soul of the poet rather than an
encounter with the rhetoric of a literary artefact – seems to come
from the same tradition as Coleridge's *Biographia Literaria*. If this
is how the 'common reader' really reads, then, given that close
reading or some version of the New Criticism is still the dominant
tradition except where it has been supplemented by post-structuralism, then the academic and common reader have drawn apart. The
marketing of contemporary poetry supports this view. Publishers
promote individual poets rather than poetry, and promotional
leaflets, posters and so on tend to 'sell' the author rather than poetry
per se or even the poems in the collection which is being promoted.
The first appearance in print of what was to be an important, and
controversial, poem, *v.*, was heralded on the front cover of the
London Review of Books by a photograph of the poet (on the set of
the National Theatre production of his *Mysteries*, standing in front of
the banner of the Bakers' Union).[96] Blurbs which focus on personality or achievement (prizes, sales), or on a non-specific lauding of the
poet's work rather than on poetic technique, could be a reflection of
publishers' belief that the province of literary criticism has been
appropriated by the literary establishment and should not be under-
taken by those without familiarity with a technical register.

Outside literary periodicals, such exposure as is accorded to
poetry in the media is likely to focus on the poet rather than the
poem. This is partly because, to feature in a newspaper or on radio
or television (apart from within the constraints of the books pages or
arts programmes), a piece must justify its general interest or its
status as an event, something that happens – news. A new publication or performance can count as such an event, and revelations
about the personality behind the poems can count as 'general interest'. Even poets' clothes can be the starting point of an article. An
Independent piece on the 1994 Poetry International Festival developed into a semiotics of poetic dress code, and made matter from
Harrison's blue socks.[97] Some articles are simply about the autobiography which is seen as unproblematically behind the poetry,

95   Trotter, *Making of the Reader*, pp. 234–5.
96   24 January 1985. Mr Harry Harrison had belonged to the Bakers' Union.
97   Michael Glover, 'Poetry's Weakest Suit', *Independent* (2 November 1994).

others move to feelings, beliefs and opinions on matters extrinsic to the poetry, analysing the poet's poems as if they were speeches, and his personality as though he were an aspiring politician. Lucas, whilst deploring Howard Brenton's 'grandiloquent and self-serving argument' that 'at a time when "some kind of evil" was stalking the land many writers at least were describing and accounting for the state of the nation's soul', argues that 'the name that ought surely to have appeared at the top of the list is that of Tony Harrison'.[98] Whilst Harrison, it is to be hoped, would point out that his concern should be with dole, not soul, Lucas is right, but there are problems about being at the top of the list. Glover's poet-wear piece briefly mentioned one poem that Harrison read ('The Lords of Life'), but described at length the tenor of his reading ('wallowing about in [...] guilt'). The rest of that part of the article concerned with Harrison was devoted to a critique of his performance as a 'celebrity':

> Harrison is not one of life's natural celebrities, and for that reason the festival got off to a muted start. He was absent from its opening reception, and he disappeared into the night immediately after his reading, having paused just long enough to sign a few books for his admirers and to complain, bitterly and repeatedly, about the quality of the wine.

Personality, or rather image, is, significantly, described as coming between the poems and their reception. Harrison, 'being a Northerner and therefore 101 per cent street-credible (especially in the South), is too far beyond the reach of sensible criticism'. We may pay lip-service to the idea that art cannot be divorced from history, and should not be regarded as merely affective and ornamental, but creators of social art which takes a radical view, if successful, trigger media coverage which inflates creator over creation, depicts the pragmatic materialist as a fascinating eccentric, and reinforces the cult of personality. Another *Independent* article suggested that the consequences of the increased popularity of poetry readings are an increase in book sales and 'a bringing to ground of what many people have regarded as an aery, abstracted discipline, the humanising of an art that has looked cold and cerebral on the page'.[99] That art is literally humanised in the supplying of a face and voice 'behind' the poems. This may lead to a more direct association

---

98   Lucas, 'Speaking for England?', p. 351.
99   Michael Glover, 'For Crying Out Loud', *Independent* (29 June 1994).

of poetic and personal subject, which in turn can lead to the kind of interview in which the poet is asked about his or her favoured brand of toothpaste. The process deflects interest from the dysfunctional society to the egotistical sublime, and if it is really successful any unhealthy dwelling on the former can be put down to anomalies in the latter – these artists are very highly strung. The process has begun with Harrison; we are frequently reminded of his nick-name, 'Northern Gloom',[100] and of his tendency to pessimism and melancholia, and the matter of the poetry, as in Glover's article, is identified with personal guilt.

More damaging than articles which attack Harrison are those which tacitly assume his acceptance as an important literary figure. 'Troublesome poet Tony Harrison has taken a golden god around Europe to make a film in rhyming couplets about our misuse of technology. It may be bonkers, but it could also be art, writes John Sweeney'.[101] This *Observer* report of a visit to the set of *Prometheus* described Harrison in terms of an institution, an established, even admirable figure whose genuine anguish is acknowledged, but whose causes are removed or obscure enough, and methods odd enough, for his work to be amusingly eccentric rather than politically effective. 'Engineering this madness is one of the usual suspects: Tony Harrison, poet, trouble-maker and lover of the Classics [. . . .] Summing up the moment, one of the crew – all of whom indulge Harrison in his vision – says: "It's completely bonkers, isn't it?"' The licensed pricker of consciences is perilously close to the licensed fool, and the grand old man of rhyming couplets is robbed of his point.

The rejection by modern critical thought of the animism of Romantic images of nature has been described as symptomatic of an inward-looking or narcissistic psychology productive of an inward-turning art. 'We may find an image for our own uncircumscribed energies in the sea or the north wind, but we are unlikely to perform sacrifices to Poseidon or Boreas. Sea remains sea for us, and wind remains wind, phenomena of an outside nature, although their mystery and turbulence may make us aware of similar energies in ourselves'. Thus, today, 'it is the inward significance which matters, as if the gods had shifted their centre of gravity from the external

---

100 Attributed to the director John Dexter by Burton, in 'Introduction', p. 17.
101 *Observer* (13 July 1997).

plane to the inner kingdom of ourselves'.[102] Day Lewis responds: 'this is true enough but is there not a sense in which it has been true, where lyric poetry is concerned, for a long time?'[103] Is the intro-spective poet, isolated by his exquisite sensibility, preoccupied with his vision, the epitome of the Romantic spirit, Hegel's *schöne Seele*, still extant?[104] If so, that much of the interest in Harrison's poetry comes from the turbulent inner kingdom of Harrison – the divided, Lo[i]ner protagonist, should not be surprising. In 1889, Yeats was complaining of the pervasiveness of this aspect of lyric in the prod-ucts of the 'Anglo-Saxon' poet:

> He is full of self-brooding. Like his own Wordsworth, most English of poets, he finds his image in every lake and puddle. He has to burden the skylark with his cares before he can celebrate it. He is always a lens coloured by self.[105]

Yeats's own poetry is described as attempting to reintegrate lyric or 'aesthetic' with narrative or 'popular' poetry, and seeking a 'Unity of Being' as Eliot sought an undivided sensibility. If, however, as Stead suggests, the 'best poets of this century have tried again to "bring the whole soul of man into activity"',[106] we should not forget that sometimes, as in *Banquet*, for example, the cares of the skylark – and the cares of society – *are* the cares of the poet.

The outsider aspect of Harrison's narrative 'I', the *metoikos*, then, is aptly named a Lo[i]ner, and that aloneness foregrounds the unique personality. In his piece on *Trackers*, Taplin writes: 'the satyrs are not part of culture, but they are not totally separate from it either: they are on the very borderline between the strange, alarming and anarchic world of the wild on the one hand, and on the other the civic Athens of democracy, of the Pantheon and, not least, of comedy and tragedy'. Taplin associates these with the poet himself. 'These borderline creatures are very Harrison. [...] In so many ways he, "the poet" is caught between two worlds, belonging to both and belonging to neither [....] There is a both-and-neither quality about [Harrison's] whole personality as well as externals.'[107] I

---

102 Quoted in Day Lewis, *Lyric Impulse*, pp. 103–4.
103 Day Lewis, *Lyric Impulse*, p. 104.
104 See Frye, *Anatomy*, introduction, and pp. 270–81.
105 W. B. Yeats, article on Todhunter in the *Providence Sunday Journal* (1889) quoted by MacNeice, *Poetry of W. B. Yeats*, p. 53.
106 Stead, *New Poetic*, p. 13.
107 Taplin, 'Satyrs', *Bloodaxe 1*, p. 461.

would suggest that Taplin's conclusion is as applicable to the fiction-alised poetic persona as it is to the 'real' man he describes. Harrison's 'I' is a 'borderline individual'.[108] Neither sitting on fences nor hedging bets is implicit in that phrase. Though he issues himself a wry *caveat* through Silenus to the effect that the 'sensitive' poet would 'probably follow, / when it came to the crunch, the laws of Apollo', he also issues, through the skinhead of *v.*, a reminder that he (Harrison) has made 'poet' '*a crude four-letter word*'[109] – an achievement upon which he should surely be congratulated. The simultaneous occupation of both sides of the various borders merely ensures that none of them becomes complacently at peace with the others.

---

108 Taplin, 'Satyrs', p. 462.
109 *v.*, p. 19.

CHAPTER 7

Art & Extinction: Greek tragedy and the black circle

Ζεύς δ'ὀλέσει καὶ τοῦτο γένος μερόπων ἀνθρώπων,
εὖτ' ἂν γεινόμευοι πολιοκρόταφοι τελέθωσιν
Hesiod, *Works and Days*, 180–11[1]

the end of dialectic is death.
Peter Forbes, 'The Bald Eagles of Canaveral', *Bloodaxe*[1]

Referring to the 'pole of misanthropic reductiveness' which Palladas sets for Harrison, and whose 'attraction Harrison's poetry and theatre work both feels and resists',[2] Jeffrey Wainwright suggests that the rejection of immortality and '"divine life" stuff' entails a quest for something to put in 'the black empty space that is such a recurrent image' in Harrison's writing. 'All the work might be said to share in an effort to populate that empty circle, fill that void – fill it with "life" certainly, but also, *pace* Plato, with meaning and significance.' The extent to which Harrison's poems belong to the tradition of consolatory narratives which offer to fill the void left by the absence of faith by scientific, philosophic, or other revelation, is, I think, debatable. While *v.* describes a personal consolation, and an uncertain vision, 'Coming', by its circular form, offers no prophecy of hope. 'Gorgon' does propose that the spirit of Heine, presiding over a meeting of ECU statesmen, might lead humankind into another way than the Gorgon's, but, again, it is only a suggestion, and it is a 'marble poet' who might 'keep new Europe open-eyed'.[3] Wainwright suggests that in modern atheistic writing there is a quest 'for what the philosopher Charles Taylor calls a "believable framework" [...] that in virtue of which we make sense

---

1 'Zeus shall destroy this race of fated men when their children are born with grey hair at the temples', quoted by Harrison, 'Facing up to the Muses', *Bloodaxe 1*, p. 431.
2 Jeffrey Wainwright, 'Something to Believe in', in *Bloodaxe 1*, p. 407.
3 *Gorgon*, p. 75.
4 Wainwright, 'Something to Believe in', p. 407.

of our lives spiritually'.[4] He finds that 'the overlapping narratives that Harrison has made in his poetry [...] are all struggling to make some framework of identity and belief that will resist the sceptical reductiveness represented by Palladas'.[5] Harrison's poetry may advocate atheism and scepticism, but it is not nihilist. Though the narrative I of many of the poems fills the void left in his identity by the breakdown of the extended family, social mobility and the fraying of family/class ties at least in part with interpersonal bonds, he does not necessarily lack a framework of belief. The black empty space of uncertainty and fear is filled by 'the thorny whys and wherefores, awkward whences',[6] the intellectual pleasures of dialectic and the necessity of challenge, which does not assume the necessity to produce answers and solutions:

> Who lives for the future, who for now?
> What good's the *cigale*'s way or the *fourmi*'s
> if both end up as nothing anyhow
> unless they look at life like Socrates
> who wished, at the very end, to learn to play
> a new air on his novice lyre. *Why?*
> said his teacher, *this is your last day.*
> *To know it before I die*, was the reply.[7]

And it is filled by the pursuit of 'life', and the resistance to all that (it is suggested) opposes it.

The 'big O' – picked out in the typography of the cover of *Continuous*,[8] dwelt on by the camera in the closing shots of the film of *Banquet*, and represented by seconds of black screen in *Loving Memory*[9] – is a motif common to many of Harrison's poems, echoing Graves as well as Faust:

> '*O per se O, O per se O!*'
> The moribund grammarian cried
> To certain scholars grouped at his bedside,
> Spying the round, dark pit a-gape below:
> '*O per se O!*'[10]

---

5 Wainwright, 'Something to Believe in', p. 415.
6 *Banquet*, p. 59.
7 'Following Pine I', *SP*, p. 225.
8 In white on the paper cover, in silver and gold on the hard cover.
9 *Loving Memory*, BBC TV, four films transmitted July–August 1987.
10 Robert Graves, 'O', *Collected Poems*, p. 287.

The black O of death's oblivion is as central to Harrison's poetry as
the life it opposes, and in a way a more powerful, because more
focused, image. In *v.* the mine under Beeston Hill Cemetery liter-
alises the void of oblivion and personal extinction, awareness, and
fear which both 'undermine' our equilibrium, yet define us.

> I've never feared the grave but what I fear's
> that great worked-out black hollow under mine.[11]

In *Banquet*, the 'I' becomes 'we':

> Feeling that life seems blasted by some blight
> we keep on yearning for some purer light
> but this, as Bertrand Russell wrote, is born
> from our deep fear of everlasting night[12]

The medium of film seems to unleash the apocalyptic strain of
Harrison's imagination, from the personal apocalypse of pieces such
as *Black Daisies* to the genocide described in the war poems, to the
global extinction predicted by *Prometheus* and the nuclear horror of
Shadow.

> 'This voice comes from the shadow cast
> by Hiroshima's A-bomb blast.
> The sound you hear inside this case
> is of a man who fans the face
> he used to have before the flash
> turned face and body into ash.[13]
> [....]
> First the conflagration of the fan
> then after it the fanning man.
>
> Before my eyes burst from the heat
> a blazing dove falls at my feet'
> [....]
>   are we all like shadow San
> facing inferno with a fan?

Harrison does not bring Freud to his banquet, but Freud's opposition
of *eros/thanatos* is a ghostly presence behind many poems, as the
ego's instinctual revulsion at the idea of not-being surfaces in an explo-

---

11 *v.*, p. 25.
12 *Banquet*, p. 59.
13 *Shadow*, pp. 3, 15, 17.

sion of libidinous energy. In 'Mother of the Muses', memory is associated with consciousness and the life-force, and thus with 'being':

> Some hoard memories as some hoard gold
> against that rapidly approaching day
> that's all they have to live on, being old,
> but find their savings spirited away.
> What's the point of having lived at all [. . . .]

> If we *are* what we remember, what are they
> who don't have memories[14]

The chilling brush with *stasis*, living death, brings a surge of lust for
life:

> but you kissed your dad, who as we left, forgot
> he'd been anything all day but on his own.
> We needed to escape, weep, laugh and lie
> in each other's arms more privately than there,
> weigh in the balance all we're heartened by,
> so braved the blizzard back, deep in despair.[15]

The long dark night of sensory deprivation as the world is muffled
by the blizzard which follows their journey back is a taste of the
coffin, *'that long thing where you lie'*,[16] from which Harrison rises
with the resolution to leave behind a record more permanent than
memories:

> I woke long after noon with you still sleeping
> and the windows blocked where all the snow had blown.
> Your pillow was still damp from last night's weeping.
> In that silent dark I swore I'd make it known,
> while the oil of memory feeds the wick of life
> and the flame from it's still constant and still bright,
> that, come oblivion or not, I loved my wife
> in that long thing where we lay with day like night.[17]

Memory and art, preserving not only individual consciousness
but the products of culture which are the vaults of our collective
memory, are part of the 'light', life, which outshines oblivion:

---

14 'Mother of the Muses', *Gorgon*, p. 42.
15 *Gorgon*, p. 44.
16 *Gorgon*, p. 40.
17 *Gorgon*, p. 44.

Memory runs a marathon, a human mind relay
from century to century to recreate our play.
Memory, mother of the Muses, freed
from oblivion the 'Ichneftes' of Sophocles.[18]

The audience draws the satyrs back into life from oblivion by speaking aloud some fragments of Greek text, rather as J. M. Barrie's Tinkerbell is restored to life by applause. The act embodies the Trackers' rebirth as functioning (as opposed to forgotten and thus defunct) signifiers, their becoming other (rather than undistinguished and indistinguishable non-significance, i.e. nothing) and their re-entrance into modern literature and modern awareness of them. Thus their literal stage entrance is identical with their re-entrance into viability, the symbolic, and life.

I have said that dialectic provides the dynamic of many of Harrison's poems, and that this dialectic involves opposed but not diametrically opposite forces which are in tension but not *stasis*. The characteristic form of the poems is not the well-ordered rhetoric of an already proven argument, or a flawless syllogism leading to an incontrovertible conclusion. More often, conclusions are conditional or absent. Harrison sets up apparently 'personal' convictions and allegiances only to undermine them by taking the opposite side or stance, giving a sense of an 'ambiguous partisan', a dichotomised or polyvalent subject. He was, however, resolutely unambivalent in his speech as President of the Classical Association in April 1988.[19]

Harrison's speech reiterated his affinity to the form of cultural capital held to be the highest to which the northern hemisphere can aspire, the art of the Classical world. Harrison is no Arnoldian. He does not prescribe the Classical ideals of the Hellenes as a cure for the social vices of Hebrews and Philistines. The Classical virtues which he wishes upon society are the willingness to look at and show suffering and death without flinching, persistence to the limit of human capability, dignity, and a propriety of social interaction and language which could have been described as 'decorum' before the word became associated with starched reserve. These attributes seem to be summed up for him in Greek tragedy, and their emblem is the tragic mask. Harrison asks his audience to 'juxtapose the naked

---

18 Part of additional lines written by Harrison 'three hours before our première [at Delphi]', partly to account for the stripping of the stage by high winds. *Trackers*, introduction, pp. xx–xxi.
19 Reprinted as 'Facing up to the Muses', *Bloodaxe 1*.

human face that you and I have with a tragic mask' in order to 'get a feel of the difference between life and theatre'.[20] He suggests that when we are confronted with real or realistically presented horrors – blood, death, violence and terror – we are stricken dumb; we close our eyes; our heads bow down.[21] When a mask gazes on the same horrors, however:

> it goes on gazing. It is created with open eyes. It *has* to keep on looking [. . . .] Words never fail it. It goes on speaking. It's created with an open mouth. To go on speaking. It has faith in the word [. . . .] the mask keeps it head upright. It is created to stay upright. It's created to present itself. In this theatre of 'obvious reciprocity' the mask is created to see, to speak, and to present itself so it can be seen. Even Oedipus has to present his bloody sockets to be seen.[22]

Much that might be taken to be sentimentality, exploitation of other people's history, and self-absorption in Harrison's own poetry could be interpreted as part of this relentless need to expose and be exposed. If the television camera is perceived as a kind of mask, then its relentless pursuit of the patients in High Royds hospital is no longer redolent of the asylum-as-entertainment.[23] Oedipus keeps his head/mask unbowed not only 'for us to see the terrible sockets' but also 'to register the carriage of survival'. Similarly, the mask of Hecuba:

> presents itself to the audience, faces up to its suffering, speaks, and carries from this first act of presentation an existential meaning that survives in the last words of the *Trojan Women*. The very final scene of the play could be said to have been prepared by this *ana, dysdaimon* [Hecuba's first words], that survives into the play's ending and brings us back full circle to the act of raising the head and facing up to the life of the future with all its horrors.[24]

Euripides uses the dramatic device of bringing Hecuba (and the Trojan women) low to the ground near the end of the play, to mirror our first sight of her prostrate on the earth, before she stirs, raises herself on one arm and commands, 'Lift your neck from the dust /

---

20 'Facing up', p. 445.
21 This could be a powerful gloss on Harrison's play *Bow Down*.
22 'Facing up', p. 446.
23 I.e. in *Black Daisies*.
24 'Facing up', p. 447. Harrison uses the Latinate form rather than the Greek Hekabe throughout this discussion.

Up with your head!'[25] According to Harrison, the playwright does this not only so that the women can take a last leave of their dead, but 'in order that they again had to raise their heads like Hecuba at the beginning of the play, and stand, in order to make an exit'. He suggests that this is crucial. 'And the bearing of that exit and the deportment of the mask are reasons why we are able to gaze on the terror and not turn to stone.'[26] In the last words of the chorus which close the play, Harrison finds a reinforcement of and commitment to Hecuba's last word, 'βιου', 'life'. (Though this interpretation may seem a little strained, as the context of the word is the phrase 'a life of slavery': 'δούλεον ἀμέραν βιου')[27]. He finds that 'these are small words, but crucial, and spoken in masks, with their necessarily upright bearing, they resonate with existential survival that is at the heart of tragedy and make it impossible to agree with Jean-Paul Satre that the play ends in "total nihilism"'.[28]

If 'there were to be only one Muse', Harrison 'would have to choose [...] Melpomene, the Muse of Tragedy [....] This is the Muse, as Macneile Dixon wrote sixty years ago, "who deals with the most monstrous and appalling that life can offer, when it turns upon us its Medusa-like countenance of frenzy and despair".'[29] The Medusa face represents the human ability to face (up to) tragedy.

> This frenzy and despair of the Fifth Age is that terror that tragedy allows us to gaze into, as Nietzsche said, 'yet' (and this is a very important yet), Nietzsche added, 'yet without being turned to stone by the vision'. In an age when the spirit of affirmation has almost been burned out of us, more than ever we need what Nietzsche also called tragedy in *Ecce Homo*, 'the highest art to say "yes" to life'.[30]

Harrison asserts that what the theatre needs for the age of nuclear terror, the Fifth Age of iron, when Zeus, it was said, would destroy humankind (significantly *meropon anthropon*, 'men who have speech'), is tragedy, and: 'this tragedy has to believe in the primacy of the word'.[31] Greek tragedy offers its vision of life as an opposi-

---

25 Euripides, *The Women of Troy*, Vellacott, *Bacchae*, p. 93.
26 'Facing up', p. 447.
27 Euripides, *Troades*, ed. K. H. Lee (London, 1976), 11. 1329.
28 'Facing up', p. 448.
29 'Facing up', p. 440.
30 'Facing up', pp. 448–9.
31 'Facing up', p. 440.

tion to the eternal silence of oblivion, which in turn is represented for Harrison in the twentieth century chiefly by nuclear war. Thus he equates the Greenham women with the muses, dancing on the anti-Helicon of the missile silo:

> The mountain that these Muses dance on is where our oblivion is stored, an extinction that even Memory, the mother of the Muses, will not survive to make our sufferings a story like those of Hecuba and the women of Troy, an extinction that will mean no going 'back to civilisation' [....] Life will have no *emphasis*, no significance. There will be no dance, no Helicon, no Muses.[32]

We are the barbarians, and our barbarity will have killed us. The only hope is to adopt the bearing of the tragic mask, for 'on the brink of the silo and the extinction it represents, this chorus of Muses of the late age of iron affirm life, and celebrate it by dancing in the face of the ultimate darkness on Helicon. Our way not back to civilisation but forward might begin by facing up to these Muses'. This chapter looks at Harrison's opposition of art and extinction, and the way in which his tragic muse outfaces 'the ultimate darkness', the black 'O'.

In the context of Harrison's opposition of enlightened Greek civilisation and twentieth-century barbarity, the encounter in *v*. takes on a new aspect. The Greek language stands for all learning and all languages other than the vernacular, which in this case, is working-class Leeds English. The skinhead's threat of violence unless there is 'no more Greek'[33] seems like a true act of vandalism. By placatingly reverting to a plainer English, Harrison puts the skinhead on the dark, blind side of an Arnoldian opposition: culture versus anarchy. As Eagleton showed, however, the skin/skald are not diametric opposites.[34] The graffiti artist is not an anarchist, nor is his writing merely narcissistic self-publicising of his name, akin to Harrison's enjoyment of his name in Broadway lights. He wants work, hope, purpose. In his way he wants to Hellenise Leeds, and he sprays not (only) to obliterate messages, but to leave his own: '*Ah've got mi work on show all ovver Leeds.*'.[35]

Despite his contempt for eloquence, the skinhead has learned

---

32 'Facing up', pp. 448–9.
33 *v*., p. 19.
34 See Eagleton, 'Antagonisms', pp. 349–50.
35 *v*., p. 22.

that words are powerful weapons. Harrison sometimes seems to endorse Yeats's 'Words alone are certain good', but he also describes them as acting for certain bad.[36] The literacy/language debate becomes analogous to the nuclear weapons debate: on the one hand, can they be trusted with all that power (i.e. those who have mastery over words, whether as teachers do or as skinheads); on the other hand, who wants a disarmed language?

'The big dichotomy in Harrison', Peter Forbes remarks, 'is between sensual celebration and the fear of extinction. It's something we all have but Harrison has it to an unusual degree.'[37] Poems such as 'Giving Thanks' and 'Cypress & Cedar' are infused with the celebration of sensuality, but it is not antithetical to death. The kumquat fruit, a realisation in miniature of the 'O' surrounded by a skin (zest) of (and for) life:

> expresses best
> how days have darkness round them like a rind,
> life has a skin of death that keeps its zest.[38]

Sensual celebration is placed in opposition to extinction in the paradigms of Harrison's work, but only language, whether as writing or as remembrance, can actively oppose extinction. Though creative, sometimes even manic, energy might seem to try to out-run death, the rhythm of the poems is both the pulse of life and the heart-beat ticking away the diminishing span of life. Death and extinction are ever-present and are both opposed and acknowledged as unfeared inevitables; the inescapable obverse to joy.

> If I had to divide the heart and the head, I would say that my head faces human history, and has a very bleak and pessimistic view of the possibilities for mankind, while at the same time I am very conscious of having a very sensual, celebratory nature: much of my work seems to be a confrontation of the two.[39]

Significantly, the only work of Virgil (whom Harrison acknowledges as an important formal model) which is explicitly named in the poems is the sixth book of *The Aeneid* – 'The World Below'.[40] As

---

36 See the discussion of 'First Aid in English' below.
37 Forbes, 'Bald Eagles', *Bloodaxe 1*, p. 491.
38 *Kumquat*, p. 193.
39 'Interview; p. 227.
40 'Study', *SP*, p. 115.

Morrison remarked of the collection *Continuous*, this poetry is obsessed 'with the same two topics, language and death'.[41] Forbes writes of Harrison, 'exploring his boundaries, weighing the whole of creation against the possibility of extinction and his own personal ark against the certainty of it'.[42] This little barque of life in Harrison's poetry is sometimes the poem, its boundaries of white page the limitless ocean of silence and annihilation, sometimes the dramatic *orchestra* of the play, and sometimes the wholehearted engagement of the senses with the material world emblematised in a 'spurt of spunk' or other concentrated burst of life-force. For Charles Segal, tragedy depends upon language. Elevated and extra-ordinary speech produces an effect of nobility which creates sympathy and suggests extraordinary responses.[43] Even though the tragic hero may be 'close to what we would consider morally bad [....] the grandeur of language that surrounds the hero is an essen-tial part of the tragic experience'. Certain passages in tragedy 'not only create in us the sense of tragic waste by depicting some quality of inner greatness, some valuable human quality, in the suffering hero, they also convince us of that greatness by enacting it in the grandeur of the poetry. The language, like the thought, rises to move us beyond the normal and carry us to the limits of the human experi-ence'.[44]

Segal quotes a line spoken by Seneca's Phaedra 'when she is about to make her fateful confession of love to Hippolytus: *curae leves loquuntur, ingentes stupent* ("Light cares are spoken; the great ones are silent," Pha. 607)', finding that, in 'this last passage the extraordinary moment of irrevocable and tragic decision is in fact enacted as a play of language: desires that must be kept repressed in silence break forth into speech, and the entire first part of the scene is in fact about speech and silence'. He believes that 'Racine takes over from Seneca this technique of highlighting the moments when terrible secrets emerge from the muted and penumbral background of conversations restrained by the *bienséance* of the Racinian conventions', and concludes, 'When translators ignore the dynamics of this chiaroscuro contrast, the results can be grotesque'.[45] Where

---

41 Blake Morrison, 'Labouring: Continuous', *Bloodaxe 1*, p. 220.
42 Forbes, 'Bald Eagles', p. 491.
43 Charles Segal, *Interpreting Greek Tragedy* (New York, 1986), p. 340.
44 Segal, *Greek Tragedy*, pp. 339–40.
45 Segal, *Greek Tragedy*, p. 340.

Racine and Seneca work from a norm of linguistic taboo and conventional decorum, Harrison, typically more ambiguous, usually depicts linguistic restraint as a negative force, and passionate, unrestrained, powerful language as liberating. Poetry speaks against the silenced as well as the silent.[46] *Phaedra* pits the code of the Raj rulers against that of India, Victorian repression against overwhelming passion, civilised interior (the governor's palace) against the outside, nature, animality, the jungle (whose function corresponds with that of the sea in the Greek tragedy). Thus, the Ayah tries to make the Memsahib speak, and relieve herself of the guilty secret which is consuming her.

> Blush, Memsahib, but blush that you stay mute
> and make your sufferings much more acute.[47]

The Memsahib resolves to preserve a British reticence:

> Better to let my heart's dark secret go
> with my dead body to the earth below.[48]

When she says,

> Don't, ayah. Stop insisting. It's no good.
> This unspeakable truth would chill your blood.[49]

the Ayah responds:

> Is truth so terrible, Memsahib? *Wai*,
> could anything be worse than watch you die?

Failure to speak is, as elsewhere in Harrison's poetry, equated with a living (as well as an ultimately actual) death.

> No time to waste. Each moment of delay
> Memsahib's precious lifeblood ebbs away.[50]

By allowing the Memsahib to think herself 'persuaded' to confess her love for Thomas, the Ayah takes upon herself the guilt of revelation. Giving way to the confessional urge can be blamed on the steamy atmosphere of India which weakens and saps western constitutions and minds.

---

46 See, for example, 'On Not Being Milton', *SP*, p. 112.
47 *Phaedra*, p. 8.
48 *Phaedra*, p. 9.
49 *Phaedra*, p. 10.
50 *Phaedra*, p. 9.

AYAH (On her knees.)
Memsahib, by these tears that wet your dress
rid Ayah of her anguish, and confess.

MEMSAHIB (After a pause.)
You wish it? Then I will [....]

I was about to die and hide away
this sordid secret from the light of day.
But your entreaties wouldn't let me rest.
I gave in to your tears and I confessed.[51]

Not to speak will lead to oblivion, but so will speaking the forbidden. Language, once unleashed, is unstoppable. Though Ayah implores:

MEMSAHIB
I couldn't bring myself to speak his name.[52]

AYAH
Forget! Forget! The great wheel we are on
turns all that horror to oblivion.[53]

Once the words are spoken there is no calling them back. The voicing of the Memsahib's passion sets the tragedy in motion. Despite the silence by which Thomas tries to 'Consign the horror to eternity', the Memsahib knows:

Such thoughts which never ought to even reach
the conscious mind I've put into plain speech.[54]

Once the thought has been aired, though Thomas might 'stay dumb', the Memsahib can't forget. Her own words prod memory and conscience, returning to torment her:

Each word I said
keeps echoing and booming through my head.
Those beastly heads his study's full of roar
as we enter *adulteress* and *whore*.
I see the hand of judgement start to scrawl
graffiti of my guilt on every wall.[55]

---

51 *Phaedra*, pp. 10–13.
52 *Phaedra*, p. 11.
53 *Phaedra*, p. 10.
54 *Phaedra*, p. 26.
55 *Phaedra*, p. 30.

Private thoughts once uttered become public. 'Death's the only answer.' Or obliteration of the guilt and shame by another suppression, more concealment. The Memsahib's accusation of Thomas, and deception of her husband through her complicity with the Ayah, seem to modern audiences worse sins than her attraction to Thomas. Thus a second silence condemns her.

MEMSAHIB
Purity put down? Innocence oppressed?

AYAH
Only keep silent and I'll do the rest.[56]

Similarly, Lilimani tells Thomas, 'Your keeping silent's suicide!', but he knows that only their unsullied love for one another makes permissible, and enables them to support, the revelation of the 'fullest horror'.

If I didn't love you would I have revealed
obscenities to *you* I'd want concealed
even from myself? [. . . .]
And even if it proves at my expense
I have to make you swear to reticence.

In this world, silence is the respect due to the social system, and its prop. Harrison's translation of the lines quoted by Segal in support of his finding modern versions of *Phaedra* 'grotesque' are, arguably, far less subtle than Racine's, and, perhaps, as heavy-handed and over-explicit, as Robert Lowell's.[57] Harrison does, however, retain the tragedy's 'coming together of strength and weakness [which] is clothed in a language that convinces us of the importance of the suffering'.[58] Significantly, the strength and weakness coincide, but do not blend.

The dialectic or dialogism in Harrison's work, and his status as an ambiguous partisan and atheist commentator, might usefully be seen in terms of the Greek *agon*.[59] The word's shift in meaning from an athletic contest to a struggle, to any conflict or anguish of mind,

---

56 *Phaedra*, p. 31.
57 Segal quotes Seneca, *Phaedra*, 710–12 and its equivalent in Racine's *Phèdre*, *Greek Tragedy*, p. 340.
58 Segal, *Greek Tragedy*, p. 341.
59 A useful survey of forms of the *agon* in Greek drama is given in Michael Lloyd, *The* Agon *in Euripides* (Oxford, 1992).

makes it applicable not only to Harrison's dramatisation of formal debate after the Classical model, for example between Kyllene and the satyrs, and between Philinte and Alceste, but also to his drama of antagonists and opposition, and his poetry of internal tension, conflict and anguish. His attempt to recreate the conditions of Greek theatrical performances (for example his thwarted plan to divide the audience of *The Oresteia* by gender) suggests an attempt to extend the *agon* from the author to the drama to the audience, as in the 'performance culture' of fifth-century Athens. Harrison's allegiance to London and the South Bank complex is not the same as Euripides's allegiance to and depiction of Athens, but there are parallels between the two. The goddess Athene, patron of Athens, appears in several Classical Greek plays, local references are scattered through Euripides's work, and Athens is the home or destination of many of his characters. 'The implication is not that she offers a refuge from tragic conflict, but quite the opposite, that the city of the audience is where the tragic tensions meet and must be confronted.'[60] *Trackers* is not a tragedy, but its National Theatre text does incorporate local references and actors playing local characters (the homeless of cardboard city) and depicts a 'real' scenario of homeless people/vandals playing football with torn and rolled- up paper which could be just the scene through which theatre-goers would pass on their way out of the South Bank. Thus, the *agon*, passed to the audience by the questions posed by Silenus, goes home with them.

Similarly, the audience of *Chorus* is 'drawn into' the action by the carol:

> Britain's not a dancing nation
> not like the ancient Greeks before us.
> But the joy of reprieved creation
> moves us as a common chorus.[61]

The historical and mythical part of the play ends with a Geordie soldier lobbing Budweiser cans over the wire, bringing the action into now, and the audience's final view of the play is of the actresses who have been playing Lysistrata and other Greek women being arrested in their 'real' (or first fictional) personae of Greenham

---

60 Rehm, Rush, *Greek Tragic Theatre* (London, 1994), p. 73.
61 *Chorus*, p. 85.

protesters. The stage directions refer to the arresting officers as 'a real POLICE INSPECTOR with POLICE and BAILIFFS',[62] and their destruction of the women's benders was an event which, at the time of the play's composition, did often happen. Having watched the enactment of the *agon* concerning war, the audience takes away an impression of a 'real' camp's destruction, and the non-resolution of a 'real' current debate. Just as in *Ion* tragic elements are followed by comic, and vice versa, and an almost farcically contrived 'happy ending' is stage-managed by Apollo,[63] in *Chorus* the success of the play-within-a-play and the singing and dancing, the shared beer-drinking and chat (as opposed to traded insults and propaganda) between the women and the soldiers is swiftly undermined by the final scene. Euripides creates a sense of unease and makes us ask: is that it? Does he (Euripides) really want us to take this at face value? What's he (Apollo) hiding? The god's fiction is foregrounded above that of the play's own, and made flawed and unconvincing; we go away, arguing with him or his author, or both. Similarly, *Chorus*, with elements of comedy and tragedy, with its own fictional devices bared, leaves a sense of unease and of continuing conflict. The pro-war camp is so palpably blind, misled, or wrong-headed; their arguments so specious – what are they hiding? Rehm's remarks on Euripides's *Ion* could, I suggest, apply equally well to much of Tony Harrison's work.

> By enjambing humour with pathos, by overlapping the ludicrous with the deadly serious, *Ion* reveals a world of disturbing complexity. Euripides does not blend the opposites in a palatable mix to be swallowed whole, but rather juxtaposes one mood against the other so surprisingly that we view both the curative powers of the comic and the deadly acts of the tragic as a form of critical re-evaluation – a way of thinking anew the gods, the myths, the politics, and the social mores that inform the world of the play.[64]

Classical drama shares or describes many of the antimonies which provide the conflict and debate in Harrison's writing, for example, high ideals and compromised actions, enlightenment and irrationality, civilisation and barbarity. Dramatic characters may take up a position on these issues, or may represent or personify

---

62 *Chorus*, p. 86.
63 Apollo sends Athene to make explanations. See Euripides, *Ion*, *Bacchae*, pp. 86–8.
64 Rehm, *Greek Tragic Theatre*, p. 142.

them, but neither debates between two such characters nor the juxta-position of two extreme types of behaviour is necessarily designed to suggest that only one of the positions or advocates is logically or ethically acceptable. Though Classical Greek drama valorises the Hellenic civilisation, it did not present the (Athenian) ideals of that civilisation as purely those of restraint, rationality and reason. 'For Greeks, "civilized" life meant controlled, orderly, proportionate life, τὸ μηδὲν ἄλαν, "No excess".'[65] To be ordered and propor-tioned, a life must have its measure of disorder. The civilised state and the civilised individual needed their uncontrolled, barbarian aspect, even if not in equal measure. 'In the great world the forces of civilization are in a heroic minority [. . . .] In a Greek city [. . .] the forces of civilization rule, and barbarism appears [. . .] as the heroic minority.' Thus

> when a community or a nation has adopted, in its political and social institutions the quality of self-control, *sophrosyne*, it soon learns that this quality belongs only in limited measure to its citizens; that the prin-ciple of barbarous excess is predominant in most individuals, so that the constant concern of government is to deal with barbarism inside the walls and in the council-chamber, as well as in foreign lands.[66]

The figure of the barbarian became both the feared outsider and the scapegoat. 'Just as in the modern world democracy, desperate to resist totalitarians, resorts to totalitarian methods, weakening its own life in the process, so the fiery Greek temperament made the menace of barbarism the excuse for its own excesses.' The virtues of restraint and control are exaggerated in Harrison's Jason, and 'joined with a calculating coldness and an unscrupulous want of feeling'. The lesson of *Medea*, like that of other Classical Greek plays, 'is that civilised men ignore at their peril the world of instinct, emotion, and irrational experience; that carefully worked-out notions of right and wrong are dangerous unless they are flexible and allow for constant adjustment'.[67] Harrison echoes this in his discussion of a line from Racine's *Phèdre*, 'La fille de Minos et de Pasiphaë', which he regards as the key to the inner struggle of Phèdre, to her essential torment (though only for those who are familiar with the genealogies of Cretan mythology).

---

65 Vellacott, *Medea et al.*, introduction, p. 8.
66 Vellacott, *Medea et al.*, introduction, pp. 8–9.
67 Vellacott, *Medea et al.*, introduction, p. 9.

As eighteenth century commentators puts it, [*sic*] this line '*semble préparer le spectateur à ce caractère mélangé de vices et de remords que le poète donne a Phèdre.*' The key word in this is *mélangé*. Many simply stress that the line signals the bad heredity of Phèdre, as if it were simply a case of the mother, Pasiphaë, though R. C. Knights tentatively suggests that 'Minos *may* perhaps stand for moral conscience.' Both elements of Phèdre's parentage are of equal importance [....] The polarities represented by Minos and Pasiphaë are those which maintain the tension of the whole play and not simply the character of Phèdre. Minos and Pasiphaë, an emblematical marriage, are the opposite poles of the human consciousness.[68]

Harrison reminds readers that Minos is 'the judge who *punishes* crime', who, 'Interiorized psychologically, as he is in Phèdre', is the part of the self which is 'judgement, prescription, that part that creates moral codes, imposes laws, fixes limites [*sic*]'.[69] Phèdre, then, represents not just individual *sophrosyne* but that aspect of us which contributes to and colludes with collective constraint, creates 'the "frontiers" of experience, defines the acceptable, and punishes transgression'. Pasiphaë, Minos's opposite, 'is the transgressor of the codes created by Minos, that part of ourselves that hungers for every experience, burns to go beyond the frontiers of current acceptability' – another Harrison blasphemer/transgressor. The balance between Apollo and Dionysus, Minos and Pasiphaë, was not a matter of the former's civilising restraint obliterating, or at least repressing, the latter's chaos, but an ideal of equilibrium, rarely realised. Thus, the Classical Greek tragedy and satyr play could be said to have constituted a single dramatic performance which, in Bakhtinian terms, was a kind of novel. That the drama/novel presented the whole picture – Medea and Jason, Minos and Pasiphaë – did not mean that it depicted a perfectly balanced society, or an ideal of humanity as emblematic of that perfection. The end of the play might appear to resolve certain loose ends and knit up the fractured society, but that coherence was not shown as sustainable. In Euripides's *Medea*, the sun, Harrison's 'common light', appears,

> vindicating the cause of passion, disorder, violent cruelty, against the cold, orderly, self-protective processes of civilised man [... A]

---

68 *Phaedra*, preface, p. viii.
69 *Phaedra*, preface, p. ix.

reminder that the universe is not on the side of civilization; and that a life combining order with happiness is something men must win for themselves in continual struggle with an unsympathetic environment.[70]

Harrison's *Medea* makes Medea and the other women the heroic minority embodying passion, while Jason is a colder, more calculating figure whose self-control is based upon self-interest. Unlike Euripides's play, Harrison's does not initially present Medea as a wronged victim deserving of our sympathy, and then, by showing her revenge to be more terrible than the crime committed against her, cause that sympathy to ebb away. Harrison's conflation of women from real news stories, Medea, and the triple goddess, makes the central character more obviously identifiable with all women, all victims of gender inequality, and thus, perhaps, a more thoroughly sympathetic character, in spite of the murders. The effect, however, could be to remove sympathy from Medea in particular and the play in general, as the audience reacts against all the parallels it is ordered to make: the texts in Greek, Latin, French, and English; the news stories from all over the world; the dragoness, goddesses 1, 2, and 3, soprano, mezzo, and contralto, Butes's wife and Medea as maiden, mother and crone, infanticides, abused wife.[71] Making explicit and reiterating:

> As part of their hostile campaign
> against the old Earth Mother's reign
> men degrade her[72]

In this way Harrison's play is closer than Euripides's to Eagleton's model of the mythological.

The parallels between Harrison's work and the Classical Greek dramatists' is not restricted to his direct translations and adaptations. Carnivalesque characters of Harrison's such as the satyrs of *Trackers*, Prometheus, and Alan of *Yan Tan Tethera* can be attributed to the positive, life-affirming side of the Dionysian instinct, while Caleb Raven and the Piper/Bad'un of *Yan Tan Tethera*, the Miller's Servant of *Bow Down*, the Memsahib of *Phaedra*, and Medea belong to its dark side. Off-stage characters such as the Ayattolah Khomeini (*Banquet*), and abstractions such as religion

---

70 Vellacott, *Medea et al.*, introduction, p. 9.
71 *Medea*, *TW*, pp. 446–8.
72 *Medea*, *TW*, pp. 431–2.

and divisive, Cold War politics ('The Chopin Express') which inhibit the individual, censor art, or break up the community and other bonds can be similarly ranked. The heroes of Harrison's dramatic poetry might seem more often to represent the Dionysian than the Apollonian side, partly because the division between temperaments is made one of class; the poor finding relief from labour and oppression in the free pursuits of singing, dancing, and/or sex. Both cults had mysteries and initiates, but the worship of Apollo was ritualistic, orderly, and located in man-made temples, while Dionysus could be worshipped in spontaneous, orgiastic festivals under the sky. To preserve this sense of a people's entertainment in his *Mysteries*, Harrison and his producer, Bill Bryden, employed a number of staging devices which removed the sense of division between actors and audience; the remove between performance and 'life'.

> Mr Bryden realised that he had to stage the plays as promenades, undermine self-consciousness with what I suppose must be called community dancing and by moving the action in and out of the crowd, and make the players mingle with the spectators at every possible opportunity.[73]

Bernard Levin asks how it is possible to turn a twentieth-century audience 'whose religion (if any) has been filleted, denatured and sterilised, into a body of men and women to whom Mary the Mother of God is as real as Mary the mother of that little red-headed pest who I'll beat the living daylights out of if he pinches any more of my apples?' The answer seems to be that it can be done by drawing the audience into participation in a Dionysian rite, by making the actors sing, dance, and above all project an energetic involvement in a shared activity. It can be done, 'by working with the actors until they are freed of the bonds of artifice and elocution, until the sword of technique is beaten into the ploughshares of truth, until they fuse into the words and characters in the terrible furnace of what and whom they are portraying'.

Levin could see the audience 'responding to the stupendous energy the cast were imbued with and expending, almost literally catching it like a fever, until they ached to be given a part themselves and play it'. He describes the performance, on stage and in

---

73 Bernard Levin, 'When Mystery was an Open Book', *The Times* (19 April 1985), reprinted in *Bloodaxe 1*, p. 328.

the auditorium, as a Dionysian outpouring which sweeps up every-one present into a state of ecstatic *furor* and a communal act of celebration. Thus the actress playing Eve:

> is part of a group which performs a dance of celebration, in form some-thing between Sir Roger de Coverly and a Morris dance. As she came round each time, I saw her face clearly; she was illuminated from within, rapt with the tremendousness of the story now moving to its climax [....] Or take the young man who plays, among other parts, Isaac. He, in turn, was part of a chorus at the funeral of the Virgin; as he too, came round again, he was singing the hymn of triumph in such roaring ecstasy that I thought the heart would burst out of his body.[74]

Such acts generate a sense of unity,

> a welding of actor, audience, play and story into one whole that gives the performance its unique quality – and I wish there were another word for performance, for it diminishes the thing that has been created, which far transcends any idea of a theatre as a place which we visit to see a play, and of a play as that which we visit a theatre to see.

The chaos of war might suggest Dionysian associations, but in Harrison's poetry war (rather than fighting) stems from the Apollonian. In the opening opposition of the educated, sneering prolixity of Fritz Haber and the demotic of Sweeper Mawes, Harrison depicts the origin of war in flawed reasoning and causes for which its ruthless instigators feel no passion, and he shows war's perpetuation as a series of intellectual problems to be solved by inventors and scientists. Once again, women represent the warm, loving aspect of the Dionysian which strives to be one with nature, and opposes the wholesale destructiveness of war.

> ### CLARA HABER
> I gave up chemistry to serve you as a wife
> now you betray our science to poison life.
> The beneficial chemistry that was our bond before
> broken when I saw science made to serve the war.[75]

Thus Dionysus takes on aspects of the Earth Mother.

Similarly, in *Kaisers*, both Apollonian Marcus Aurelius and Dionysian (in the sense of uncontrolled and sensual) Commodus are to blame for the bloodshed of the later Roman Empire, and it is

---

74 Levin, 'When Mystery was an Open Book', p. 329.
75 *Square Rounds*, pp. 41–2.

Faustina, wife and mother, who is the voice of compassion, like the
Chorus of mams from *Big H* and the absent women of the ancient
play *Halosis Miletou* from *Labourers*.[76]

> Dad's
> not the most inspiring of Dionysian ads.[77]

But his son is a fine ranting Herod, a 'proper intemperate, unrepen-
tant boozer' whose comic relish for his reign of terror enables
Harrison to refuse to let the audience avert their minds from the realities of the past by swallowing the Disneyfied version.

> It's good to smell fresh gore, and we've only just begun.
> Why did I kill this fool? I'll tell you why.
> Because this is a place for watching people die.
> So far as I know, there has never been a
> poetic play performed in this arena.
> and yet this sign says it was. Oh why
> this modern squeamish need to Disneyfy
> this space that was made for men and beasts to die?[78]

The vehicle of Commodus is even turned upon Harrison's beloved
Greek theatre.

> It was Greeks who played around in masks like these,
> spouting their Aeschylus and Sophocles
> We got rid of the verbiage and hacked
> our villains and our beasts in actual fact.
> Where Greek choruses bewailed their woes
> became for Rome a place where real blood flows.
> Where the Greeks did death it was all pretend;
> here beasts and bastards come to a real end.[79]

Dionysus and the Dionysian seem to me to have special significance for Harrison's work. Dionysus represented the instinctive side
of human nature 'which by its simplicity by-passes all the errors of
rational man, enjoys the life of the senses without the ability or
desire to analyse it, is vividly conscious of unity with the animal
world, and contains within itself that potential of divinity and supernatural power which Greeks always recognized in animals'.[80] For

---

76 See *Kaisers*, pp. 97–102, and *Labourers*, pp. 126–7, 143–7.
77 *Kaisers*, p. 71.
78 *Kaisers*, p. 75. The full point after 'arena' is followed by lower-case 'and'.
79 *Kaisers*, p. 76.
80 Vellacott, *Bacchae*, introduction, p. 30.

Vellacott, 'the first rise of [the Dionysian cults ...] was an instinctive reaction of the healthy, freedom-loving mind and flesh of
humanity against the curbs applied by the spread of civilized
communities and law'. He finds that 'Greek common-sense recognized the necessity of such reaction, and provided a safety-valve by
sanctioning Dionysian rites at certain periodic festivals'.[81] Far from
being an inescapable force, the Dionysian impulse is shown to be
kept in check by the Apollonian side of human nature. 'Each side of
man's nature tends to fear and despise the other; birth may be mani-
fested at different times in the same person or the same society.
When the civilized grows arrogant and masterful, it is betrayed from
within by the bestial, as Pentheus is betrayed by his own instinctive
fear and violence.' Only in the Arcadian Golden Age, however, is
the balance depicted as having been maintained for long, within
either the individual or society as a whole. Humanity is a state of
internal and external tension.[82]

The 'I' of the longer non-dramatic poems, as poet, kumquat-
grower, snake-preserver, and lover, might be seen as a Dionysian
hero, but that 'I' is also an intellectual, scholar, and translator. He is
both the Dionysian raider of high culture in 'Them & [uz]' and the
Apollonian poet, conscious of his craft and its worth, in 'The Heartless
Art'. He does not embody a perfect mingling of opposing attributes but
is a site of struggle, a personification of the *agon*. *Fire-Gap* was
composed long after the time remembered in *v*. when the young
Harrison came down on the side of Dionysus, and the Apollonian side
had been dominant for some time. Though the company of red-necks,
'Bible-belters', and alligator-killers provokes Harrison to feats of
competitive manliness, it also makes him exaggerate and withdraw
into his persona of erudite contemplative. In this poem the subject, and
thus the normative standard, is Apollonian. The Other is the Dionysian
rattle-snake, representing elemental nature, sex, mythical/mystical
resonance and the wild. The poet intellectualises the snake:

> I've tried at last to come to terms
> and deal only through my craft
> with this laithliest of laithly worms[83]

---

81 Vellacott, *Bacchae*, introduction, p. 32.
82 The Apollo/Dionysus is not, of course, the only dyad used in Greek drama,
   which might equally be described in terms of, for example, Stoicism and
   Hedonism.
83 *Fire-Gap*, p. 216.

Though he responds to its beauty, and can enumerate its associations for different cultures, it still evokes terror:

> with poison fore, grim music aft
> that makes my heart jam up my throat
> and fills me with fear and wonder

Walking to the shrine of art and intellect, the writing shed, through the tamed, man-made clearing of the fire-gap, past the primaeval wilderness, the epitome of civilised man is

> so scared that I mistake
> the rattle of my thermos ice
> for the angry rattlesnake[84]

The passing of the rattle-snake not only leaves small signs on the environment but also, like that of Pan or the triple goddess, generates a powerful, involuntary reaction in those nearby.

> Is it perverse of me to start
> each morning as I pass the hole
> with a sudden pounding of my heart,
> my fear out of control,
> My Adam's apple in a vice [. . . .]
>
> I've started when a pine twig broke
> or found I'd only been afraid
> of some broken branch of dead live-oak
> zig-zagged with sun and shade.
> But if some barley starts to sway
> *against* the movement of the breeze
> and most blades lean the other way

Like Robert Graves, Harrison describes an experience in purely physical and tangible terms, yet manages to endow it with a sense of the uncanny and other-worldly which combines the fearful and erotic.[85] The snake, then, is the Other, the strange, silent, inhuman Wild which is waiting 'to get' Harrison the city-dweller. It is also sacrosanct, mysterious: 'it seemed gross sacrilege to kill' it. Harrison's heart is 'mysteriously stirred' if he has 'a glimpse of tail or head' or thinks he hears the rattle of the tail. The terror becomes a kind of holy awe, and the frightened man becomes also a kind of votary or priest.

---

84 *Fire-Gap*, p. 215.
85 See Robert Graves, 'On Portents', *Collected Poems*, p. 107.

I go past the deep-dug gopher hole
where I hope my snake will stay
and stay forever if it likes.
I swear no one on this land will kill
the rattlesnake unless it strikes[86]

By the end of the poem he is identifying with the snake as an accursed outcast whom the Bible-belters would exorcise, a fellow emblem of (ironically) hot blood, blasphemy and passion.

Once you cross my boundary line
the Bible-belters exorcize
all traces of the serpentine,
from Satan plain to demon drink
the flesh you're blamed for keeping hot,
all earth-embracing snakes that slink
whether poisonous or not,
the fairy, pacifist, the Red,
maybe somebody who loves the Muse
are all forms of the serpent's head
their God tells them to bruise

The *agon* takes place as Harrison recalls an occasion when the poet who appreciates the snake's beauty and grace was pushed into the background by the father who defends his children.

I killed snakes once, about a score
in Africa and in Brazil[87]

Even while he recollects the frightened children and 'all our lives at stake', he remembers:

yet they filled me with such awe
it seemed gross sacrilege to kill.

The impulses struggle. 'The snake and I swayed to and fro'; the practical man and father wins:

I jabbed the broom. She rode the blow
and I hacked off her hooded head.
Then I lopped this 'laithly worm'
and sliced the creature into nine
reptilian lengths that I saw squirm
as if still one connected spine.[88]

---

86 *Fire-Gap*, pp. 217–18.
87 *Fire-Gap*, p. 215.
88 *Fire-Gap*, p. 216.

As soon as the snake is dead, however, and the immediate danger past, the Dionysian poet resurfaces, and so do the poetic associations:

> the gaps between the bits I'd lopped
> seemed supple snake though made of air
> so that I wondered where life stopped
> and if death started, where?

The snake becomes an emblem of the older religions trodden under the heel of the new.

> The sainted heroes of the Church
> beheaded serpents who stood for
> the Mother whose name they had to smirch
> to get their own foot in the door.[89]

The poet identifies himself with the newer faiths/enlightenment:

> We had to fight you to survive:
> Darkness versus Light!

In the very next line, however, his sympathy has returned to the snake, or he draws the snake into his own symbolic system, and his persona returns to the familiar anti-Christian.

> Now I want you on my land alive
> and I don't want to fight.
> Smitten by Jehovah's curses:
> On thy belly thou must go!
> I don't think Light is what you're versus
> though the Bible tells me so.

Poet becomes the 'unlikely ally' of rattler when he sees the snake as an emblem of conjoined opposites.

> I've seen you basking in the sun.
> I've seen you entering the earth.
> Darkness and Light to you are one.
> You link together death and birth.

– which leads to a further link:

> The Bible has another fable
> that almost puts us on a par,

---

89 *Fire-Gap*, pp. 216–17.

how God smote low ambitious Babel
for trying to reach too far.

Harrison's social ascent via diversity of (forked) tongues is equated
with the fate of both the Tower of Babel and the serpent of Eden.
Thus:

From being once your mortal foe
and wanting all your kind to die
because the Bible told me so,
I now almost identify.

Thus the poet claims exemption from the rattler's fangs because he
is pursuing that which the snake embodies.

I'm walking to my shed to write
and work out how they're linked
what's called the Darkness and the Light
before we all become extinct.
Laithly, maybe, but Earth-lover,
unmolested let me go,
so my struggles might discover
what you already know.

From feared Other, the snake has become totem animal; from
terrified killer, the poet has become protector and shaman, mysti-
cally linked to the snake.

I fear they're not the sort to see,
these Christians of the South,
the only real eternity
is a tale (like your tail) in the mouth.[90]

Harrison comes off rather better from his encounters with the snake
than D. H. Lawrence did in the poem which is one of the models for
Fire-Gap. Harrison's first encounter ended in the killing of the
snake, but, abhorrent though it is, we excuse it as the act of a father
protecting children. Lawrence, experiencing his own *agon*, allows
the 'voices' of his education and masculine vanity to over-rule his
respect and admiration, breaks the sacred law of hospitality, and
commits an act which even he recognises is paltry, vulgar, and
mean. He throws a log at the water-trough:

---

90 *Fire-Gap*, p. 219.

And so, I missed my chance with one of the lords
Of life.
And I have something to expiate;
A pettiness.[91]

Because he has his own dark sides; has explored his own black holes; Harrison's poet-voice, which identifies with the snake, is the loudest in his *agon*. He feels no horror, therefore, but only fascination when the snake leaves the light for the dark, and can respect, admire, and leave in peace his 'lord of life'.[92]

It may seem contradictory to insist that Harrison is not a modernist writer while suggesting that Dionysus, who has been described as the personification of modernism,[93] can provide insights into Harrison's work. Dionysus, not only one side of the debate and one pole of an opposition, but in himself the site of contradictions and oppositions, is well described by Segal as 'a threat not merely to the psychological coherence and integration necessary for Pentheus' successful passage from childhood to adulthood but also to that system of polarities on which Pentheus' rigid, authoritarian order rests'. Dionysus, then, is not only a symbol of that which Pentheus has repressed, 'the latent animality that turns back against himself in the god's tauriform epiphanies', but also a disrupter who 'breaks down all the familiar mediations, dissolves differentiation on every level into sameness, and through his function as the god of tragedy and the tragic mask also challenges the capacity of myth and language to mediate contradictions'. In the Dionysian realm, as in Freud's unconscious, 'fusion replaces boundary, and the mutually exclusive opposites of our everyday logic disturbingly coexist'.[94] This accords with Harrison's admiration for the Greek use of the mask, whose functions Rehm associates with Dionysus. Masks, as Rehm points out, allow an actor to merge or lose his or her self in alternative identities, 'fitting for a servant of Dionysus, the God of ecstasy (ek-stasis), literally "standing outside" oneself'. They also 'confront the audience with ambiguities of appearance and change, instantiating the conflicting urge to schematize and to personify'. In this way they 'enable the playwright to

---

91 D. H. Lawrence, 'Snake', *Selected Poems* (London, 1950), pp. 98–101.
92 He had even named a poem after them. See 'The Lords of Life', *SP*, pp. 209–13.
93 See, for example, Spears, *Dionysus*, p. 35.
94 Segal, *Greek Tragedy*, pp. 284–5.

present characters in terms of social role and type, rather than as the sum of personal characteristics', but as well as discriminating between individuals, they may also 'blur the lines between a group (grasped by recognizing similarities) and separate individuals (identified by isolating differences)'.[95]

The realm of Dionysus in Harrison's version of the Phaedra story is transferred from the sea to the jungle, an other-place of the wild, dim, tangled and mysterious. A product of neither modernist outsiderly ontological uncertainty, nor postmodernist refusal of distinctions such as in/outside, Harrison blurs boundaries in a way that suggests Dionysus's position as an anomalous figure resistant to commonplace definition. In *The Bacchae*, Dionysus 'enters Thebes as an outsider, a stranger from a barbarian land', yet he is not merely an outsider, as Segal shows.[96] Violently resisted by the king of Thebes, he is also a native of the city:

> with a legitimate claim on the city's allegiance. He combines his Olympian birth with the bestial forms of bull, snake, or lion in which he appears to his worshippers. his personal appearance fuses male and female characteristics, and his geographical associations join both Greek and barbarian, both local and universal attributes. as a kind of eternal adolescent, he stands between the child and adult. As a god of wine he embodies the life-giving forces of the earth, the moisture and sap of new vegetable growth; but he can also call the destructive power of the earth into his service when he shakes Pentheus' palace.

Dionysus is the personification of a spirit of disruption whose presence on stage as an actor in the drama, according to Segal,

> not only calls attention to the way in which tragedy and tragic myth open the secure structures of the society to the fluidity and changefulness inherent in the god, but also shows tragedy itself, as it were, demarcating before our eyes what Victor Turner calls the 'liminal space', a space between order and disorder, a realm of disturbing but also potentially fruitful disintegration of familiar boundaries and identities.

Greek mythology provides many models of dispossession and liminality, in particular, perhaps, Tithonus.[97] Tithonus gains immortality but not eternal youth. He lives neither on earth nor Olympus, and dines not only on ambrosia but also grain. Aeneas, son of mortal

---

95 Rehm, *Greek Tragic Theatre*, p. 39.
96 Segal, *Greek Tragedy*, p. 285.
97 In, for example, *The Homeric Hymn to Aphrodite*.

Anchises and immortal Aphrodite (a union which, as Segal remarks, 'hovers ambiguously between the pure lust of seduction and the sanction of marriage') himself 'hovers ambiguously between recognition by his parents and concealment by his parents'.[98] He spends his early years in a forest, between the city and the wild, where his nurses are nymphs who live on earth but eat 'immortal food', who are not immortal but have a lifespan measured by the lives of forest trees. Such dispossessed and estranged yet characteristically self-possessed figures appear to transcend the social, political, geographical, and historical limitations imposed by collective identities, and Dionysus is the most potent of all. As Segal says, in shattering the 'secure limits and well defined polarities of Pentheus' world, Dionysus reveals the hidden truth of the king's identity as both man and beast, both confident ruler and chaotic, bestial madman, both the celebrant and the sacrificial victim'.[99] The god is also the spirit of solidarity, the spirit of the collective, which could cut across the usual distinctions of class and status. Whereas Apollo demanded that his followers act their appointed role in their appointed stations, remaining within the cell of their respective individuality, the ecstatic worship of Dionysus broke down the divisions between people.

> Dionysus offered freedom: 'Forget the difference, and you will find the identity; join [us], and you will be happy today.' [....] Apollo moved only in the best society, from the days when he was Hector's patron to the days when he canonised aristocratic athletes; but Dionysus was [...] a god of the people.[100]

(We can see why Silenus is so misplaced in his servitude to Apollo in *Trackers*.) This social function of Dionysus was two-edged. Whilst his rituals dissolved barriers and promoted a sense of collectivity – oneness – and were thus liberatory and communal, they also dissolved any sense of uniqueness, of individuality, and were thus destructive and repressive – or useful and therapeutic, depending upon your point

---

98 Segal, *Greek Tragedy*, p. 60.
99 Dionysus expelled Cadmus, who had migrated to civilised Hellenic Thebes from barbarous Sidon, and founded the race of Thebans from the sown teeth of the serpent he had slain. Cadmus was driven into the wild, 'transformed into the "savage form" [...] of a snake, the creature he killed in his initial founding act. He who left barbarians for Greeks is condemned to lead barbarian hordes against Greek shrines and cities'. Segal, *Greek Tragedy*, p. 285.
100 E. R. Dodds, *The Greeks and the Irrational* (Berkeley, 1966), p. 76.

of view. Dionysus is 'the god who by very simple means or by other means not so simple, enables you for a short time *to stop being yourself*, and thereby sets you free' – for Dodds the secret of his appeal to the Archaic Age. This was not only because 'life in that age was often a thing to escape from, but more specifically because the individual, as the modern world knows him, began in that age to emerge for the first time from the old solidarity of the family, and found the unfamiliar burden of individual responsibility hard to bear'.[101] Dodds regards Dionysian (among other) rites as cathartic and purgative, purely temporary, therapy to promote psychological balance – 'social hygiene'.[102] In this light, the function of the cult of Dionysus is to relieve the individual of social responsibility, 'to satisfy and relieve the impulse to reject responsibility, an impulse which exists in all of us and can become under certain social conditions an irresistible craving'.[103] The aristocratic Apollo, then, is opposed to this daemon of collective irresponsibility as a kind of benign despot or feudal lord, exercising the responsibility of power, protective *and* oppressive of his people – truly a cowherd. To attribute to Harrison's work a Dionysian motif which can be equated with class solidarity and socialism is perhaps to reinterpret the myth. In Harrison's work, however, Dionysian groups such as the Greenham women do produce the voice of (social and ecological) responsibility, while those vested with authority exercise and abuse power without regard for the long-term effects of their actions.

The 'demoniac chant of the multitude' which Nietzsche contrasts with the 'thin, monotonous harp music' of Apollo[104] reappears in Harrison's *Trackers* as the disembodied voices of eight thousand spectators at the Pythian Games.[105] 'The essence of Dionysus, Nietzsche says, is the shattering of the *principium individuationis* for which Apollo stands: in Dionysiac rapture and awe walls are broken down and the bonds between man and man and between man and nature are re-forged.' Thus, the individual 'forgets himself in the Dionysiac vortex'.[106]

---

101 Dodds, *Greeks and the Irrational*, pp. 76–7.
102 Dodds, *Greeks and the Irrational*, p. 79.
103 Dodds, *Greeks and the Irrational*, p. 77.
104 F. Nietzsche, *The Birth of Tragedy* (1872), trans. Francis Golffing, in *The Modern Tradition*, eds Richard Ellman and Charles Fieldelson (New York, 1965), p. 555.
105 *Trackers*, Delphi text, pp. 22, 28, 29, 30, 63, and 70.
106 Spears, *Dionysus*, p. 36.

Harrison is not, of course, alone or even unusual in adopting Dionysian themes. In a section which stretches the definition almost to breaking point, Spears finds that they are

> increasingly frequent from Blake on. The bourgeois are shocked and liberal humanism rejected at varying levels of profundity, from Blake's repudiation of everything Newton and Locke began and Sir Joshua Reynolds finished through many forms of Satanism, neo-paganism, and aestheticism to Dowson, Wilde, and the other Decadents of the 1890s; and from them the line is clear to Yeats and Pound.[107]

Harrison is different in that his work is neither wholly on the side of the Dionysian, like Blake's, nor moving from the Dionysian to Apollonian, like Yeats's.[108] Rather, it embodies the tension between intellectual and ethical systems combined with personal *sophrosyne* – in, for example, his restrained classical metre – and intoxication or passion leading to excess – in, for example, his use of dialect, the 't'' and ''s' form, and invective. Thematically, the work could be said to embody the Apollo–Dionysus dyad, weighted toward the Dionysian, but this is not to identify the Harrison 'I' with Dionysus. As Spears emphasises, Dionysus is not an artist, which is 'symbolically appropriate, for the drive beyond art to the apocalyptic and eschatological has been a central one'.[109] Particularly in his Gulf War poems, Harrison resembles the modern artists described by Spears, characteristically apocalyptic and eschatological even when they are atheistic and anti-clerical, and obsessively concerned with the Last Things: Death, Judgement, Heaven, Hell (or their secular equivalents). These tend to suggest:

> not only that the era that began with the Renaissance is ending, but that the whole human enterprise is likely to end at any moment, or to continue only in some fearfully inhuman mode [...] this catastrophism (one of the themes explored in Kermode's *Sense of an Ending*) begins with the hopes and fears arising toward the end of the last century (when, as the early scientific romances of H. G. Wells show so clearly, many people foresaw not only *fin de siècle* but *fin de globe*) and has since been fed by the emotions and apprehensions associated with the

---

107 Spears, *Dionysus*, p. 48.
108 Spears quotes from a letter of 1903 from Yeats to John Quinn, in which the poet hopes that he has 'got rid of that wild god Dionysus', and 'that the far-Darter will come in his place'. *Dionysus*, p. 48.
109 Spears, *Dionysus*, p. 40.

fact that the present century will mark the end of the second millennium A.D.[110]

While Harrison's poetry is concerned both with personal extinction and the apocalypse, he is not entirely misanthropic and pessimistic, with 'little interest in keeping the ship afloat, seeing that life goes on in the City'.[111] Though in his bleaker moments, 'prone as I am to despair',[112] he consigns humankind and its works to perdition, his expression of 'the anxiety of meaninglessness'[113] is tempered by the warmth of the tribe, and by hope, however tenuous, for the future.

> Most of my life I've wanted to believe
> those words of Luther that I've half-endorsed
> about planting an apple tree the very eve
> of the Apocalypse; or the Holocaust.[114]

Meaning is given to existence both by the intellect:

> Who lives for the future, who for now?
> What good's the *cigale*'s way or the *fourmi*'s
> if both end up as nothing anyhow
> unless they look at life like Socrates
> who wished, at the very end, to learn to play
> a new air on his novice lyre. *Why?*
> said his teacher, *this is your last day.*
> *To know it before I die,* was the reply.

– and, of course, by 'the ones we choose to love' who become 'our anchor'.[115]

> I will what's still a hedge to grow less slow,

> and be tall enough to mask the present view
> of you watering the saplings as you spray
> rainbows of fig-trees planted 2-1-2
> and both of us still nude at break of day.
> A morning incense smokes off well-doused ground.
> Everywhere you water rainbows shine.

110 Spears, *Dionysus*, pp. 53–4.
111 Spears, *Dionysus*, p. 53.
112 'Cypress & Cedar', *SP*, p. 233.
113 Paul Tillich, 'The Courage to Be', *Modern Tradition*, quoted in Spears, *Dionysus*, pp. 54–5.
114 'Following Pine', *SP*, p. 224.
115 *v.*, p. 31.

This private haven that we two have found
might be the more so when enclosed with pine.[116]

This enclosed private Eden is exclusive, a consolatory present rather
than a promise of redemption, and the image, earlier in the poem, of
the post-apocalyptic world dominated by insects, snakes, and
rodents, though in its way a consolatory vision of the continuance of
life, is based upon the anticipation of humanity's horrific end:

> it's often said that what will come off best
> once, step by step, we've reached All-Systems-Go,
> of all life on this Earth,'s the lowliest [. . . .]

> Even the love bugs, randy and ridiculous,
> coupling regardless of death close behind
> could still be fucking after all of us
> are merged in the molten mess made of mankind.[117]

'Cypress & Cedar' explicitly denies that art, or the single artist, is
the bright spot of hope for mankind's future:

> Let the candle cliché come out of the chill –
> 'the flickering candle on a vast dark plain'
> of one lone voice against the state machine,
> or Mimi's on cold stairs aren't what I mean[118]

Art does provide consolation, optimism and a quasi-religious experience, however, which enable the participator to transcend the
barriers of his or her skin to achieve communion not with god, but
other people. In a neat circularity, Harrison describes Greek drama
as a life-enabling, life-enhancing force of light (equated with life and
memory in Harrison's work) which confers a kind of immortality
upon its themes and characters; as a link between its Classical
Athenian and contemporary audiences which transcends temporality.
Yet the poet himself rescues Greek drama from the oblivion of the
forgotten (and, in *Trackers*, of the rubbish pit), and restores it to
light and life, a resurrection which extends to the play's author,
Sophocles, who is given a curtain-call.[119]

   The social function of art, the 'Big O' of the dramatic *orchestra*,
is opposed to the pessimism of the modernist, the cruelty and aggres-

---

116 'Following Pine', *SP*, p. 229.
117 'Following Pine', *SP,* p. 227.
118 'Cypress & Cedar', *SP*, p. 234.
119 *Trackers*, Delphi text, p. 71.

sion of the Dionysian, the nihilism of the atheist. The suspension of difference which the circle generates lasts only for the duration of the performance. Art does not provide solutions, it embodies struggle.

> Looking into that circle I once thought of it as the nightsky globe totally devoid of stars, an annihilated universe [....] It looked like this when my imagination couldn't cope with the twentieth century [....] I began to learn to people that scorched orchestra only after an immersion in the drama of the ancient Greeks. Things just as 'dark' occurred in this orchestra of Dionysus but it was lit by the sun and was surrounded by a community as bonded in their watching as we had been by our celebratory blaze.[120]

Shared participation in this struggle bonded the community. The

> 'light common to all' [...] is the first essential of ancient drama [...] it is not only the illumination in the sense of the lighting that unites audience and performer in a shared experience but also in the sense of spiritual understanding. Things are brought, as Oedipus says 'εις το φως', to the light, or as we might say, 'to the light of day'. Shared space and shared light.[121]

In this sense, literary art is in Harrison's work distinguished from the manipulation of language, and the poet from the scholar/linguist. The former is depicted as recording past failures of human compassion and understanding, and predicting future catastrophe, the latter is a putative agent of oblivion. Harrison's poems protest the right of all social groups to eloquence, both in the sense of the right to 'own' and to master the common language, and of the right of the dialect voice to have the same status as the 'literary' or privileged form, but they also issue a caveat about the consequences of mastery of the language system. 'First Aid in English' suggests that the study of grammar, the abstraction of the underlying regularities (*langue*) from utterances (*parole*) is a dangerous enterprise.[122] Divorcing language from context, distancing it from its application, can (literally) dehumanise and kill meaning – and people. School children chanting count and mass nouns which have been 'drilled into' them are 'parrots', giving no thought to the animals they name. The reader may infer that learned collective names for the human animal

---

120 *Trackers*, introduction, pp. vii–viii.
121 *Trackers*, introduction, p. ix.
122 *Gorgon*, p. 15.

– 'Nazi', 'Japanese' – are likewise robbed of resonance, becoming abstract signs signifying only within systems of (lexical) differences. The poem extends the concept of the de-association of words and living things by suggesting that the process can, finally, lead to extinction, oblivion. When animal species become extinct their names are redundant; the signifier has no significance without a referent. The word for the 'dodo couple' became 'in the last one's lifetime, obsolete'. When the human species becomes extinct, however, it is the destruction of the signified which will destroy the signifier, and all signifying. There is 'no aid in English [or any other language]' for genocide. Thus the splitting of the sign, the crucial ability to symbolise which, it could be argued, is definitive of imaginative, linguistic humankind, is equated with the splitting of the atom, the other end of the process wrought by human intellect:[123]

> Cats in their clowder, lions in their pride,
> but there's no aid in English, first or last,
> for a [Fill in the Blank] of genocide
> or more than one [Please Tick] atomic blast.

Language is not accused of causing extinction and genocide, but it is shown as standing helplessly, even callously, aside from the process. Unlike Patience Kershaw (in 'Working'), humankind will not be resurrected from the slagheap of the post-nuclear holocaust by a poet's embodiment in language, because there will be no poets. Those who are more concerned with reductive semiotics than the living functions of language are shown as dehumanising, and associated with a literal, apocalyptic dehumanisation. Harrison's poetry seems to suggest that it involves something other than the manipulation of signs. He implies a 'real presence' in his poetry, as though the dodo, the fritillary and the flambeau were in some sense 'there' behind the signifiers in the poet's imagination. Within that implication, however, is contradiction. Just as the collective in, for example, *Trackers* represents the social and egalitarian, and in 'First Aid in English' represents the de-individualised and atrophied, so poetry, which gives life to and celebrates the extinct dodo, oryx, and great auk, and almost-gone manucode, pygmy hippo and oviparous toad,[124] also records 'the whole fatuity of the belief that writing poetry will *do* anything' in the face of 'all the gale-force winds of

---

123 This theme is also developed in *Square Rounds*.
124 See 'Art & Extinction 6: t'Ark', *SP,* p. 189.

what negates' it: 'social indifference, self-destructiveness, time, nothingness'.[125]

> A language near extinction best preserves
> the deepest grammar of our nothingness.

Jeffrey Wainwright infers that 't'Ark' presents poetry, itself endangered, as the most suitable medium for a record of the obliteration of languages and cultures.[126] This reading – poetry as embattled and under-valued yet redemptive – would seem too obviously characteristic of Harrison's work to need elaboration, but a later poem, 'Killing Time', perhaps records a more ambiguous and complex conception of language. Looking into a display case at JFK airport, Harrison sees, together with Hawksbill Turtle, scrimshawed spermwhale bone, the Margay of the family *Felidae*, a reflection of 'the poet preserved beneath deep permaverse'.[127] Is this a bitter realisation that while poetry is a preserve, in both senses of the word, it preserves only to distance and to ossify, like a glass case? Or is it another realisation of the divisiveness of high art, and of the price Harrison pays; a suggestion, pre-empting *v.*'s accusations, that these days the poet is a removed, unreal figure, an exhibit behind glass?

It is in this simultaneous fascination with and mistrust of language that, I suggest, Harrison has his closest affinity with the Greek dramatists. In Classical times, 'the role of language in the production of meaning, in the development of thought, in the uncertainties of reference, is a regular source of debate not only at the level of philosophical enquiry or literary self-consciousness, but also in the more general awareness of the possibilities and dangers of the tricks and powers of words'.[128] Taking the *Oresteia* as his model, Simon Goldhill finds that 'the use of language constitutes one of the important themes' of Greek tragedy, justifying his description of this genre as the 'drama of logos'.

> The powers and dangers of language are essential to the narrative of revenge through the repeated acts of deceitful persuasion. The workings of language are traced and discussed through the different scenes of message-sending, sign-reading, interpretation and manipulation. The

---

125 Harrison 'in an interview in 1982', quoted in 'Introduction', p. 14.
126 See Jeffrey Wainwright, 'The Silence Round All Poetry', review of *School, Poetry Review*, 69, no. 1 (July 1979), pp. 57–9.
127 'Art & Extinction 4: Killing Time', *SP*, p. 187.
128 Simon Goldhill, *Reading Greek Tragedy* (Cambridge, 1986), p. 2.

search for the right word, the desire for accurate prediction and prophecy, the effects of blessing, curse and invocation are all linked to the understanding of the workings of language.[129]

Harrison's poetry similarly focuses on language as rhetoric – language in terms of its effect (its ability to move or convince).[130] Messages which are misunderstood or mis(re)interpreted, or which deceive, either because of their inherent ambiguity or a mis-match of linguistic codes, provide much dramatic matter.[131]

Goldhill could be describing *Chorus* or *Trackers* when he writes of tragic texts which associate social with linguistic confusion:

> which depict and analyse the tensions, uncertainties and collapse of social order, return again and again to the shifting, distorting qualities of language [....] repeated doubts and misgivings about the sense and usage of words [....] Lack of security and misplaced certainty in and about language form an essential dynamic of the texts of tragedy.[132]

If language is an agent and index of disruption and break-down, however, in Harrison's work it also represents salvation, and this, too, echoes Greek tragedy. 'As much as the earlier transgressions of the trilogy are committed through the misuse of language, the ending of the *Eumenides* attempts to right that disorder through the powers of the word.'[133] In speaking of the disruption of his early family life: 'I've being trying to create new wholes out of that disruption ever since. They're not reconcilable, it seems, in the kind of class system we have in England; they are reconcilable in the kind of emotion I would momentarily grant in certain poems' – Harrison appears to claim for his work a Classical emotive hedonism. He does not, however, suggest that his poems can produce permanent (re)solutions. The reconciliation, like the emotional response, is 'momentary' – 'I have to take it away in the next poem'.[134]

Earlier in the same interview, Haffenden noted this duality in Harrison's juxtaposition of language and extinction. 'You are on

---

129 Goldhill, *Reading Greek Tragedy*, p. 5.
130 See, for example, Athene's speech, which averts the Furies' curse. *Oresteia*, *TW*, pp. 286–9.
131 See, for example, the dialogue between skin and skald in *v.*, the description of Hugh Gaitskell's electioneering in the same poem, *v.*, p. 20, and the Ayah's message to the governor in *Phaedra*, p. 106.
132 Goldhill, *Reading Greek Tragedy*, pp. 2–3.
133 Goldhill, *Reading Greek Tragedy*, p. 5.
134 'Interview', p. 246.

record as having said elsewhere that "a poem is a momentary defeat of pessimism", which suggests that you share Robert Frost's sense of a poem being "a momentary stay against confusion", except for the fact that "pessimism" is the operative word for you.'[135] Harrison's reply makes clear that this duality is confrontation rather than conjunction:

> however dark and pessimistic the content of the poetry, the act of confronting it with a poem was itself a denial of the pessimistic beginning. If I had to divide the heart and the head, I would say that my head faces human history, and has a very bleak and pessimistic view of the possibilities for mankind, while at the same time I am very conscious of having a very sensual, celebratory nature: much of my work seems to be a confrontation of the two.

The suggestion is that while confrontation – dialectic, dramatic *praxis*, argument – continues, while the tragic mask keeps looking and the tragic poet keeps clashing together opposed elements, communication, and thus life, will continue, but the end of dialect is death.

---

135 'Interview', p. 227.

CONCLUSION

Harrison's articulation

Between the two
the gauge went almost ga-ga
'Wordlists'

I suggested that Harrison's oppositional poetry could be seen as a 'compromise equilibrium' such as that within which, in Gramsci's model, the texts and practices of popular culture move. To read Harrison's work through Gramscian hegemony theory would entail an interpretation of its depiction of (for example) popular versus high culture not as a balance of opposites but as the terrain of struggle. The field of popular culture

> consists not simply of an imposed mass culture that is coincident with dominant ideology, nor simply of spontaneously oppositional cultures, but is rather an area of negotiation between the two within which – in different particular types of popular culture – dominant, subordinate and oppositional cultural and ideological values and elements are 'mixed' in different permutations.[1]

Appropriately, as John Storey finds, 'The key concept in this use of the neo-Gramscian perspective is the concept of *articulation*' – a key concept also for Harrison's work, not only in its meaning of 'to utter (intelligibly)', but also in its meaning of 'united by a joint' or 'composed of segments united by joints'.[2] In the 'School of Eloquence' poems, the articulation of thought in language is a product and touchstone of the articulation of people and power in society, and a means of exhibiting the interpenetration of the segments of that society. Just as popular culture 'is said to be

---

1 Tony Bennet, 'Introduction: Popular Culture and The Turn to Gramsci', in Tony Bennet, Colin Mercer and Janet Woolacott, eds, *Popular Culture and Social Relations* (Milton Keynes, 1986), pp. xv–xvi, quoted by Storey, *Cultural Theory and Popular Culture*, p. 13.
2 Interestingly, also 'To charge, bring a charge against', *OED*.

marked by what Chantal Mouffe calls "a process of *disarticulation-articulation*",[3] so the themes and forms of other of Harrison's poems are concerned with the temporary linkages of articulation and their severance – disarticulation – in the personal, inter-personal and social. Harrison often uses 'private' or introspective and 'popular' forms of literature which are the traditional reading material of Smith's 'audience': readers who 'were generally considered to be incapable of participating in the body politic, and who intended to gain more social and political standing'.[4] This literature 'might express ideas about political events', but 'was not regarded as an attempt to participate in public life'. By using it for statements about public life and the (sick, sick) body politic, he challenges the presentation of the personal, political and social, as distinct realms of experience, and suggests that they are interpenetrative.

I suggest that some contradictions in Harrison's poetry come from its apparent invitation to two opposed kinds of reading. One is based upon the abstract individualism premised on essentialism which distinguished the individual from the social group, privileging the former and making it the origin and focus of meaning. The 'I' implicitly 'behind' the work seems to refer back to a subject and a subjectivity which, though multiple and diverse, constitutes an unproblematic human essence. The existence of so many supplements to Harrison's poetry – interviews, blurbs, notes, and certain critical pieces – suggests that our readings of the poems benefit from, or even need, extraneous material, and invites us to read the poems for autobiographical, 'real' information. Harrison's voice, auditory and conceptual, is so distinctive that it could easily become associated with the narrative voice of his verse. This in turn could lead readers to look for the 'whole story' – autobiography and portrait. Incompleteness and contradiction, while frustrating this expectation, also add to the pleasures of deferral. Such a reading is entirely along the humanist grain, of course, and to read poet and poetry alike as skeins of discourses neither necessarily continuous nor contiguous would be to read against that grain. I would not suggest either that 'every poem should be a self-contained, self-referential artefact or "verbal icon", and that any outside references or contextualisation are not only extraneous but positively harmful',

---

3 Mouffe, 'Hegemony and Ideology in Gramsci', in Bennet, Mercer, and Woolacott, *Culture, Ideology and Social Process*, p. 14.
4 Smith, *Politics of Language*, preface, p. ix.

or that we should impose upon Harrison's work the tradition for which 'there is no society, no history, just a succession of pure literary formations'.[5] I would, however, suggest that readings which ignore the production of the poem at each moment of reading, and the effects of that poem in the history of its re-readings, in favour of the parthenogenetical 'birth' of the poem from the author, and vice versa, are limiting. Such readings would be perverse for the work of a poet who is not only autonomous, sensitive soul, but also social being; who prides himself upon his sense of political and historical struggle; who has shown 'how the sign is a terrain of struggle where opposing accents intersect, how in a class-divided society language is a cultural warfare and every nuance a political valuation'.[6]

Harrison's ambiguity, doubt, and despair do not amount to nihilism. His cosmological anxieties and metaphysical uncertainties do not undermine the coherence of the implied 'presence' behind the poetry – the Big H in the O – but reinforce it. Angst and self-reflection are, the poetry seems to suggest, defining characteristics of the human condition. The personality depicted in so many of the poems is itself a compromise equilibrium whose several aspects are in negotiation, and those poems are made from the tension between such aspects. Harrison's poetry acknowledges that the self is constructed by forces extrinsic to its notion of itself – is in negotiation – yet it retains the notion of an integrated, autonomous personality which can reflect upon those forces. Though the voice of the Harrison 'I' produces and is produced by many discourses, one remains dominant.

Conversely, the poetry could be taken to invite a form of cultural materialism which replaces such individualism with the totality of social relations. Some of the social themes of Harrison's drama, especially its opposition of (for example) the autocratic individualist 'villains' Apollo and Kyllene and the collective *ichneutae* 'heroes', might be taken as indications of a Brechtian enterprise, refusing a representation of humanity as a stable, fixed entity emanating from a transcendent essence, and instead creating protagonists who are 'like an empty stage on which the contradictions of our society are acted out'.[7] The fetishisation of individualism in

---

5 Worpole, 'Scholarship Boy', *Bloodaxe 1*, p. 68.
6 Eagleton, 'Antagonisms', *Bloodaxe 1*, p. 349.
7 Walter Benjamin, *Understanding Brecht*, trans. Anna Bostock (London, 1977), p. 17.

Harrison's work, however, is shown as a luxury which only the privileged can afford, while 'the social being' is less a matter of organic socialism than of the dumping of the voiceless poor into the communal lime-pit of historical anonymity.

In conclusion, I would suggest that Harrison's oppositions, contradictions, and boundary-straddling are best seen as part of a project to reaffirm 'the power of the word', an affirmation he finds in 'some of the best poetry in the world' which is 'in some of its drama from the Greeks onwards'.[8] In his case this means the power of living speech, with or without aspiration, and its record in memory and art, to survive the threat of the black O of silence and oblivion, or the fire-filled O of war. Tennyson described geology and science as the new 'terrible muses' of poetry; Harrison's 'terrible muse' is the high-tech fire which could consume poetry and life alike. He exploits the power of the word to 'make it new', to make us look afresh; he reminds us that 'Ezra Pound said that literature is news that stays news'.[9] He also harnesses the power of the word to keep us looking: 'poetry, the word at its most eloquent, is one medium which could concentrate our attention on our worst experiences without leaving us with the feeling, as other media can, that life in this century has had its affirmative spirit burnt out'.[10] That word, 'eloquent', carries the history of all the 'Schools of Eloquence' which monopolised articulacy: exclusive education which taught the inferiority of the Rhubarbarian working class, prescriptive grammars designed to eradicate dialect and impose the Big H. Opposing those are the schools which have attempted to reclaim the power of words in general and poetry in particular for the inarticulate. These include that School of Eloquence run by the London Corresponding Society in the eighteenth century,[11] and *The School of Eloquence*, and other poems, which use the products of the exclusive schools – poems written or 'dubbed' into RP[12] – and appropriate them as touchstones for the other side. It is, then, characteristic of Harrison's work that it harnesses the word at its most eloquent to make its point, and embeds that inspired/inspiring eloquence in the strained and difficult diction which makes each poem an act of labour.

---

8 *Bloodaxe 1*, preface, p. 9.
9 'Conversation', p. 237.
10 *Bloodaxe 1*, preface, p. 9.
11 See prose note, *SP*, p. 109.
12 See 'Them & [uz]', *SP*, pp. 122–3.

SELECT BIBLIOGRAPHY

WORKS BY TONY HARRISON

Published Books and Pamphlets

Earthworks. Leeds: Northern House, 1964.
Newcastle is Peru. Newcastle-upon-Tyne: Eagle Press, 1969.
The Loiners. London: London Magazine Editions, 1970.
The Misanthrope. London: Rex Collings, 1973.
Newcastle is Peru, second edn. Newcastle-upon-Tyne: Northern House, 1974.
Palladas: Poems. London: Anvil Press, in association with Rex Collings, 1975.
Phaedra Britannica. London: Rex Collings, 1975.
Phaedra Britannica, third edn, with introductory essay. London: Rex Collings, 1976.
Bow Down. London: Rex Collings, 1977.
From 'The School of Eloquence' and Other Poems. London: Rex Collings, 1978.
Continuous: Fifty Sonnets from 'The School of Eloquence'. London: Rex Collings, 1981.
A Kumquat for John Keats. Newcastle-upon-Tyne: Bloodaxe Books, 1981.
The Oresteia. London: Rex Collings, 1981.
U.S. Martial. Newcastle-upon-Tyne, Bloodaxe Books, 1981.
Selected Poems. London: Penguin Books, 1984.
Dramatic Verse 1973–1985. Newcastle-upon-Tyne: Bloodaxe Books, 1985.
The Fire-Gap. Newcastle-upon-Tyne: Bloodaxe Books, 1985.
The Mysteries. London: Faber and Faber, 1985.
v. Newcastle-upon-Tyne: Bloodaxe Books, 1985.
Theatre Works 1973–1985. London: Penguin Books, 1986.
Anno 42. Scargill Press (imprint of Michael Christopher Cain), 1987.
Selected Poems, second edn. London: Penguin Books, 1987.
Ten Sonnets from 'The School of Eloquence'. London: Anvil Press, 1987.
v., second edn. Newcastle-upon Tyne: Bloodaxe Books, 1989.
The Trackers of Oxyrhynchus. London: Faber and Faber, 1990.
A Cold Coming. Newcastle-upon-Tyne: Bloodaxe Books, 1991.
The Common Chorus, a Version of Aristophanes' Lysistrata. London: Faber and Faber, 1992.
The Gaze of the Gorgon. Newcastle-upon-Tyne: Bloodaxe Books, 1992.
Square Rounds. London: Faber and Faber, 1992.
Black Daisies for the Bride. London: Faber and Faber, 1993.

Select bibliography

Poetry or Bust. Saltaire, Bradford: Salt's Mill, 1993.

The Shadow of Hiroshima and Other Film/Poems. London: Faber and Faber, 1995.

Plays 3: Poetry or Bust, The Kaisers of Carnuntum, The Labourers of Herakles. London: Faber and Faber, 1996.

The Prince's Play (*Le Roi s'amuse*). London: Faber and Faber, 1996.

with James Simmons, *Aikin Mata*. Ibadan: Oxford University Press, 1966.

with Philip Sharpe, *Looking Up*. Malvern: Migrant Press, 1979.

Translations in Peter Jay, ed., *The Greek Anthology*. London: Allen Lane, 1973.

POEMS PUBLISHED ONLY IN PERIODICALS

'When Shall I Tune My "Doric Reed"?', *Poetry and Audience*, 4, no. 11 (25 January 1957).

'What Plato Might Have Said', *Poetry and Audience*, 4, no. 15 (22 February 1957).

'When the Bough Breaks', *Poetry and Audience*, 4, no. 15 (22 February 1957).

'Plato Might Have Said', *Poetry and Audience*, 4, no. 22 (22 May 1957).

'Two into One': 'The Beast with Two Backs' and 'Grog', '*Guardian* New Poetry', *Guardian* (12 January 1994).

'Deathwatch Danceathon', *Guardian* (12 October 1994).

'A Celebratory Ode on the Abdication of Charles III', *Guardian* (11 January 1995).

'The Cycles of Donji Vakuf', *Guardian* (15 September, 1995).

'The Bright Lights of Sarajevo', *Guardian* (15 September, 1995).

PROSE

'Dryden's Aeneid', in Bruce King, ed., *Dryden's Mind and Art*. Edinburgh: Oliver and Boyd, 1969.

[?] unsigned editorial, *Poetry and Audience*, 7, no. 1 (17 October 1959).

'English Virgil: The Aeneid in the XVIII Century', *Philologica Pragensia*, X (1967).

'Shango the Shaky Fairy', *London Magazine*, new series, 10, no. 1 (April 1970).

'New Worlds for Old', review of four collections of Latin-American poetry, *London Magazine*, new series, 10, no. 6 (September 1970).

'Beating the Retreat', review of poems by Clifford Dyment, P. J. Kavanagh, George Macbeth, Hugh MacDiarmid, and Donald Davie, *London Magazine*, new series, 10, no. 8 (November 1970).

'All Out', review of *The Penguin Book of Socialist Verse*, *London Magazine*, new series, 10, no. 12 (March 1971).

Select bibliography

Television Films and Interviews

Arctic Paradise. BBC 2 'World About Us Series', October 1981.
The Big H. BBC 2, December 1984.
Loving Memory. Four-film series BBC 2, July–August 1992.
  Letters in the Rock (July 1992)
  Mimmo Perrella Non è Piu (July 1992)
  The Muffled Bells (July 1992)
  Cheating the Void (August 1992).
v. Channel 4, November 1987.
The Blasphemers' Banquet. Byline Series, BBC 1, July 1989.
The Gaze of the Gorgon. BBC 2, October 1992.
Black Daisies for the Bride. BBC 2, June 1993.
Maybe a Day in Kazakhstan. Channel 4, May 1994.
Prometheus. (film) 1998.

WORKS CONTAINING MATERIAL ON TONY HARRISON'S POETRY

Books

Acheson, James, ed., *British and Irish Drama Since 1960.* London: Macmillan, 1993.
Astley, Neil, ed., *Bloodaxe Critical Anthologies 1: Tony Harrison.* Newcastle-upon-Tyne: Bloodaxe Books, 1991.
Beer, Gillian, *Open Fields: Science in Cultural Encounter.* Oxford: Clarendon Press, 1996.
Byrne, Sandie, ed., *Tony Harrison: Loiner.* Oxford: Clarendon Press, 1997.
Crawford, Robert, *Devolving English Literature.* Oxford: Clarendon Press, 1992.
Easthope, Antony, and Thompson, John O., eds, *Contemporary Poetry Meets Modern Theory.* London: Harvester Wheatsheaf, 1991.
Kaiser, John R., ed., *Tony Harrison: A Bibliography 1957–1987.* London: Mansell Publishing, 1987.
Peach, Linden, *Ancestral Lines: Cultural Identity in the Work of Six Contemporary Poets.* Bridgport: Seren, 1995.
Peer, Willie van, ed., *The Taming of the Text: Explorations in Language, Literature and Culture.* London: Routledge, 1988.
Schmidt, Michael, *Reading Modern Poetry.* London: Routledge, 1989.
Spencer, Luke, *The Poetry of Tony Harrison.* London: Harvester Wheatsheaf, 1994.
Thwaite, Anthony, *Poetry Today: A Critical Guide to British Poetry 1960–1984.* London: Longman, 1985.

Select bibliography

Wilmer, Clive, ed., *Poets Talking: The 'Poet of the Month' Interviews from Radio 3*. Manchester: Carcanet, 1994.

PERIODICALS

Cluysenaar, Anne, review of *The Loiners, Stand,* 12, no. 1 (1970).

Dodd, Philip, 'Lowryscapes: Recent Writing about the North', *Critical Quarterly,* 32, no. 2 (summer 1990).

Eagleton, Terry, 'Antagonisms: Tony Harrison's *v.*', *Poetry Review*, 67, nos 1 and 2 (June 1986).

Egleton, Terry, Review of *The Gaze of the Gorgon*, *Poetry Review*, 82, no 4 (winter 1992/3).

Wainwright, Jeffrey, 'The Silence Round All Poetry', *Poetry Review,* 69, no. 1 (July 1979).

Woodcock, Bruce, 'Classical Vandalism: Tony Harrison's Invective', *Critical Quarterly*, 32, no. 2 (summer 1990).

INDEX

Note: 'n' after a page reference indicates a note number.

Index

Index

Leeds Grammar School
themes 5–21
war as theme 77–8, 84–6, 134–9,
148–51, 161–2, 193, 197–8,
210
Harrison, Tony, books and/or
performed works
Aikin Mata 8, 10, 26n.24,
101n.54, 166
Arctic Paradise 73
The Big H 22, 35n.66, 82, 84,
129, 148, 166, 178, 211
Black Daisies for the Bride 52,
57–9, 193, 197
The Blasphemers' Banquet 18,
19, 45, 57, 58, 60–5, 66,
70, 88–9, 121, 178, 192,
193, 208
censored 60n.1
Bow Down 18, 114n.106, 165,
208˙
A Cold Coming 121 *see also
under* poems
A Common Chorus 77–8, 117,
126, 148–9, 151, 156–7,
166, 204–5, 227
cover copy 148
Continuous 43, 44, 45, 54,
108–9, 126, 192
Earthworks 7, 8–9, 12, 101
The Fire-Gap see under poems
The Gaze of the Gorgon 121; *see
also under* poems
The Kaisers of Carnuntum 88,
165, 184, 210–11
*A Kumquat for John Keats see
under* poems
The Labourers of Herakles 148,
211
The Loiners 8, 12, 78–9, 101,
163, 177
*Loving Memory: The Muffled
Bells; Mimo Perrella Non è*

*Piu; Cheating the Void;
Letters in the Rock* (BBC TV
films) 20–1, 192
A Maybe Day in Kazakhstan
178n.58
Medea: A Sex-War Opera 79–80,
87–8, 166
The Misanthrope 63, 81–2, 86–7,
105, 146, 158–60, 162
The Mysteries 45, 46–52, 114,
209
Newcastle is Peru 101n.54; *see
also under* poems
The Oresteia 46, 79–81, 130,
148, 155, 166, 204, 226–7
Phaedra Britannica 2, 34, 43,
158–9, 166, 167–8, 201–3,
208, 227n.131
Poetry or Bust 19–20, 56
Prometheus (forthcoming
film/poem) 188, 208
*From 'The School of Eloquence'
and Other Poems* 37, 43–4;
see also poems, 'The
School of Eloquence'
(sequence), *and individual
poem titles*
Selected Poems, second edn 8,
12 dedication 175
The Shadow of Hiroshima 84,
193
Square Rounds 20, 75, 76–7,
148, 166, 210, 225
The Trackers of Oxyrhynchus 3,
5–6, 19, 36, 46, 51, 52, 69,
70–1, 84, 96, 99, 126,
151–2, 161, 172, 204, 208,
220, 223, 225, 227, 231
U.S. Martial 45
v., Channel 4 film 67–70, 90,
130–3; *see also under* poems
Yan Tan Tethera 1, 112,
114n.106, 166, 208

239

Index

Index

'Them & [uz]'
'Long Distance I' 140, 180
'Long Distance II' 40
'The Lords of Life' 51, 72, 73,
    75, 174, 217
'Manica' *see* 'The White Queen'
'Marked with D' 39, 95n.28
'Me Tarzan' 19, 35, 41, 108–9
'The Morning After I' 179
'The Mother of the Muses' 58,
    194
'National Trust' 22–3
Newcastle is Peru 7, 13, 18, 19,
    35, 101, 173, 174
'Next Door I' 44–5
'Next Door IV' 39, 45
'The Nuptial Torches' 75, 101
'An Old Score' 95n.28
'Old Soldiers' 178
'On Not Being Milton' 37, 39,
    56, 201
'Pain-Killers II', 123
'The Pocket Wars of Peanuts
    Joe' 165
'Poetry Lesson' 181
'The Pomegranates of Patmos'
    69, 73, 137, 165n.8, 170,
    176, 184
'Prologue' for the National
    Theatre's Olivier Stage
    opening 128–9
'The Promised Land' 141
'Punchline' 40
'The Queen's English' 45
'The Railroad Heroides' *see* 'The
    White Queen'
'Remains' 55–6
'The Rhubarbarians I' 30, 39,
    43, 106
'The Rhubarbarians II' 105, 106
'School of Eloquence' (sequence)
    7, 43, 45, 108, 123, 132,
    177, 229, 232

*see also under individual poem
    titles*
'Schweigermutterlieder' 139,
    170n.25
'Self Justification' 169
'Snap' 85
'Social Mobility' 53, 54
'The Songs of the PWD Man' (I
    and II) 163–4, 178
'Still' 53, 95n.28
'Study' 37, 41n.90, 199
'Summoned by Bells' 106–7
'Them & [uz] I' 14, 23, 31 32,
    36, 44, 104, 232
'Them & [uz] II', 56, 168–9, 212
'Thomas Campey and the
    Copernican System' 8–9, 101
'Timer' 102, 123, 139
'Two into One': 'The Beast with
    Two Backs' and 'Grog' 169
    see also 'Beast with Two
    Backs'
v., 1, 2, 22, 29, 54–5, 67–70,
    73n.55, 90, 134, 142–3,
    144–6, 166–7, 169, 174,
    178–9, 186, 190, 193, 198,
    222, 227n.131: *see also
    under* books and/or
    performed works
'What Plato Might Have Said' 34
'When the Bough Breaks' 34
'When Shall I Tune My "Doric
    Reed"?' 7, 34
'The White Queen' 8–12, 101,
    178
'Wordlists ' (three poems) 26
'Wordlists I' 38, 41
'Wordlists II' 38, 53
'Wordlists III' 43
'Working' 41, 102, 225
'Y' 53, 54, 179
'*from* The Zeg-Zeg Postcards'
    see 'The White Queen'

241

Index

Index

Index